tab

2001 GUIDE

on MONEY PENSIONS AND TAX

tab

Taxation Advice Bureau
Eagle House, Wentworth, Eblana Villas, Dublin 2.
Telephone: (01) 6768633. Fax: (01) 6768641

GW00361248

Minister's Foreword

I would like to congratulate the Taxation Advice Bureau on the latest version of their *Guide to Money Pensions and Tax.*

This is the sixteenth year that the guide has been published. As was the case with previous editions it is a concise, user-friendly publication that provides advice on almost all aspects of taxation and finance that the average family would encounter. It brings clarity and simplicity to matters that without such a publication could appear complex and inaccessible.

A lot of progress has been made in reforming the tax system in recent years and the change to tax credits has made the system easier to understand. While a great many people have been taken out of the tax net at the same time there has been an enormous growth in numbers employed in this country. So there is a greater need than ever for a guide to financial topics that is aimed at ordinary people and that helps them to optimise their personal financial arrangements.

From 1 January 2002 we in Ireland will move to a calendar year basis for taxation which is the way that taxation is organised in most countries. Therefore, our next tax year is a 'short' year which will conclude at the end of 2001. In this respect I am pleased to see that the guide is fully up to date as indeed it is regarding the other changes that I announced in the recent budget on 6th December.

Once again I compliment the authors for the excellent service that they give to the general public in producing this *Guide to Money Pensions and Tax.*

Charlie McCreevy TD
Minister for Finance

1

A Message From Sebastian Devlin

- Creator of the Tab Guide

This is a very important issue of the Tab Guide.

Not only does it capture all the far-reaching changes and benefits of the December 2000 budget, but I am very conscious that we are entering a completely new era for Irish tax payers.

The tax 'year' commencing 6th April 2001 will operate for a short nine month period only. It terminates on the 31st December 2001. And from 1st January 2002 onward our income tax year will be exactly the same as the calendar year.

That's why I took a decision with my fellow authors, **Jill Kerby** and **Sandra Gannon** to increase the size and contents of this year's Guide so that we can carefully guide you step by step through all the many changes that are taking place in matters relating to money, pensions and tax in Ireland.

Ours is a challenging task! Because what you are now holding in your hands is the definitive "Tab Guide" which for its accuracy and clarity has been described by **Gay Byrne** as ...'one of those books that should be in every home in Ireland'.

Each year as I pen this little message to our readers I ask myself 'have we lived up to this somewhat daunting challenge"?

This year, I genuinely believe we have!

Sebastian Devlin

Sebastian Devlin

*This book has been prepared as a general
guide for use in the Republic of Ireland and is
based on our understanding of present law
and practice. While every effort has been made
to ensure accuracy, neither the publisher nor
editor are liable for any errors or omissions.*

Published by
THE TAXATION ADVICE BUREAU,
Eagle House, Wentworth,
Dublin 2.
Telephone: (01) 6768633
E-mail: tab@eircom.net
Web Site: www.tab.ie

ISSN No: 0790 9632
ISBN No: 0-9522553-8-3

Produced by Siobháin Usher / BCS Ltd.

Printed by Typeform Ltd., Dublin.

Now that we've joined up, your future is safer than ever.

How do you improve on the services offered by the safest hands in the business?

By linking up with other service providers, with other areas of expertise – and together presenting the most comprehensive and competitive Life and Pensions portfolio on the market.

Together, CGU, Norwich Union and Hibernian manage more than £5.5 billion, from savings and investments to pensions and life assurance. And now the expertise of all three organisations is available as one, to all Hibernian Life & Pensions customers.

So whatever the task in hand, you can be sure you're safest in ours.

HIBERNIAN

Hibernian Life & Pensions, 60/63 Dawson Street, Dublin 2. Tel: 6178000 Fax: 6710803

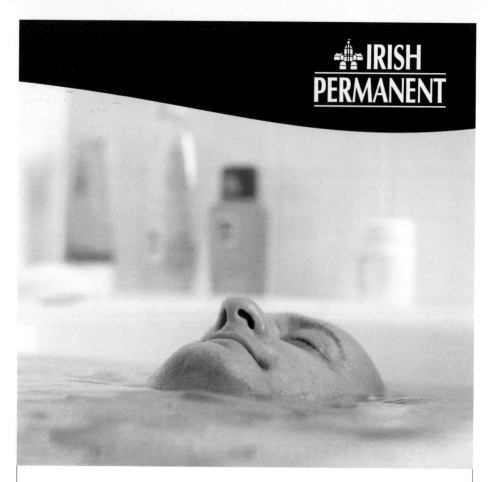

you know when
You're Home

We all want somewhere of our own, where we can be ourselves. Where we feel comfortable and relaxed. This is how people feel when they come to Irish Permanent. More Irish families have made their home with an Irish Permanent mortgage than any other. They enjoy competitive rates and of course our range of flexible options too. Test the water and you'll soon find plenty of reasons to breath easier.

For details of our mortgage options call in, call direct on 1850 500 121 or log onto www.irishpermanent.ie You're home with Irish Permanent.

call into any branch and ask about your mortgage options or phone 1850 500 121 (lines open mon-fri 8.30am-9pm) **or log onto www.irishpermanent.ie**

Table Of Contents

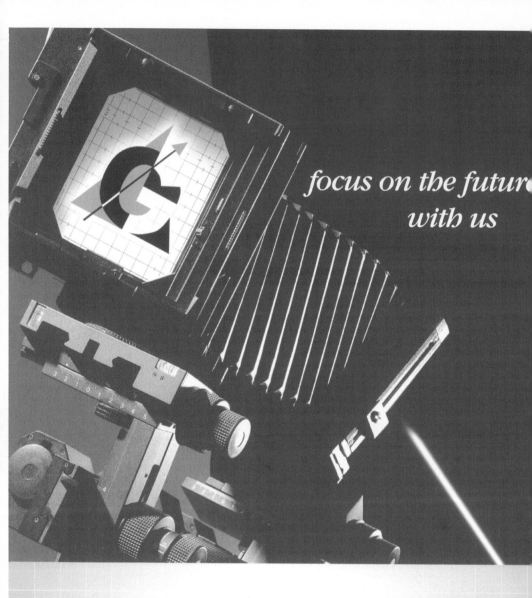

finance2u.com
Finance & Insurance Direct Online

Because Choice Is Everything

Now you can get Information, Quotations and even Apply Online. Forget about endless queuing and hours on the telephone.

Why not let finance2u.com do the hard work for you?

You can compare products and services from Ireland's top financial and insurance companies and get the deal that best suits you.

Insure your car, get a mortgage, get a loan, plan your own personal finances, convert currencies, plan your retirement and much much more.

finance2u.com provides you with the most comprehensive personal finance and insurance service available in Ireland today.

1

The Euro

The European Single Currency the euro, formally came into being on January 1st 1999 and the transition from various national currencies to the euro will be completed on January 1st 2002 when euro notes and coins will be put into general circulation. Until the transition is complete, the euro has a value of £0.787564 against the Irish pound, or inversely, the pound is worth €1.269738 euros.

So far, eleven of the European Union member states – Austria, Belgium, Finland, France, Germany, Ireland, Italy, Spain, Luxembourg, the Netherlands and Portugal have joined the euro. The United Kingdom has decided to wait until certain conditions are met before it decides whether to join. Denmark voted against euro membership in a referendum last year while Greece was judged not to have met the necessary conditions.

While euro notes and coins do not come into circulation until next year, the euro has been useable for cashless transactions like cheques, direct debits and credit transfers. Put simply, until January 1st 2002, cash transactions in Ireland will continue in Irish pounds while cashless transactions can be carried out either in Irish pounds or euros.

Already, the euro is trading as a currency on international capital markets, readers will doubtless be aware that since its inception the euro has weakened steadily against both the dollar and sterling. In the case of the dollar, the euro began its life with an exchange rate of $1.17 to the euro. By December 2000, that value had fallen to $0.85 to the euro.

When euro notes and coins do come into circulation and the transition is completed, there will be notes in denominations of 5, 10, 20, 50, 100, 200 and 500 euros while euro coins will be denominated in units of 1, 2, 5, 10, 20, and 50 cents and 1 and 2 euros.

When changeover day arrives in January 1st 2002, accounts in Irish pounds will be automatically converted to euros at the six-digit conversion rate of £0.787564, free of charge. Non-cash transactions involved credit and debit cards and cheques will be denominated in euros. Lodgements, whether in cash or non-cash form will be in euros. ATM machines will begin to dispense euro notes, State payments such as social welfare payments will be in euros, wages and salaries will be paid in euros and change in retail outlets will be in euros. It is expected that within two weeks of the changeover, the bulk of transactions will be carried out in euros.

By now, most goods and services show a dual pricing in both Irish pounds and euros, mainly as part of a public information campaign conducted by the Euro Changeover Board, a section within the Department of Finance. Bills and invoices increasingly show the euro equivalent of the Irish pound amount while the banks have also displayed closing balances on bank statements in both currencies.

In addition, any banking service required in euros – other than euro notes and coins is available and, in general, financial institutions will on request provide accounts in euros or will enhance existing accounts to operate in euros. Further information on these types of services is available from your bank or building society. Loan and deposit balances will be in general denominated in Irish pounds with the euro equivalent until January 1st 2002 when the final changeover takes place and balances will be denominated in euros.

Pensions will be paid in Irish pounds until January 1st 2002 and then changed over to the euro. If somebody, however, has a foreign pension which is paid, for example, in sterling or US dollars, it will be converted into Irish pounds at the exchange rate of the time. From January 1st 2002, the foreign pension will be converted into euros at the exchange rate at the time of conversion.

Since the euro came into being, interest rates have not been determined by national central banks or national Governments, but by the European Central Bank based in Frankfurt. Since the inception of the euro, Irish interest rates have fallen sharply although there have been a series of interest rate increases by the ECB in the past year in an effort to support the value of the euro.

Lower interest rates is the upside for Irish borrowers, as the Irish Central Bank no longer determines Irish interest rates. It is fair to say that had the Irish Central Bank still have the power to raise interest rates, it would have done so by now in an effort to curb rising Irish inflation.

Banks and building societies

Irish banks and building societies through their representative organisations, the Irish Bankers Federation and the Irish Mortgage and Savings Association have published a standard of good practice on bank charges for conversion to the euro.

Since January 1st 1999, any banking service required in euro – other than euro notes and coins – have been available and will continue to be available until January 1st 2002. While most wholesale banking transactions are being initiated and settled in euros since January 1st 1999, the pace of the changeover in retail banking is being determined by customers.

Banks and building societies will process lodgements and payments expressed in either Irish pounds or euros regardless of the denomination of the customer's account . Customers are being encouraged to use electronic means in making or receiving euro payments, but cheques and credit transfers in euros are also available. Charges for domestic transactions in euros are the same as charges for identical Irish pound transactions.

Cross-border payments between euro member states, non-participating member states such as the UK and non-EU countries – including credit transfers, telegraphic transfers, money orders etc. as well as a number of newer, speedier and cost-effective options are available in euros. In contrast, domestic cheques – whether they are in Irish pounds or euros - will remain a slower and more costly means of making cross-border payments because there is no Europe-wide clearing system. Customers should consult their bank or building society on the optimum payment method to suit their particular needs.

The stock exchange

One area where the euro is most visibly at work in on the stock markets, where shares of companies in the participating countries are now denominated and have traded solely in euros since the beginning of 1999. The financial pages of the newspapers currently carry the Irish pound equivalent but this is merely a convenience for their readers.

For example, people who bought Eircom shares last year may have paid for their shares in Irish pounds, but their shares are listed in euros. Likewise, public companies now publish their accounts in euros, the dividend they pay shareholders is denominated in euros, but until the financial changeover is completed the actual payment of the dividend to shareholders is usually in Irish pounds.

While share prices are denominated in euros, most stockbroking firms will translate euro equities transactions into Irish pounds for clients who wish to transact in Irish pounds. The Irish pound transaction, however, will still be based on the price in euros of the relevant equity.

Prior to the introduction of the euro, Irish investors in, for example, German and French shares had to take a risk on the exchange rate against German and French currencies when they invested. Now they can do so without such an exchange rate risk. Irish stockbrokers are increasingly offering their clients the opportunity to invest in European public companies. This has given Irish investors a much broader investment horizon and many Irish investors have, for example, put money into flotations such as Deutsche Telekom and other major European companies.

Insurance

Since January 1st 1999, insurers will deal in euros on request, although the vast majority of people are paying premiums, making investments and making claims in Irish pounds. At present, claims are settled in Irish pounds.

Many insurers are providing dual currency information on headline figures in life and non-life insurance policies, while euro-denominated savings and pensions products are being increasingly introduced. From January 1st, 2002, all insurance transactions will be carried out in euros.

2

Turning risks into rewards

Your personal finances involve more than putting a little money aside every week, or buying a life insurance policy to ensure a decent burial. Irish people are becoming increasingly sophisticated about how their money is earned, taxed, spent, saved and invested, and the huge range of financial products on the market is testimony to this general rise in spending power and awareness.

What is often lacking, however, is personal financial planning. Many people spend more time planning a summer holiday than they do planning for their retirement - which could last 20 years or more. The hours spent choosing a new car would be just as well spent looking for the right education investment scheme for your children.

Proper financial planning doesn't take place in a vacuum: a young person starting their first job may not be ready to think about a pension plan, but does need to find the best finance package for a first car or the right savings account to accommodate the deposit for an apartment or house. What are the most tax-efficient ways to be paid or to spend their surplus income? Does it make financial sense to work abroad for a few years?

Young married couples are always looking to the future: they may be planning a family, moving house, taking on all kinds of responsibilities. They need to make their Wills, get the best finance deal for their new house, make sure they have insured each other's lives (especially for when the baby arrives) and they need to set up a viable family budget.

Children bring enormous joy - and bills. If the mother (or father) does not stay at home with the baby, someone else may have to be hired to provide childcare; either way there is going to be a significant cost incurred.

Since your child is going to have to be fed, dressed, educated and amused for the next two decades, the sooner you start planning for all these costs the better - it is best to start putting aside even a modest amount of money each week or month. Taking out a savings policy two or three years before secondary or third level school fall due is usually about 10 years too late. Now is also the time to consider starting a tax-efficient pension fund or AVC (Additional Voluntary Contribution) if you don't have one at your work, and to review your life and health insurance policies. Debt management should also be a priority.

The financial needs of someone in their middle age are very different from a single person or a young parent. Though your monthly outlay may be high, there is light at the end of the childrearing tunnel; ideally you are earning more and have built up some equity in your home and in other savings or investment funds. You may still have 15 or 20 years before retirement, but do you have a pension plan and if so, is it being fully funded?

For the over 60's, retirement can be a blessing or a burden. Without an adequate pension or other assets, day to day spending may have to be curtailed and outstanding debts may provoke a serious financial crisis. For the financially secure, retirement can provide exciting new opportunities to enjoy life at your own pace. But whether you work for someone else or have your own business you need to take stock of your financial position, including, your assets and debts, plus your short and long term health care provisions.

Death comes to us all, and this book also takes you through a number of financial issues that must be dealt with when somebody dies: Wills, Inheritance Tax, Probate, Intestacy and the tax adjustments that come with widowhood.

Financial planning is best done with a trusted advisor, whether an accountant, broker or a bank manager. But independent, objective advice is by far the best option and the fee you pay such a person may be one of the best investments you will ever make.

Risks and rewards

Everyone takes chances at some time in their lives. One of the ingredients of success, aside from talent and luck, is the ability to take a few risks to achieve a difficult task or goal.

Taking risks with your money can be difficult to handle, especially if it has been hard-earned or if there is any history of poverty in your family. Yet, higher risk will give greater potential for higher rewards, long term.

Financial institutions recognise this reluctance on the part of many people to take chances with their income or savings and offer a range of interest earning products with little or no risk and thus low long term rewards.

Low growth/low risk

Deposit-based bank, building society and Post Office accounts carry the security of vast capital-based institutions of the State. But with virtually no associated risk the interest paid is a fraction of a percent on the most basic deposit accounts. Savings accounts, which may require a minimum deposit amount and savings term will pay higher interest rates, but not much above the level of inflation long term.

Higher returns reflect risk and if you want a high reward, you need to first look at your ability to deal with risk: taking into account your age, your general financial circumstances and your ability to absorb any losses. For example, an elderly widow, relying on a state pension for her income is not a suitable candidate to invest her savings in the stock market, no matter how buoyant the performance of shares may appear to be.

A younger person with a steady, rising income or a professional with existing assets and excellent earning potential is a good candidate to take some short or long term risk, whether by investing directly in the stock market, by buying property or international managed funds.

Living with risk

To establish your own level of risk, you need to ask yourself the following questions:

- Can I afford to lose my money? Will I be able to meet all my regular, day-to-day obligations if it disappears?

- Am I prepared for the fact that investment markets are cyclical and values are likely to go down as well as up?

- Can I wait for investment markets to recover, if they do go down?

If you answer negatively to these questions, then you probably have a relatively low risk threshold and investing directly in the stock market, or even in unitised funds or in property - which all require relatively long term investment periods - may not be for you.

Risk also needs to be related to age. A young person taking out a pension plan which will mature in 40 years should take some risk with the underlying investments in the fund in the early years while someone in their 50's investing in a pension needs to be more cautious, especially if retirement is coming up in just five to ten years. Parents of young children who want to save for their education need to take fewer risks than a long term pension investor since, again, time may not be on their side.

Matching the risk

Post office Savings Certificates, Bonds and Instalment Savings Plans, Special Savings Accounts and higher yield deposits are good options for low risk savers (like pensioners) or people with short term funding needs, but the biggest danger associated with deposit type products is that they are not always inflation proof. If you leave all your money on deposit for a long period, it could get eaten away by the inevitable rise in the prices of everyday goods and services.

Unit Linked or with-profit bonds, low cost PIPS and PEPS and tracker bonds are more suitable for low to medium risk personalities who wish to save on a regular or lump sum basis for up to 10 years or so. For people prepared for more of a roller-coaster ride, they can start with domestic or international managed equity funds, where the risk is spread, and work their way towards direct stock market or property investments.

Independent financial advice

Unless you are a financial expert yourself, the huge variety and types of savings and investment products on the market may make it very difficult for you to know which one is suitable for your particular needs and circumstances. An independent financial advisor could be of great assistance in helping you choose which deposit account to open, which savings policy, pension or stocks and shares to buy.

Independent financial advice is not available from the Post Office, banks or building societies, stock brokers or life assurance companies since they all want you to buy their company's products: the bank official is not going to recommend that you take out a Post Office Instalment Savings Plan, even if it happens to pay more interest than the bank's equivalent scheme. The credit union will not recommend you borrow from the building society, even if the society's interest rate is lower. A life assurance company wants you to buy into their managed equity fund, not go directly to the stock market.

Unfortunately, finding truly independent financial advice is very difficult because there is a shortage of financial experts who operate on a fee basis.

Commissions are paid by financial institutions as a sales reward to the broker or sales agent when you opt to buy one of their products. The size of the commission will vary in size from institution to institution and also depends on whether you are contributing a lump sum or are making regular monthly or even weekly payments.

Many people advertise themselves as 'independent' financial advisers on mortgages, general and life assurance policies, pensions, deposit accounts and investment funds. Yet nearly all of them accept commission payments from the institution. Those institutions which do not pay broker commissions - the Post Office, some banks and building societies (depending on the product), are unlikely to be recommended by a broker or salesperson who relies solely on commission for their remuneration.

No disclosure

Although there is no requirement for financial advisors or brokers, or the companies they deal with, to disclose the size of the commission paid, legislation is expected to be operative from 1st January 2001 which will require such disclosure at point of sale in the case of many financial products. The Government is also considering the creation of a central financial regulator, one of whose roles will be to investigate consumer complaints about misselling, as well as the setting of standards under which financial services companies and their intermediaries will operate.

Avoid misselling

Until then, the best way to reduce the danger of being missold an expensive financial service or product is to seek advice from a genuinely independent financial advisor, who ideally is paid a fee. Knowing that their time and expertise is being rewarded, regardless of whether you buy a product, your wider financial situation will more likely be taken into account and the chance that you will be sold an unsuitable product should be lessened.

Such advisors may be specialist life and pensions brokers, mortgage brokers and/or investment brokers, accountants and management consultants who deal with the personal finances of their private clients. Since there is currently no register of fee-based brokers, the onus is on the consumer to establish whether an independent broker or advisor is genuinely fee-based or not.

If you prefer to deal with a commission-based advisor rather than pay a fee, make sure they explain why they are recommending one product or policy over another and satisfy yourself they are not being influenced by the size of the commission they are being paid.

3

What you should know about saving

There have never been so many outlets for your savings, whatever your age or financial position. Whether you are 80 or 8, choosing the right savings outlet, and the most tax-efficient one depends on:

• Why you are saving

• How accessible you want your money to be

• The interest rate on offer

and

• Security.

An Post

Savings Bonds are a three year investment and require a minimum investment of £100. At the end of the three years, you will currently earn 8% or an annual compound rate of 2.6%. An individual is restricted to holding no more than £60,000 worth of bonds or £120,000 for joint holdings. Since the interest is cumulative and increases towards the latter part of the savings period, you should avoid encashing savings bonds early. Withdrawals are subject to seven days notice.

"Flexible savings and investments give us great freedom."

Lump Sum Investments

Regular Savings Accounts

Prize Bonds

Choose from the range
of Savings and Investment
options from your
local Post Office.

The Post Office. Helping you do more.

FreeFone 1800 30 50 60
or call into your Post Office

Investment of £1,000	£	€
After 1 Year	£1,020	€1,295
After 2 Years	£1,042	€1,323
After 3 Years	£1,080	€1,371

Savings Certificates are another very tax-efficient way to save your money, at no risk. Purchased in £50 lots, savings certificate pay 16% interest guaranteed and tax-free over a five year and six month period. This is the equivalent of an average annual compound interest rate of 2.74% per annum.

The following table illustrates how an investment of £1,000 grows every six months:

	£	€
After 6 Months	£1,008	€1,280
After 1 Year	£1,017	€1,291
After 1 Year & 6 Months	£1,027	€1,304
After 2 Years	£1,038	€1,318
After 2 Years & 6 Months	£1,050	€1,333
After 3 Years	£1,063	€1,350
After 3 Years & 6 Months	£1,077	€1,368
After 4 Years	£1,092	€1,387
After 4 Years & 6 Months	£1,110	€1,409
After 5 Years	£1,132	€1,437
After 5 Years & 6 Months	£1,160	€1,473

An individual can hold up to £60,000 worth of savings certificates or £120,000 for a married couple. Saving Certificates can pay a regular half-yearly income, by encashing units every six months. Since the rate of interest is lowest in the early years and highest in the later years you should try to avoid encashing early.

National instalment savings

To join An Post's Instalment Savings Scheme, the saver - who must be at least age seven - must make regular monthly payments for at least one year, of between £20 and £300. Left for another five years, your accumulated savings will then earn 15% tax free, or a typical compound rate of 2.58%, including the first 12 month contribution period, when no interest is paid.

Instalment Savings are a popular - and tax free way - to watch savings grow over the medium to longer term and are a good way to save for a child's education, and other domestic goals. Many mothers take advantage of the automatic facility on offer which deposits the monthly child benefit allowance (now worth £67.50 a month per child for the first two children and £86.00 for third and subsequent children) directly into the Instalment Savings Scheme (as well as into Savings Certificates and other An Post accounts).

The following table illustrates the annual growth rates of National Instalment Savings from the first to fifth years after the 12 month contribution period has been completed:

	%
After one year on deposit	2.0
After two years on deposit	4.0
After three years on deposit	6.0
After four years on deposit	10.0
After five years on deposit	15.0

Deposit accounts

An Post has a number of deposit accounts on offer, such as the Instant Access Deposit Account on which interest is calculated daily and added to your account on December 31st each year. Similar to bank and building society demand accounts, the interest rate is very low and these are not very suitable as saving vehicles, even if all you want to do is match the rate of inflation.

Typical rates for demand deposit accounts and 30-day notice accounts are as follows;

Amount on deposit £	On demand
Less than £5,000	0.25%
More than £5,000	0.50%

Amount on deposit £	SSA 30 days notice account
Less than £40,000	2.0%
More than £40,000	2.5%

Children's accounts

Most of the banking institutions have special children's saving clubs or accounts which pay modest rates of interest, but may also supply the child with a toy savings bank to bring home and fill up, a membership card, savings book and a special joining gift. Some send out bi-annual kids club magazines or posters. Teen and student accounts can be interest bearing and include access to an ATM card for easy withdrawals.

Because interest rates are so low, depositors may be charged fees soon to operate such accounts and you may want to look at the range of higher interest bearing accounts available from the building societies and, to a lesser extent, the retail banks. These include:

Fixed term accounts

These accounts require that you leave your money with them for an agreed period of time - usually from one to 12 months. The interest is higher than is paid on deposit or "share interest" accounts from the building society. The downside of these accounts is that you cannot access your funds until the maturity date.

Regular savings accounts

These accounts reward the regular saver with a slightly higher - interest rate (usually about 0.5% more) than is paid by a share or demand deposit account. For this, you must agree to save a set amount over a set period of months.

Regular income accounts

These are ideal for someone who needs a regular income, though they usually require a minimum initial deposit. Interest rates can be quite low, but some societies offer a high rate if you agree to certain restrictions on the amounts you can withdraw at any one time. The income may vary if interest rates go up or down.

Guaranteed interest accounts

A sort of savings bond, these accounts are extremely popular and involve the building society guaranteeing to pay a fixed amount of interest for a minimum sum over a specific period. The following table shows the different SSA rates that were available in November 2000 for £10,000 deposit:

Deposit term	3 months		6 months		12 months	
	Gross %	Net %	Gross %	Net %	Gross %	Net %
A.I.B.	3.73	2.98	4.06	3.25	4.80	3.84
Anglo Irish Bank	4.47	3.58	4.47	3.58	4.48	3.58
Bank of Ireland	3.28	2.62	4.00	3.20	4.25	3.40
E.B.S.	5.00	4.00	5.13	4.10	5.25	4.20
First Active	4.27	3.42	4.32	3.46	4.38	3.50
ICC Investment Bank	4.50	3.60	4.50	3.60	4.50	3.60
ICS	2.22	1.77	2.22	1.77	2.23	1.78
Irish Nationwide	5.12	4.10	5.00	4.00	5.25	4.20
Irish Permanent	4.67	3.74	n/a	n/a	3.35	2.68
Lombard & Ulster	4.57	3.66	4.61	3.69	4.67	3.74
TSB	4.00	3.20	4.75	3.80	5.00	4.00
Ulster Bank	2.50	2.00	2.75	2.20	2.75	2.20

Net = Net of 20% DIRT

Special savings accounts

When Special Savings Accounts were first introduced in 1993, interest rates were high and the DIRT tax was just 10%, making them one of the best savings options around. Today, the DIRT rate has risen to 20% and, while they offer considerable security and competitive interest rates for higher sums, SSAs have lost much of their attractiveness.

Certain conditions need to be met before you can open such an account:

- The account must be designated by the institution as an SSA.

- You need to be over 18 or married when you open the account.

- You or your spouse must be the person entitled to the interest earned; you cannot open an SSA for someone else.

- You cannot make a withdrawal in the first three months.

- You need to give 30 days notice of a withdrawal.

- Fixed interest rates must not apply for longer than 24 months.

- You can only have one SSA at a time and must limit your deposit to £75,000 (£50,000 before 5th April 1999). A married couple can have two separate SSAs of up to £75,000 each (£50,000 before 5th April 1999).

Wealth warning

Your SSA will also be taken into account if you wish to open any of the Special Investment Accounts or Investment Portfolio Accounts. See Page 45.

Investment certificates

Similar to An Post Savings Certificates, some of the building societies/banks now offer Investment Certificates which pay tiered interest rates on a six monthly basis, usually over a six year period. The following table shows how £1,000 would grow with EBS Sure Certs, from which 22% DIRT (20% from 6th April 2001) is withheld, compared with An Post Savings Certs which are paid tax-free.

	EBS Sure Certs		An Post Savings Certs	
	Gross £	Net £	Gross £	Net £
6 Months	£1,013	£1,010	£1,008	n/a
€	€1,286	€1,282	€1,280	n/a
1 Year	£1,032	£1,025	£1,017	n/a
€	€1,310	€1,301	€1,291	n/a
1 Year 6 Months	£1,051	£1,040	£1,027	n/a
€	€1,334	€1,321	€1,304	n/a
2 Years	£1,072	£1,056	£1,038	n/a
€	€1,361	€1,341	€1,318	n/a
2 Years 6 Months	£1,096	£1,075	£1,050	n/a
€	€1,392	€1,365	€1,333	n/a
3 Years	£1,121	£1,094	£1,063	n/a
€	€1,423	€1,389	€1,350	n/a
3 Years 6 Months	£1,147	£1,115	£1,077	n/a
€	€1,456	€1,416	€1,368	n/a
4 Years	£1,175	£1,137	£1,092	n/a
€	€1,492	€1,444	€1,387	n/a
4 Years 6 Months	£1,205	£1,160	£1,110	n/a
€	€1,530	€1,473	€1,409	n/a
5 Years	£1,243	£1,190	£1,132	n/a
€	€1,577	€1,511	€1,437	n/a
5 Years 6 Months	£1,284	£1,222	£1,160	n/a
€	€1,630	€1,552	€1,473	n/a
6 Years	£1,329	£1,257	-	n/a
€	€1,687	€1,596	-	n/a

Credit Unions

The Credit Union movement has two million members who save regularly at 533 different Credit Union offices. Credit Unions are essentially savers' co-ops in the community or at the saver's place of work. Members come together to save on a regular basis and to provide loans to each other from the collective savings fund.

Every pound you save is the equivalent of a single share in your local Credit Union and shares pay a dividend or interest at the end of each year. The size of the dividend can vary between Credit Unions but has averaged at about 5% in recent years. Members are usually restricted to their local credit union on the basis of geography or work, so you are unlikely to be able to choose to save with a credit union in a different neighbourhood or town simply because they pay a higher dividend.

You can withdraw your Credit Union savings at any time, as long as they are not pledged as security against a loan.

If you are a shareholder in the Credit Union, depending on your age and state of health, your dependants will benefit from the free Life Savings Insurance Scheme which matches the value of your shares up to a maximum of £10,000 pounds in the event of your death if you are under age 55. If you are between 55-59 it pays an additional 75p for every share; between 60-64 it pays an extra 50p for every share and between 65-70, 25p extra for every share.

Example

If you were under age 55 when you died and had £5,000 pounds worth of shares in the Credit Union, as a member of the life savings insurance scheme, your estate would be entitled to an additional £5,000 pounds tax-free. If you were 69, the savings insurance benefit reduces to £1,250.

All Credit Union dividends and interest is taxable at your relevant rate of tax. However no tax is deducted at source. If you are in receipt of a dividend or interest from a credit union you are obliged to include this amount on your income tax return.

Budget 2001 change: In the 2001 Budget it was announced that interest on deposit interest received from Credit Unions will be liable to DIRT @ 20% and will be exempt from any further tax.

Members may opt to have their dividends taxed either;

- As at present;

- By having DIRT @ 20% applied to the dividends;

- By placing their shares in special 3 or 5 year savings accounts where the first £375 p.a. (£500 p.a. for 5 year accounts) will be tax exempt and DIRT at 20% will apply to the balance.

Life assurance

With the exception of Irish Life's Credit Club, and a new savings and loan product from First Active Bank in which savers put away a set amount each month in order to eventually borrow a multiple of their built-up fund, there are few suitable true "saving" options from life assurance companies.

Other life assurance plans and investments are generally high risk where the potential is for a higher return over the longer term, but the return is related to the performance of the underlying Bonds, Property, Domestic and International Equity Funds etc.

Summing up

Deposit accounts will never be a way to get rich quick. In the current climate they are barely able to maintain the value of your assets. However, what cash deposits do offer is safety and ready access to your money. So it makes sense to use them:

- To provide cash reserves for emergencies.

- When you know you will need money for a particular purpose soon (for a new car, wedding etc.).

- When you think other types of investments are particularly risky and you want to play safe.

Tax

Irish interest

In most deposit based accounts DIRT will be deducted at source;

* 20% DIRT will apply to special savings accounts.

* 22% (20% from 6th April 2001) DIRT will apply to other accounts.

While no further tax is payable, interest earned from a non special savings account should be included on your tax return as it may be liable to the 2% health levies. Interest earned from a special savings account should only be returned on your tax form if you are entitled to a refund of DIRT, see page 32.

UK interest

Where the UK tax has been deducted at source, the tax will be repaid in full from the UK Tax Authorities on completion of the appropriate form **IRL/Individual/Int**. The gross interest is taxed in Ireland under Case III Schedule D.

Other interest

Other interest arising abroad for Irish residents will be taxed whether or not it is remitted to this country. Any tax paid abroad will generally be available as a credit against tax payable here.

Tax rebates

If your income is so low that you don't pay any income tax and you are either permanently incapacitated or 65 or over, you are entitled to claim back any DIRT you have paid on deposit interest. The Income Exemption Limits are listed on page 198.

4

Take advantage of your investments

If you have spare cash each week or month and want to put it away for a rainy day, there are plenty of secure, accessible savings outlets: the post office; bank or building society and the credit union. These savings can normally be withdrawn or even borrowed against at any time.

Other people with spare cash or a windfall whether an inheritance, a gain from the sale of a capital asset (a house, car, antique) or perhaps even a retirement or redundancy lump sum - often want more than a modest, guaranteed return. They want to see this money earn more significant returns, - they want an investment.

Investments come in three basic forms:

• Bonds

• Stocks & shares

• Property

Historically, high quality shares have, on average, tended to give greater returns than any other class of investment, beating property, bonds and deposits, as illustrated in the long-term returns table 34.

Annual returns from Irish investments					
	Bonds	Stocks & shares	Property	Inflation	Cash deposits
	%	%	%	%	%
30 yrs	12.14	16.97	15.64	7.95	10.24
25 yrs	14.85	22.16	15.06	7.39	10.42
20 yrs	14.42	20.43	13.92	5.66	10.20
15 yrs	13.49	16.94	14.00	2.77	8.51
10 yrs	10.33	16.26	15.37	2.30	7.47
5 yrs	11.56	24.91	23.89	1.90	5.18

The above chart provided by Bank of Ireland Asset Managers details the returns achieved by various Irish asset classes from 1969 to 1999. Returns do not reflect any charges or taxes which would reduce the returns.

Bonds

Beyond the security of the bank and building society deposits, lie a whole family of fixed-income assets, which are dependent on fluctuations in the national and world economies for their day to day values.

If you understand how they work, bonds can be a very useful instrument for investment purposes.

Bonds are long-term fixed-interest debt. They are issued by companies and governments - particularly governments. What happens is that companies and the government take your money now and promise to repay you sometime in the future.

Nominal value

This is the value guaranteed to be repaid to you by a Government or company at maturity. The price of a particular Bond is normally quoted in terms of £100 nominal value of the stock. For example, a price of £115.35 for the 11.75% Capital Stock 15th April 2004, means that £100 of the nominal value of the stock could be bought today for £115.35.

Maturity date

Most Bonds have a maturity date, i.e. the date at which the nominal value of the stock is guaranteed to be repaid to you by a government or company. Remember that the guaranteed payment at maturity is not the original sum you invested, but the nominal value of the stock you hold.

There is a wide choice of Bonds available - with maturity dates that may only be a few months away or as much as 20 years or more away.

Gilts

Because they've always been regarded as being extremely safe, government bonds are often called 'gilt-edged' securities, or simply 'gilts'.

However, it is important to notice that, unlike bank or building society deposits, bonds are only completely safe if you're willing to hold them until they mature. If you need to get at your money earlier you can sell your holding in the 'gilts market'. Gilts are traded in much the same way as shares and, as in the case with shares, the price fluctuates daily.

Coupon

The "coupon" is the term used to describe the rate of interest payable on a gilt. It is expressed as a % of the nominal value of stock. In the case of the 11.75% Capital Stock 15th April 2004, the coupon is 11.75%. So, that if you buy £1,000 nominal value of this stock, the annual payment guaranteed by the Government is £117.50 p.a.

Bond prices

What determines the market price of a bond? Let's suppose that the market rate of interest is 10% per year, and that it's expected to remain 10% per annum forever. If the government issues a 20 year bond with a 10% annual coupon it can sell a £100 bond now for every £100 it promises to repay in 20 years' time.

For as long as the present and expected rate of interest stays at 10%, £100 will remain the market price of the bond.

Suppose the market rate of interest decreases to 8%. What is your bond worth then? Remember, it promises to pay you £10 a year every year for the next 20 years and then to pay £100 back at the end. Your question really is: what would a new purchaser be willing to pay you for this flow of guaranteed future income now? £10 per annum is 8% of £125. So, if there was going to be no capital gain or loss on the bond, the new buyer would be prepared to pay £125. Then this investment would yield 8% each year, in line with the market rate of interest.

However, we know that the bond will be redeemed for £100 in 20 years' time. So, if the new buyer did pay £125 he would suffer a capital loss of £25 and that would detract from the total return or the redemption yield would be lower than the income yield.

In practice, the price of your bond will rise to a bit less than £125: or to approximately £119.80. At this new price, the income yield is higher than 8% per year (about 8.35%) and it will be higher by just enough to offset the capital loss that a new buyer will suffer when the bond is eventually redeemed for £100 as opposed to the £119.80 you received. The key point is that the price of the bond today adjusts so that the total return or redemption yield that the new buyer gets equates with prevailing long term interest rates.

Stock types

Gilts are generally categorised by reference to their maturity dates:

Short term gilts: The maturity date of the stock is within the next 5 years.

Medium term gilts: The maturity date of the stock is more than 5 and less than 15 years away.

Long term gilts: The maturity date of the stock is more than 15 years away.

Ex div/cum div

In general, interest payments are made on gilts at six monthly intervals.

To facilitate these payments, the Register of gilt owners is closed 31 days before a dividend is due to be paid and each registered owner on this closing date is paid the upcoming dividend.

If you buy stock before this closing date you are said to buy it "cum div" and you will be entitled to receive all of the next dividend payment when it becomes due. If you buy a stock after this closing date you are said to buy it "ex div" and you will not receive the upcoming dividend.

Tax

If you sell a government stock "cum div" however, the price you receive will reflect an interest element, which the purchaser will receive and this interest element can also be taxable in your hands, under Case III Schedule D.

Example

Mary purchases £20,000 6% Guaranteed Stocks on 7th July 2000 and she resold the stock on 28th November 2000 for £21,000. The details were as follows:

Last dividend date	01/07/00
Ex dividend date	02/12/00
Next dividend date	01/01/01

Mary held the stock for 145 days and received no interest payment. However, the following interest will be deemed to have accrued and may be taxable.

$$£20,000 \times 6.00\% \times \frac{145}{365} = £476.71$$

This amount may not be taxable if:

• The stock transfer was between Mary and her husband or,

• The stock had been held by Mary for a continuous period of two or more years.

If Mary is deemed to be trading in "gilts", the full gain will be taxed as income.

Other interest received from gilts will be taxed in the normal way under Case III Schedule D on a current year basis.

If you made a capital gain on a gilt, no tax is payable unless you are deemed to be trading in gilts.

Scope.
The simple way to invest in shares.

(All great ideas are simple ones.)

With Scope you can take advantage of a range of share investment options which are also simple to understand.

To find out more about Scope, talk to your broker, ask your Irish Life Financial Advisor, call into any Irish Permanent branch, or freephone 1850 30 60 90 for a copy of our brochure. It's the simpler way to make your money work harder. **www.escope.ie**

Shares made simple

Irish Life

UK gilts

Where the UK tax has been deducted at source, the tax will be repaid in full from the UK tax authorities on completion of the appropriate form IRL/Individual/Int. The gross interest is taxed in Ireland under Sch D Case III.

Stocks and shares

Suppose that at the end of 1919 one of your relatives had invested £1,000 on the London Stock Exchange. This portfolio would now be worth over £7,970,980*. Of course, £1,000 doesn't buy what it used to in 1919 -in real terms the purchasing power of the £1,000 then would have turned into something like £211,432 now. However, the £1,000 investment on the London Stock Exchange in 1919 would have increased your real wealth, by a factor of more than 37.7.

Although returns from the stock market have not been good over the past year, it is very good long term performances that explains why there is so much interest in stocks and shares as investments.

When you buy stocks and shares, you become a part owner of the company and entitled to a percentage of its profits by way of a dividend. Dividends are normally paid twice a year. Unlike the income from a bank or building society, share dividends are not directly related to the money you invest but, instead, are linked to the growth in the company's profits and its dividend policy. When you invest money in shares, you may be more interested in capital growth or the increase in the relevant stock market valuation.

Buying shares is a risky business and there is always the possibility of a bad investment and of losing some, or all, of your money. This risk of loss usually diminishes over time, provided you choose wisely and spread your risks.

However, if you are going to need your money next month or next year, shares are not for you and you would be better off putting your money in a more secure place. On the other hand, if you can wait for five, ten or even twenty years for your investment to "mature" and can cope with the "crashes" along the way, then shares are likely to give you a very good return.

* *Source* - NCB Stockbrokers.

If you decide to invest in shares, you may want to keep an eye on their performance by reading the financial pages of your daily newspaper. At first sight these can be puzzling but they do contain a lot of useful information. A typical section of a financial page will look like this;

High	Low	Company	Price	+ -	Div. yld.	P/E	Times cover	NTA
827	571	BOI	690xd	+ 10	6.3	21.64	1.67	457
2100	1075	CRH	1675	+ 16	4.06	12.11	2.71	1129
420	310	Jurys	405	- 4	7.41	10.84	1.66	245
1	2	3	4	5	6	7	8	9

High and low

The first column usually gives the highest price paid for that individual share in the current year and the second column gives the lowest price. The idea is to buy as close as possible to the lowest price and sell as close as possible to the highest price.

Company

The next section gives the relevant company or stock name.

Share price

The share price in column four is usually the previous day's closing price.

Ex-dividend

As we said earlier, companies usually pay dividends twice a year. About six to eight weeks before a dividend is paid, the company announce what the next dividend will be. A week or two after this announcement the company's share register is temporarily closed; upcoming dividends will be paid to the registered shareholders on this date. The company's shares will then go ex-dividend and are marked "xd" in the paper. So, if you buy shares marked xd you will not get the upcoming dividend.

Rise or fall

Column five gives the difference between the opening and closing prices of each share in the previous day's trading.

Dividend yield

The dividend yield is the ratio of the annual dividend from a share to the share price. Column six gives the gross dividend yield i.e. the dividend yield before tax.

Price earnings ratio (p/e)

Traditionally, many people related a share price to a company's net asset value. Another way of valuing a share is to relate the share price to the company's flow of profits. The price earnings ration in column seven is calculated by dividing the company's share price by the after-tax earnings due to each share over the company's most recent financial year. This ratio can also be calculated using expected rather than historical earnings. A high price-earnings ratio shows that investors have a lot of confidence in that company's future prosperity. A low P/E ratio can mean an investor is getting earnings "cheap" or can imply a lack of confidence in that company's future prosperity.

Times cover

The times cover is the ratio of last year's profits to the dividends paid. In the case of C.R.H. it is 2.71. In other words, if C.R.H. had paid out all of its profits to shareholders, the dividend would have been 2.71 times higher.

N.T.A.

Column nine gives the Net Tangible Assets (NTA) per share. This is an important indicator of a company's financial standing and is obtained by dividing the company's net assets by the number of shares. If a company's share price in the market is below its net tangible asset value, it is vulnerable to take-over as its break up value may be greater than its stock market valuation.

Investments clubs

Investments Clubs are another way to invest directly in stocks and shares, but at the same time spreading your risk and keeping your costs down. A product of the

Internet age, these clubs are growing in popularity in Ireland and involve a group of like-minded people (usually no more than 20) getting together once a month to pool their cash and their respective skills to research and buy stocks. Most clubs limit the monthly contribution to about £50 a member and wait until they have a few thousand pounds before they make a purchase. Having larger sums to play with means you can open an account with an Irish stockbroker who will charge a percentage of the deal or a minimum cash fee, depending on which is the larger. Some clubs, with access to the Internet, are opting to deal through Internet execution only brokers, based in London and/or New York.

Investment clubs tend at first, to buy well-known blue chip stocks where capital values are more stable. When they gain confidence and expertise, they often spread their interests to smaller listed or overseas companies.

The investment club concept isn't going to diminish the impact of the volatility of stock markets - but with only modest stakes at risk, it can reduce your personal liability if the market takes a downturn.

Expensive seminars and workshops are held periodically on investments and investment clubs, but a UK company called ProShare Investment Clubs, a not-for-profit organisation funded by the London Stock Exchange and private industry, has produced a manual for Stg. £25 which gives a comprehensive step-by-step formula for the successful running of such clubs. They can be reached at 0044 171 394 5200.

Tax

Buying and selling shares can give rise to two taxes:

• Income tax on dividends you receive

• Capital Gains Tax on investment gains

Irish resident companies

Dividend Income is liable to income tax under Schedule F. Prior to the 6th April 1999, when you received a dividend from an Irish resident company a tax credit would also apply. However, tax credits on dividends were abolished with effect from 6th April 1999.

Now, if you receive a dividend from an Irish Resident company after 6th April 1999, the standard rate of tax (22% in 2000/01, 20% in 2001) is deducted by the company. If the amount of tax withheld exceeds your total tax liability you can claim a refund. However, if you are a higher rate taxpayer you will have to pay the difference between the standard rate and the higher rate.

Example

John a 44% tax payer, received a dividend of £1,000 in November 2000. Dividend withholding tax of £220 (22%) was withheld by the company. John's tax liability will work out as follows:

		2000/01	
		£	€
	Irish Dividend Gross	£1,000	€1,270
	Tax @ 44%	£440	€559
Less:	Withholding Tax	£220	€279
	Additional Tax Payable	£220	€279

UK dividends

When you obtain your dividend from a UK company it will normally show:

(a)   The net dividend

      and

(b)   A tax credit which is equivalent to 1/9th of the net dividend.

For dividends received after 5th April 1999, only the net dividend received is taxable in Ireland, i.e. the cash amount received exclusive of any tax credit.

Under the existing agreement between Ireland and the UK, the dividend can be taxed in the UK at a rate not exceeding 15% of the gross dividend (net dividend and tax credit). This liability will be reduced to an amount equal to the tax credit which currently stands at 1/9 th. If you receive a UK dividend you will suffer UK tax equal to the tax credit. From 6th April 1999, you are not entitled to a refund of this tax credit.

Example

If you get a net dividend from ICI of £180, the voucher will also show a tax credit of £20 (1/9th). You will pay Irish tax as follows, assuming that your top rate of tax is 44% in 2000/01 and ignoring the rates of exchange.

	2000/01	
	£	€
UK Dividend (£180 net)	£180.00	€228.55
Irish Tax @ 44%	£79.20	€100.56

The tax credit of £ 20 deducted in the UK by ICI is not refundable.

Capital gains tax

All realised gains in excess of your annual exemption limit (£1,000) will be liable to Capital Gains Tax at 20%. See page 283.

Special Portfolio Investment Accounts (SPIA)

Obviously, if you could invest in shares and only pay 20% tax on the dividends and capital gains, your net returns would be higher. Special Portfolio Investment Accounts operated by designated stockbrokers allow you to do just this.

- You must be over age 18.

- You must be beneficially entitled to all shares.

- You must sign a declaration certifying that you are complying with all requirements.

If your lazy lump sum sits there doing nothing

move your assets.

How they work

A designated stockbroker buys the relevant shares or government securities in a nominee account on your behalf. The maximum investment in a SPIA for a single person is £75,000 (£150,000 for a married couple). These limits will, however, interact with special savings accounts and other special investment products as outlined on Page 65.

If you wish to transfer shares you already own into a SPIA account, it will be necessary to sell the shares in the normal way and reacquire them under a SPIA.

Tax

Tax is calculated at 20% on the net gain achieved within your SPIA account on the 5th April each year. The taxable net gain takes into consideration tax credits due on dividends received, administration costs paid and any capital losses incurred. Losses accumulating within a SPIA may be offset against future gains.

There is no need to include details of a SPIA investment on your tax returns, as designated stockbrokers will supply the Revenue Commissioners with all the relevant data. The cost of operating a SPIA with a designated stockbroker is approximately £250 per annum.

Property

There are three reasons why most people think property is a good investment:

- Buying property has been, for most people, the only way to borrow large amounts of money cheaply

- Rapid increases in property prices in recent times

- Tax incentives relating to property investment

Borrowing money cheaply

Suppose you buy a property for £100,000 and its price rises by 3% in real terms each year for the next 20 years. At the end of that 20 years the property will be worth £180,600 in real terms. You make a real profit of £80,600 (after accounting for inflation).

Now, suppose that instead of putting up the whole £100,000 yourself, you borrow £90,000, over 20 years, and rent the property. We also assume that the rent you will receive from the property will be sufficient to repay the loan and also pay all interest charges, expenses and tax bills associated with the property over the next 20 years. This is roughly equivalent to what has happened in the marketplace.

After 20 years, your stake in the property will have gone up from £10,000 to £180,600 and your new profit is £170,600. Now, because your original investment was low, your stake has increased by a factor of 17 in real terms (£170,600 ÷ £10,000). That's a good investment by any standards.

The ups and downs of property prices

Although property prices have steadily increased in this country over the past 30 years - these increases, as the figures below will highlight, have not always been consistent.

The following chart, illustrates how the average three bedroom semi- detached house in Dublin 6 has increased in price over the past 30 years.

Average price of 3 bed semi, Dublin 6.		
Year	£	€
1970	£5,500	€6,984
1980	£27,000	€34,283
1990	£70,000	€88,882
2000	£225,000	€285,691

Commercial property

The value of commercial property is normally directly related to the rental income it can generate. In the table on page 49, we highlight how rental income from commercial properties has been increasing at different paces over the years. This illustration outlines the average cost per square foot of commercial properties in the Dublin area over the past 30 years.

Year	Average office rental cost per sq. ft. £	Average retail rental cost per sq. ft. (shopping centres) £	Average industrial rental cost per sq. ft. £
1970	£2.50	n/a	n/a
1980	£6.00	£12.00	£1.75
1990	£12.00	£60.00	£4.50
2000	£36.00	£135.00	£8.59

So, when it comes to investing in property it's always wise not to lose sight of both the current and long-term potential return on your investment.

(The above figures relating to property were provided by Insignia Richard Ellis Gunne Research)

Property in Own Name or Company

Your home

If your home is bought through a company, Capital Gains Tax (CGT) relief on principal private residence relief will be lost and Benefit in Kind will be assessable on the annual value of the relevant benefit to you. Thus a main residence should always be purchased personally or in a trust.

• **Rental Properties**

Many who purchase rental properties have substantial incomes so the rate of tax on rental income will generally be high (42% tax plus 2% levies).

The rate of Corporation Tax on rental income is 25%. Undistributed rental income in a closed company is liable to surcharge of 20% so the effective Corporation Tax rate can be as high as 40%. After the Second Bacon Report no relief is available on interest paid on money borrowed to purchase a residential property personally or in a company.

Tax on disposal

When a property is sold the taxable proceeds will normally be subject to CGT at 20%, so, if you own the property personally you retain proceeds less 20% CGT. If the property is owned by a company it also pays CGT at 20%, however there will be further personal tax liability if you wish to gain access to the cash within the company. If you access the cash by way of salary or dividend the rate could be as high as 42%. The other option is to liquidate the company; this will give rise to a new CGT liability or what is commonly known as the double "hit".

Example

Mary set up "A" Limited ten years ago with ordinary share capital of £ 2. "A" Limited bought a property for letting for £100,000. "A" Limited sells the building now for £ 500,000. Here we assume indexation of 50% for CGT purposes and that the company has no other assets or liabilities. Mary's tax position is also illustrated if she bought the property personally.

	Personal purchase		"A" Limited	
	£	€	£	€
Sale Proceeds	£500,000	€634,869	£500,000	€634,869
Less: Cost of property plus indexation	(£150,000)	€190,461	(£150,000)	€190,461
Taxable Amount	£350,000	€444,408	£350,000	€444,408
CGT on £350,000 @ 20%	£70,000	€88,882	£70,000	€88,882
Available for distribution			£430,000	€545,987
CGT on liquidation of A Limited £430,000 @ 20%			£86,000	€109,197
Net personal proceeds	£430,000	€545,987	£344,000	€436,790
Total Tax payable	**£70,000**	**€88,882**	**£156,000**	**€198,079**

Property tax incentives

Property Tax incentives fall into two main areas:

- Capital allowances relating to Industrial buildings

- Tax incentive relating to designated areas

Qualifying Industrial Buildings

Section 268 TCA 1997 sets out the type of industrial buildings or structures, which qualify for relief. These are, a buildings or structures in use:

- For the purposes of a trade carried on in a **mill, factory or other similar premises**, or a laboratory the sole or main function of which is the analysis of minerals in connection with exploration for or extraction of such minerals.

- For the purposes of a dock undertaking.

- For the purpose of growing fruit, vegetables in the trade of market gardening.

- For the purpose of the trade of **hotel-keeping**.

- For the purpose of intensive production of cattle, sheep, pigs, poultry, or eggs in the course of a trade, other than farming.

- For the purpose of a trade which consists of the operation or management of an airport and which is an airport runway or an airport apron used solely or mainly by aircraft carrying passengers or cargo for hire or reward.

- For the purpose of a trade which consists of the operation or management of a **qualifying nursing home**.

- For the purpose of a trade which consists of the operation or management of an airport.

- For the purpose of a trade which consists of the operation or management of a qualifying **convalescent home** (such convalescent home must hold a certificate from the relevant Health Board) for the provision of medical and nursing care or persons recovering from a treatment in a hospital which provides treatment for acutely ill patients.

Type of allowances available

Initial Allowance

An initial allowance is available in the case where a person incurred capital expenditure on the construction of an industrial building or structure which is occupied for the purpose of a trade.

The initial allowance is available to both owner occupiers and lessors. These allowances were severally restricted over the years and were eliminated for capital expenditure incurred after 31st March 1992 expected in certain cases. e.g. buildings in designated areas.

Annual Allowance

An annual allowance is available generally to persons holding an interest in an industrial building or structure. The rate varies between 4% and 15% depending on the type of trade for which the industrial building or structure is being used. The annual allowance is available to both owner-occupiers and lessors of buildings.

Hotels, nursing homes, convalescent homes and **crèche facilities** will normally qualify for a 15% annual allowance on qualifying expenditure for the first six years and 10% in year seven.

Holiday Cottages registered with Bord Failte will qualify for an annual allowance calculated annually at 10% of qualifying expenditure, over a 10 year period.

Most other industrial buildings will normally qualify at an annual rate of 4% p.a. over a 25 year period.

Designated Areas

In 1986, areas were designated in each of the five cities-Cork, Dublin, Galway, Limerick and Waterford. Areas are designated by order of the Minister for the Environment and Local Government, with the consent of the Minister for Finance under the Urban Renewal Act, 1986. These urban renewal schemes were subsequently extended to include areas in many of Ireland's major towns.

1994 Urban Renewal Scheme

The 1994 scheme was more focused than its predecessor, concentrating on those areas where dereliction was most severe and providing for greater remedial works and measures to conserve existing urban infrastructure. More emphasis was placed on residential development in inner urban areas to provide a better mix of social and private housing and a greater use of vacant upper floors.

1999 Urban Renewal Scheme

Following an in-depth consultancy study on the operation of urban renewal schemes, the Government introduced a major new urban renewal scheme in 1999. Phase 1 of the new urban renewal scheme (residential incentives) commenced in March 1999. Phase 2 (commercial and industrial incentives) was introduced in July 1999. The scheme, which will benefit five cities and thirty-eight towns represents a more targeted approach to urban renewal incentives, concentrating not just on areas of physical development but also on issues of local socio-economic benefits.

Town Renewal Scheme

Town Renewal Schemes is based on a similar approach to that which applies in relation to the 1999 Urban Renewal Scheme. Designations are based on Town Renewal Plans (TRPs) which in turn were based on the principles of promoting the physical renewal and revitalisation of towns, enhancing their amenities and promoting sustainable development patterns.

Rural Renewal Relief

This relief was introduced in the 1998 Finance Act. It designated parts of Cavan, Roscommon and Sligo and the administrative county of Leitrim and Longford.

Tax summary

Below we summarise the tax incentives available to owner occupiers and investors for urban, town and rural renewal schemes.

Residential - **owner occupier**	• Construction: 5% deduction against total income for 10 years. • Refurbishment: 10% deduction against total income for 10 years
Residential - **investor**	• Section 23- type relief in respect of expenditure on the Construction, conversion or refurbishment expenditure.

Non residential - **owner occupier**	• Free depreciation - 50% • Initial allowances - 50% • Annual allowance for 12½ years - 4%
Non residential - **investor**	• Initial allowance - 50% • Annual allowance for 12½ years - 4%

Example - Residential owner occupier

John is single and bought a new home for £130,000 in a designated area: - site cost £20,000 - first time buyer's grant of £3,000.

	£		€	
Purchase Price		£130,000		€165,066
Less: Site Cost	£20,000		€25,395	
Government Grant	£3,000	£23,000	€3,809	€29,204
Qualfying Expenditure		£107,000		€135,862
Annual Allowance				
(5% of £107,000 over 10 years)		£5,350		€6,793

Note: This annual allowance will be granted at John's marginal rate of tax.

Residential - Investor
Section 23/27

Section 23/27 type relief is available on the construction, conversion and refurbishment of certain residential premises in designated areas.

The minimum floor area for a house is 35 square metres and the maximum area is 125 square metres. The minimum floor area for a flat or maisonette is 30 square metres and the maximum area is 90 square metres.

The property must be used solely as a dwelling and cannot be owner-occupied within ten years of the first letting. If, however, within the ten year period, the property ceases to be a qualifying premises e.g. is sold or owner-occupied, all the allowances already given will be clawed back.

If a qualifying property is sold within the ten year period and is then rented, the purchaser will be entitled to the same allowance as the original owner. There is no restriction on the amount of rent which may be charged. The property must be let under a Qualifying Lease. i.e.

• The lease must be a genuine rental agreement with regular payments by way of rent.

• The tenant cannot be granted an option to buy the property at less than market value.

Qualifying expenditure

If you buy a qualifying property in a designated area, the site cost together with a portion of the builder's profit is not allowed as qualifying expenditure. Qualifying expenditure is arrived at by applying the formula:

$$\frac{\text{Purchase Price x Builder's Development Cost}}{\text{Site Cost x Builder's Development Cost}}$$

Example

	£	€
Cost of Site	£20,000	€25,395
Development Costs	£80,000	€101,579
Builder's Profit	£20,000	€25,395
Purchase Price	£120,000	€152,369

Qualifying expenditure is as follows:

$$\frac{£120,000 \text{ x } £80,000}{£20,000 + £80,000} = £96,000$$

This £96,000 is available to offset against all taxable rental income as follows;

	Without section 27		With section 27	
	£	€	£	€
Taxable Rental Income	£25,000	€31,743	£25,000	€31,743
"Section 27" relief	-	-	£96,000	€121,895
Tax Payable @ 44%	£11,000	€13,967	Nil	Nil
Rental Loss to be carried forward to the following year	Nil	Nil	£71,000	€90,151

Buying a second hand "Section 27" property

If you buy a property where the qualifying expenditure has already been claimed, all relief already granted to the original owner will be clawed back and passed on to you, provided you rent a property and the property is less than 10 years old.

Example - Non residential

John bought a site in a designated area for £100,000. The qualifying building expenditure at December 2000 was £600,000. John's tax rate is 44%.

John's tax savings are as follows;

	£	€
Development Cost	£600,000	€761,843
Capital Allowances 50% in Year 1	£300,000	€380,921
Tax Saving @ 44%	£132,000	€167,605

John will also get £ 12,000 Annual Allowance for years 2 to 13 years and an annual allowance of £ 6,000 in year 14. These annual allowances will be granted at John's marginal rate of tax.

Double rent allowance for traders

A trader is entitled to a tax allowance of double the rent payable for an industrial or commercial building in a designated area if the lease has been negotiated during the qualifying period. The allowance is available for a period of 10 years. The relief does not apply unless the building is let on bona fide commercial terms to an unconnected person.

Restriction on capital allowances

From 3rd December 1997, the maximum amount of capital allowances which you can offset against your total income has been capped at £25,000 in any one year for investors. This cap does not affect owner occupiers.

Tax

Property Investment can give rise to three;

- Income Tax on the Rental Income.

- Capital Gains Tax on investment profits. See Page 283.

- Anti Speculative Property Tax.

Income tax

Rents are taxed under Schedule D Case V on the basis of the actual year's income - e.g. rents arising in the year ending 05/04/01 are assessed to tax in the income tax year 2000/01.

The following expenses can normally be deducted from the gross rents for tax purposes.

- Interest paid on money borrowed to purchase new residential property. (See page 59)

- Rent payable on the property.

- Rates payable on the property.

- Goods provided and services rendered in connection with the letting of the property.

- Repairs, insurance, maintenance and management fees.

- Capital Allowance of 15% of the value of the fixtures and fittings for the first six years and 10% in year seven can be claimed.

Be sure to keep all receipts, especially for repairs and maintenance, as your Inspector of Taxes may wish to examine these.

Interest paid for residential properties

As a result of the second Bacon Report, the government introduced changes regarding interest paid on money borrowed to purchase residential properties.

Tax relief is not available for interest on money borrowed on or after 23rd April 1998 for the purchase, repair or improvement of residential premises, unless the property is acquired before 31st March 1999 under a contract entered into before 23rd April 1998.

Also, if you rent your sole or main residence after 23rd April 1998, interest on your existing mortgage cannot be offset against rental income.

These restrictions will not apply to interest paid in connection with certain designated seaside resort areas or designated rural development areas. In the case of foreign residential properties interest restrictions apply to properties purchased after 2nd May 1998.

Interest paid prior to the first letting is not tax deductible; however, any losses incurred can be carried forward and can be offset against future rental profits.

It is a good idea to include with your tax return a rental statement similar to the one outlined on page 60, showing your gross rental income and the allowable expenses. Enter the net taxable rent on your tax return.

Budget 2001 change: "Rent a Room Scheme" - where a room or rooms in a person's private principal residence is let as residential accommodation, gross annual rent of up to £6,000 will be exempt from tax. Room rentals coming within the scope of this scheme will not trigger a clawback of any stamp duty relief nor will it effect the CGT relief on your principal private residence or mortgage interest relief.

Residential property
Rental statement

NAME: **RSI No:**_____

Y/E: _____

		Before Second Bacon Report		After Second Bacon Report	
		£	€	£	€
	Rents Received	£9,000	€11,428	£9,000	€11,428
Less:	Allowable Expenses				
	Rates/Ground Rents Payable	£100	€127	£100	€127
	Insurance on premises	£300	€381	£300	€381
	Repairs and Renewals	£750	€952	£750	€952
	Light, Heat and Telephone	£300	€381	£300	€381
	Cleaning and Maintenance	£1,000	€1,270	£1,000	€1,270
	Agency and Advertising Charges	£550	€698	£550	€698
	*Interest on Borrowed Money	£4,900	€6,222	-	-
	Sundry Expenses	£250	€317	£250	€317
	Total Expenses	£8,150	€10,348	£3,250	€4,127
	Net Rental Income	£850	€1,079	£5,750	€7,301
Less:	Capital Allowances on Fixtures & Fittings £7,000 @ 15%	(£1,050)	(€1,333)	(£1,050)	(€1,333)
	Taxable Rental (Loss) Income / After Capital Allowances	(£200)	(€254)	£4,700	€5,968
	Tax - assuming a 44% rate of tax.	Nil	Nil	£2,068	€2,626

* *Note:* Interest relief will be allowed on money borrowed to buy residential property before 23rd April 1998 or if a contract was entered into before 23rd April 1998 and the property was acquired before 31st March 1999.

Anti-Speculative Property Tax

Anti speculative property tax was introduced after the publication of the third Bacon Report. It applies to residential property in Ireland which is acquired on or after 15th June 2000 and which is not your principal private residence.

An exemption from this tax also applies where:

- the property was acquired by the current owner as an inheritance,

- the property was acquired as a gift so long as the donor owned the property prior to 15th June 2000,

- the property is let and the landlord has complied with the registration, rent books and standards regulations provided for under the Housing (miscellaneous provisions) Act, 1992,

- the property is held by a charity,

- the property is comprising of the trading stock of a trade.

- the property is:

    - a building which is intrinsically of significant scientific, historical, architectural or aesthetic value and to which reasonable access is afforded to the public or which is in use as a tourist accommodation facility.

    - 'section 23' type properties under various tax incentive schemes. The properties in question are rented residential properties, the expenditure on the construction, conversion or refurbishment of which qualify for a deduction against rental income.

- Bord Failte registered holiday cottages throughout the country together with Bord Failte registered apartments and other listed self-catering accommodation throughout the country (e.g. listed holiday cottages and listed apartments)

Anti-speculative property tax is a self assessment tax which will last for 3 years.

The first year is due to be paid on 1st November 2001 in respect of property owned on 6th April 2001.

The tax due for each of these three years is 2% of the market value of all non-exempt residential property owned by the person on the 6th of April in that year but where the property was acquired and fully paid for before 6th April 2001, the price paid is taken as the market value of the property on that date.

Managed funds

As the name implies "Managed Funds" are where investors pool their resources to create a common investment fund which is controlled by professional managers. The two main benefits of this collective approach are that it allows for more efficient and economical investment management, plus it provides greater security to investors, as the risk is spread over a diverse range of investments. Managed Funds are normally marketed under a number of headings:

- Life Assurance Products

- Pips and Peps

- Investment Bonds / Unit Linked Funds

- Tracker Bonds

- Offshore Investment Funds

- UCITS

Life assurance products

Many people invest in life assurance policies, which can either be unit-linked or with-profits plans. The first involves the purchase of units of value in a range of assets, such as stocks and shares, government stocks (i.e. 'gilts'), property and cash. These assets are then managed by the company's fund managers. The units you buy have a daily value, which can go up or down as market demand for the assets rises or falls.

With-profit investment plans also invest the policy holder's money in various assets. However, instead of your money being subject to the daily movement of the investment markets, the company sets out a minimum guaranteed value for your policy and then, as profits are earned, an annual bonus is declared and added to your policy. Once declared, these bonuses cannot be taken away. The aim is to pay a bonus that relates to market growth but one that can also be sustained if the market falls. Some companies pay a higher proportion of performance growth in the form of a final bonus than others. This can penalise policyholders who encash their policies early and reward those who stay the course of the contract.

The smoothing-out effect of the bonus system protects the customer's with-profit fund from the volatility that is part and parcel of the marketplace. But ultimately, with-profits policies cannot buck the market: the values that are paid out will reflect the overall performance of the stocks and shares, property, gilts and cash investments that underpin them.

Tax

The returns from unit-linked and with-profits funds are paid tax-free. All tax which is due on profits earned will have already been deducted and paid by the fund managers to the Revenue Commissioners.

The current position is that the income and gains accruing to policy holders are taxed within the fund on an annual basis at the standard rate of income tax and the policy holder is not liable to any further tax on maturity or encashment of a policy.

For new policies issued after the 1st January 2001 no annual tax will be imposed on policy holders funds, however the life assurance company will have to deduct tax on the investment income within the policy at the standard rate of income tax plus three percentage points on encashment on maturity. This tax will be a final liability tax, for Irish residents. No tax will be deducted from payments to a person who is neither resident nor ordinarily resident here provided they have complied with the declaration requirements.

PIPS & PEPS

Up until recently, life assurance investment funds to which contributions were made on a regular basis (i.e. monthly or annually) carried high initial charges. Because of this, many of these funds did not break even for 7-10 years after you commenced the plan and many policyholders were bitterly disappointed by the poor value they received.

The new generation of unit-linked managed-funds have, for the most part, resolved this problem. Low-cost, unit-linked PIPS and PEPS have been specifically designed to meet reasonable investment expectations within a 10 year savings frame, though neither capital nor profits are guaranteed.

Most PIPS (Personal Investment Plans) require a minimum monthly contribution of between £50-£80 and profits are taxed at the standard rate within the fund. PEPs, (Personal Equity Plans) are a special type of Investment Policy in which the fund manager now pays tax also at 20%. Investors in PEPs must meet requirements similar to those for investors with Special Savings Accounts (SSAs):

- The investor must be over 18 or married and the policy must be issued only to the individual who is beneficially entitled to all amounts under the policy.

- Except in the case of a married couple, the policy may not be a joint life policy.

- The investor must sign a Declaration certifying that he or she is complying with all the requirements.

- The investor can have only one special investment product - either a Special Investment Policy or a Special Portfolio Investment Account with a designated stockbroker (see page 45).

There is an overall investment limit of £75,000 (£150,000 for a married couple). However, this maximum also interacts with SSAs. The following summarises those limits for a single person:

Special investment products			Special saving accounts	
£	€		£	€
£25,000	€31,743	and / or	£50,000	€63,487
£50,000	€63,487	and / or	£25,000	€31,743
£75,000	€95,230	and / or	Nil	€Nil
These limits are doubled for a married couple				

Investment bonds

Aimed at the lump sum investor, bonds come in different guises, such as

• Unit-linked and with-profit bonds

• Tracker bonds

• Special Investment bonds

Life assurance bonds are among the most widely sold and have provided good value for money invested over the past number of years. Nearly all require a minimum investment of £5,000 and at least a five year investment time frame. Ideally, these should be regarded as medium to long-term investments to allow a good maturity value to build-up. Entry costs are usually between 3%-5% and annual management charges are usually 0.75%.

Tracker bonds

Tracker bonds are a relatively safe way of participating in international stock markets, such as the FTSE-100, the DOW and Japanese Nikkei, without many of the associated risks. A popular investment option since the early 1990's, most tracker bonds last from three to six years and require minimum investments of £3,000 to £5,000.

Tracker bond fund managers are not buying actual stocks and shares, just the options on the performance of shares represented by a particular stock market index. In order to guarantee the safety of the investor's capital - a strong selling point for tracker bonds - a large portion of your investment must be put on deposit.

Up until recently, many tracker funds guaranteed the return of virtually the entire capital so long as the investors left their money untouched. With interest rates so low, the cost of this guarantee has risen, and recent tracker bonds are not achieving the same kind of returns that were enjoyed by people in the early nineties.

Offshore investment funds

Irish investment managers are as competent, professional and lucky (or unlucky) as their counterparts in the UK, America or Japan. Some concentrate solely on the Irish market; others buy and sell equities and other assets in far flung parts of the world. Certainly all the larger investment companies here offer a selection of domestic and international equity funds (such as UK, American, Japanese, European, Developing Economies and Sectoral Funds) to their clients as well as fixed asset funds such as government gilts or currency funds.

One of the perceived advantages of buying an investment from a larger player is that it will usually have considerably greater access to research and analytical resources, often directly on the ground in the country where the investments are directed. This insider knowledge has produced consistently good results for many of the big international players familiar to Irish investors, such as Fidelity, Gartmore, HKSB, Invesco and others.

UCITS

'Undertakings for Collective Investments in Transferable Securities' are very popular and tax efficient with investment mainly in equity funds. UCITs are highly regulated by EU authorities, the unit prices are highly transparent as are charges. The tax treatment of UCITs means that there can be a greater overall potential for growth.

Tax

Where an Irish resident receives the proceeds of foreign investment products on or after 1st January next, the same tax rate will apply to such proceeds as will apply where an Irish resident invests in an Irish life assurance company or Irish investment fund, provided certain conditions are met. In the case of existing foreign products, the investor must declare the investment to Revenue and pay the tax due on the proceeds under the self-assessment income tax rules. In the case of new foreign products, the investor and, where it applies, the intermediary must inform Revenue - when making the investment and on receipt of the investment proceeds. The tax will be paid under the self-assessment income tax rules. If these conditions are not met, the investor will be liable for tax under the current rules i.e. 40% CGT or in the case of certain offshore funds, the investor's marginal income tax rate.

5

Borrowing wisely

"Neither a borrower nor a lender be" may be sound advice, but few of us can afford to be so virtuous. Yet borrowing money can be a perilous activity since there are so many things that can go wrong when it comes to repaying the loan - illness, unemployment, other unexpected events, even happy ones like having a baby and having to interrupt a career.

Before you take out a loan, whether a term loan from the bank, a mortgage or even a credit card limit, you need to consider the following:

- The amount.

- The type of loan.

- The interest charge.

- The duration of the loan.

- Your ability to pay, even if interest rates rise.

- Your personal circumstances.

- Borrowing outlets.

Loans

Banks, building societies, credit unions, finance houses and moneylenders are all willing to lend you money, if you meet their criteria which is usually based on your age, income and credit record.

Borrowing money for a long term purpose, such as a mortgage or to finance a business is very different from borrowing to buy a car, household goods or even a holiday. For one thing, the interest rate you pay and the repayment period are going to be very different. It is best from the start to try and match the loan with the right lender.

If you want to borrow money for a home, go to a building society or bank. If you want an overdraft that you dip in and out of you must stick with the bank or building society from which you have your current account. The lending pool for personal loans widens to include finance houses, credit unions and even life assurance companies if you happen to hold a valuable with-profits policy. But moneylenders, who are the keenest of all to lend , should be avoided by all but the most desperate because of the crippling interest rates they can charge.

The cheapest interest rates are provided by mortgage lenders, who are counting on you borrowing for many years; the most expensive interest rates are charged by credit card providers and moneylenders whose lines of credit are designed to be paid off - ideally in a short amount of time. Credit card "loans" are ideal for people who can pay off the amount borrowed each month since they will incur no interest at all.

An upward change in interest rates will not normally change the amount most personal borrowers pay back each month, even if the rate is a variable one, but any adjustments that have worked against you over the period will have to be settled up at the end - usually with a final balance payment(s).

Variable rate mortgages don't work this way. Any rate hike or fall is usually applied to the homeowners next repayment. If rates go up by a half per cent, you will have to pay more each month until they go down again. Fixing your personal loan or mortgage interest rate is one way to avoid this kind of volatility, but it is difficult to predict interest rate movements: if you fix your rate and interest rates fall, you must continue to pay the fixed rate for the agreed term or incur penalties to break the contract. Many term loan borrowers are keen to stretch their repayments over a number of years because the monthly repayment is smaller. But they forget that ultimately they will pay more for the loan.

Example

If you borrow £5,000 for three years and the interest rate is 10%, you will pay back nearly £161 a month or a total of £5,790. If you borrow the same amount for five years, however, the repayments drop to £106 a month, but you will have paid back £6,360. The effect is more dramatic with a mortgage. Borrow £50,000 at

5% over 20 years and the monthly repayment will be £380 per month. The total repayment is £78,080. Extend the loan by five years and your monthly repayment drops to £292 a month but total repayments rise to £87,600, a difference of over £8,500 in just five years, money that you could put to a better use.

Bank and Building Society Loans come in all shapes and sizes.

Term loans

Before you take out a term loan with a bank or building society you need to determine the real cost of the loan, the Average Percentage Rate (APR) and the total repayments. The APR is the true interest rate and is calculated based on the duration of the loan and any fees that may fall due. The APR is inevitably higher than the published flat rate. Along with the APR rate you should also ask for the cost per thousand per month which will tell you how much every £1,000 borrowed will cost. You then multiply this amount by however many thousands of pounds you borrow and by the number of months over which you are repaying the loan. This is your total repayments.

Overdrafts

Arranged on your current account, overdrafts are a cheap and simple way to arrange extra credit as you need it. Interest rates are usually the same as the personal lending rate and payable only as you use the facility. If you overspend your overdraft limit, without permission, the bank is entitled to charge extra interest and a "referral charge". This charge range from £3.50 to £5.00 per offending transaction.

Revolving credit

Also known as a budget account, this is a type of overdraft which smoothes out the annual cost of running your current account by allowing you to borrow a multiple of your monthly pay cheque (paid directly into the account) to cover large once-off outgoings like school fees in September, Christmas spending in December or the cost of a summer holiday in July. Interest is charged only as you draw down the facility.

Credit Unions

Credit Unions do not seek collateral before lending money - your record as a regular saver and whether you are employed or not, is how they judge your ability to repay. The loan amount is usually a multiple of the value of shares you hold. Credit unions tend to show more flexibility about repayment schedules than conventional lenders and calculate the interest on the diminishing balance basis. Credit unions are set up on a geographical location basis - whether by neighbourhood, village, town, place of work or affinity group. They are self-help organisations managed and run for the benefit of all their members in the 32 counties.

Life assurance

Life assurance companies may seem like an unusual place from which to borrow money, but there is provision for lending up to 80% of the cash value of a with-profits policy. Interest rates are usually quite competitive and borrowing against the fund value is nearly always better than encashing the policy. Investment policies like this should always be allowed to run their course - since a significant part of the total value of the policy may be paid in the form of a final bonus which only comes into effect on the maturity of the policy.

Life assurance policies are frequently used as security against conventional loans - if you renege on your debt the bank will simply cash in the policy. Pension plans, because of their tax and legal status, cannot be used as security for loans.

Credit and charge cards

These are among the most expensive but convenient forms of borrowing. Designed for short-term purchases, the APR can be as high as 22% for those card holders who don't clear their monthly balances in full. Disciplined cardholders can take full advantage of the 50 plus days of free credit available, but those who don't can run up large balances very quickly. The most popular credit cards are VISA and Mastercard which now come in different guises - such as Affinity cards for professional groups who can benefit from a slightly lower interest rate and a donation to their college or charity or in the form of a loyalty card with which you can build up cash discounts with a series of retailers. With charges, conditions and interest rates varying so much, it is a good idea to shop around for the best rate and conditions.

If you have a sufficiently high income you may be entitled to a prestigious Gold Card from your credit or charge card company. Gold card membership entitles you to a higher spending limit, unsecured overdrafts, increased cash withdrawal facilities and a better range of insurance benefits. These can include holiday insurance and 90 day purchase insurance, which protects items you purchased with your card from theft, loss or damage.

Charge/Store cards

These include the likes of American Express and Diners Club as well as popular store cards like Arnotts, Clery's, Debenhams or Marks and Spencer. Charge cards involve an annual membership and require you to clear your balance monthly or within a set time frame or face hefty interest penalties. Unlike store cards, however, American Express and Diners do not have spending limits. The store cards are handy and convenient but interest rates are very high (sometimes higher than ordinary credit cards) if you do not clear your balance monthly.

Credit Card Charges

Financial institution	Card type	Interest rate payable ✔ %	Annual charge + £	Minimum fee on cash withdrawals £	* Interest charged from
ACC Bank	Visa	18.57%	Nil	£2.00	Statement Date
AIB	Gold	15.9%	Nil	£1.50	Transaction Date
	Standard	18.9%	Nil	£1.50	Transaction Date
Bank of Ireland	Mastercard/ Visa	18.8%	Nil	£2.00	Transaction Date
EBS	Visa	18.9%	Nil	Nil	Transaction Date
Irish Nationwide	Visa	20.9%	Nil	£1.50	Transaction Date
National Irish Bank	MasterCard /Visa	18.2%	Nil	Nil	Transaction Date
TSB Bank	Visa	18.9%	Nil	Nil	Statement Date
Ulster Bank	MasterCard /Visa	17.9%	Nil	£2.00	Transaction Date
MBNA	Standard	18.9%	Nil	£1.50	Transaction Date
	Gold	17.9%	Nil	£1.50	Transaction Date

*   If the full amount is not paid by due date
+   Excluding Government Tax   ✔ As at December 2000

Savings
that really
add up.

EBS have a range of savings and investment options to suit every need and every amount of money.

For more information about EBS savings and investments, drop into your local branch or call **<<EBS *DIRECT*>> 1850 654 321**

EBS
BUILDING SOCIETY
You're better off in the long run.
www.ebs.ie

6

Home buyer's options

For most people, buying a home is their single biggest investment and it can be an anxious time, especially if the property market is experiencing a boom, as it has done in Ireland in the last few years. To buy a home, you need some capital, usually at least 10% of the purchase price. Banks and building societies are prepared to lend up to 90% mortgages, but better interest rates are available to buyers who have more than 20% of the purchase price.

Start saving

If an average new home costs £150,000, you will need a minimum of £15,000 as starting capital. Many savers choose a good interest-yielding account in the Post Office, bank or building society to start the process, though you do not need to be saving with any particular institution in order to secure a mortgage from them at a later date.

The DIRT rate is 20% on a Special Savings Account, but no health levies (2%) are payable so it may help accelerate your savings fund, however you will have to fulfil certain SSA conditions when you open such an account. (See also page 28).

Choosing a lender

Once you have the appropriate minimum capital and have found the home of your choice, you need to start shopping around for the best mortgage. The property supplements of the major newspapers publish updated mortgage interest rates from all the leading lenders. These lists also include a column which shows the cost per thousand pounds borrowed so that you can quickly calculate the monthly repayment of the mortgage you have in mind.

Income conditions

All lenders require certain income conditions before they will give you a mortgage. A rule of thumb is that the loan must not exceed three times your income, and if you are joint applicants, two and a half times the higher income plus 100% of the lower income. A self-employed person will usually need to provide proof of average taxable earnings over the past three years. A couple earning £30,000 and £15,000 respectively can expect to borrow up to £90,000 in total.

Budget 2001 change: "Rent a Room Scheme" - where a room or rooms in a person's private principal residence is let as residential accommodation, gross annual rent of up to £6,000 will be exempt from tax.

First time buyers grant

A grant of £3,000 may be claimed for a new home if you meet the following conditions:

- Your new home is built in accordance with good building practice.
- Your home is built by a contractor registered for VAT who holds a current Form C2 or tax clearance certificate from the Revenue Commissioners. In the case of a home built on your own site ("selfbuilt"), VAT registered work of not less than £15,000 must be undertaken by a registered contractor(s).
- The floor area of the house must not exceed 125 square metres and must be not less than 38 square metres.
- You or your spouse, either individually or jointly, must not previously have purchased or built another property for your own occupation.
- You must occupy the property as your normal place of residence.

How to claim
Apply for provisional grant approval when you place a deposit on your new home and when you move in, complete the back of this provisional grant approval and forward it to the Department of the Environment for payment. Payment will be made directly to you unless you assign it to the builder.

Home purchase related costs

There are other costs which may be related with home purchase: application or arrangement fees, legal and valuation fees, administration fees, indemnity bonds and stamp duty as well as the cost of furnishing your new home.

Stamp duty

Newly built homes are still exempt from stamp duty so long as the home is under 125 square metres (or 1,346 sq. ft.) in size and you occupy the property as your place of residence for the 5 years after the date of purchase.

Budget 2001 change: From 6th December 2000, a site transferred from a parent to a child, for the purpose of the construction of the child's principal private residence, is exempt from stamp duty (limited to one site with a value of £200,000 per child).

From 15th June 2000 the rates of stamp duty for a first time buyer are as follows;

Purchase price £	Stamp duty first time buyers %
Up to £150,000	Nil
Over £150,000 up to £200,000	3%
£200,000 up to £250,000	3.75%
£250,000 up to £300,000	4.5%
£300,000 up to £500,000	7.5%
Over £500,000	9%

A first time buyer is a person, (or where there is more than one buyer each of such persons):

• Who has not on any previous occasion, either individually or jointly, purchased or built on their own behalf a house or apartment, in Ireland or abroad;

• Where the property purchased is occupied by the purchaser, or a person on his behalf, as his/her only or principal place of residence;

• And where no rent is derived from the property for five years after completion of the current purchase.

From 15th June 2000 the stamp duty rates for an Owner Occupier who is not a first time buyer are as follows;

Purchase price £	Stamp duty owner occupiers non first time buyers %
Up to £100,000	Nil
Over £100,001 up to £150,000	3%
£150,001 up to £200,000	4%
£200,001 up to £250,000	5%
£250,001 up to £300,000	6%
£300,001 up to £ 500,000	7.5%
Over £500,000	9%

An Owner Occupier is a person who purchases a property which is to be occupied by the purchaser, or a person on their behalf, as their only or principal place of residence and no rent is derived from the property.

The rate for investors is 9% regardless of the consideration paid for the property.

Legal fees

The Law Society recommends to its members that they charge 1.5% of the purchase price, plus £100.00, plus 21% VAT. On a £150,000 home purchase, the total legal fee could amount to £2,843.50.

Lenders vary considerably in the way they apply charges and you need to shop around to find the most competitive deal. Some, for example, insist on charging you their legal costs, calculated as a percentage of the loan up to a maximum amount. It could amount to as much as £200 - £300. If a lender's fees seem low in comparison to another, take a good look at the interest rates being charged, both in the first year when a discount of half to one percent may usually apply and over the longer term, when you will revert to the normal variable interest rate.

Mortgage indemnity bond

If you borrow more than 70% - 75% of the value of your home, you may also have to buy a Mortgage Indemnity Bond from the bank or building society. These bonds guarantee the total repayment of your loan in the event of your home being sold for less than the outstanding loan amount. Indemnity bonds usually cost

3.5% of your borrowings above the specified limit and, while the cost can be absorbed into your 20 or 25 year mortgage term, it is more cost efficient over the longer term to pay it at the outset.

The following is a typical list of charges your could pay when buying a £180,000 home with a mortgage of £162,000. (Assuming you are a first time buyer).

	£	€
Stamp Duty	£5,400	€6,857
Search Fees	£150	€191
Survey Fees	£150	€191
Legal Fees	£3,388	€4,302
Mortgage Indemnity Bond	£945	€1,200
Total Charge	£10,033	€12,741

Relocation costs - relating to employment.

Strictly, the cost of relocating your home is a personal expense, however, if it is a requirement of your job to move home and certain procedures are followed, your employer may compensate you for these costs in a tax free manner.

The types of expenses covered are:

• Auctioneer's fees, solicitor's fees and stamp duty arising from moving home.

• Furniture removal costs.

• Storage charges.

• Insurance of furniture and items in transit.

• Cleaning stored furniture.

• Travelling expenses on removal.

• Temporary subsistence allowance while looking for new accommodation.

Formal Requirements

- Prior approval must be obtained from the tax office before the payment is made.

- The cost must be borne directly by the employer in respect of actual expenses incurred by you.

- The expenses must be reasonable.

- The payments must be properly controlled.

Receipts must be provided (apart from temporary subsistence), and your Inspector of Taxes must be satisfied that moving home is necessary for your job.

Mortgage interest relief

Tax relief on mortgage interest paid is now available at the standard rate of tax only (20% in 2001).

From 6th April 2001 first time mortgage holders , for the first five years can claim 100% tax relief on the interest paid within the following limits ;

£5,000 for a married couple, who are jointly assessed for tax
£5,000 for a widow(er)
£2,500 for a single person

Non first time buyers can claim 100% tax relief on interest paid within the following limits;

£4,000 for a married couple who are jointly assessed or a widowed person.
£2,000 for a single person.

Example

John and Mary, 42% taxpayers, will pay mortgage interest of £6,500 in the 2001 tax year. Mortgage interest relief will be granted as follows:

A.   Assumes that John and Mary have claimed mortgage interest relief for the first time less than five years ago.

B.   Assumes that John and Mary have claimed mortgage interest relief for the first time more than five years ago.

	2001			
	Less than 5 years mortgage holders		**More than 5 years mortgage holders**	
	£	**€**	**£**	**€**
Mortgage Interest paid	£6,500	€8,253	£6,500	€8,253
Maximum interest allowed for tax purposes	£5,000	€6,349	£4,000	€5,079
Tax relief @ 20%	£1,000	€1,270	£800	€1,016

Bridging loan interest

Additional tax relief is allowed for interest on "bridging" loans obtained to finance the disposal of your main residence and the acquisition of another residence. This relief is confined to a period of 12 months from the date the loan is obtained. It is subject to the same restrictions as mortgage interest. However, both reliefs may be claimed at the same time.

Example

In 2001 John and Mary pay mortgage interest of £4,400 on their new home which they bought on 1st April 2001. The sale of their old home is due for completion in October 2001 and the interest payable on the second loan will amount to £2,000. Their tax allowance for 2001 will work out as follows:

Mortgage interest will be restricted to £4,000 on the new home.

As the bridging loan was for a period of 6 months, the maximum amount of bridging loan interest will be restricted on a time basis to £1,000 (£2,000 x 6/12 = £1,000).

	Interest paid		Interest allowable	
	£	**€**	**£**	**€**
Mortgage Interest	£4,400	€5,587	£4,000	€5,587
Bridging Loan Interest	£2,000	€2,539	£1,000	€1,270
	£6,400	€8,126	£5,000	€6,349

Interest rates and the cost of borrowing

The cost of borrowing for a mortgage has been steadily coming down in recent years, but interest rates are cyclical and are likely to vary by a few percentage points either way over the 20 or 25 years. The important thing now is to take account of as many unforeseen circumstances as possible.

Although many couples are both earning incomes, an unexpected event, like illness, redundancy or even the arrival of a new baby, can put considerable strain on a family budget. A typical £130,000 mortgage being repaid at 5% interest will result in monthly repayments of £856.50.

A 1% rise in interest rates to 6% will increase the payment to £930.51 a month, or another £888.12 a year.

Choose lender carefully

Choosing a lender that offers the best, long-term interest rates is very important. By carefully shopping around, you may be able to save yourself a considerable sum of money over the term of your loan. No lender will guarantee that their rate will always be the most competitive, but certain lenders have better track records than others for offering consistently lower rates and charges. Check them out.

Below we illustrate the typical monthly repayments on £100,000 loan, assuming annual interest rates of 5%, 6%, 7% and 8% p.a. over 20 and 25 years.

Annual interest rate	Monthly repayments over 20 years		Monthly repayments over 25 years	
	£	€	£	€
5%	£659	€837	£584	€742
6%	£716	€909	£644	€818
7%	£775	€984	£706	€896
8%	£836	€1,062	£771	€979

The longer your mortgage term, the cheaper the monthly repayment will be. But when the total cost of repayments are added up, an extra five or ten years will cost you several thousands pounds extra.

Example

Whereas a £130,000 loan arranged over 20 years at 5% interest will cost £856.50 per month, the same loan stretched out five years will cost £759.20 a month, a "saving" of £97.30. The extra five year lending term, however, will amount to an extra £22,200 in mortgage payments overall.

Anyone who arranges a 25 or 30 year mortgage would be advised to accelerate their payments after a few years, when their income has increased and the high, early costs associated with home ownership have diminished.

Designated areas

If you buy, build or restore a dwelling in a designated area, you are entitled to offset against part of the development cost against your income. An annual deduction of 5% in the case of construction expenditure and 10% in the case of refurbishment expenditure may be claimed each year for 10 years. To claim this relief, you must be the first owner-occupier of the dwelling after its construction or refurbishment. You will not be entitled to this relief for any year in which the dwelling is not your sole or main residence.

Example

John is single and bought a new home for £130,000 in a designated area; - site cost £20,000 - first time buyer's grant of £3,000, - mortgage was £105,000 - income was £35,000 p.a.

	£		€	
Purchase Price		£130,000		€165,066
Less: Site Cost	£20,000		€25,395	
Government Grant	£3,000	£23,000	€3,809	€29,204
Qualifying Expenditure		£107,000		€135,862
Annual Relief				
(5% of £107,000 over 10 years)		£5,350		€6,793

Note: This annual relief will be granted at John's marginal rate of tax.

Mortgage repayment methods

Annuity mortgage

The annuity method is the most common way to pay off a mortgage, you may also know it as a repayment mortgage. Annuity mortgages involve the payment each month of interest and some of the principal of the loan. In the early years, the bulk of the payment is interest, which will be the subject of mortgage interest tax relief.

As the years progress, you will pay less interest and more capital until eventually your entire loan will be cleared. A typical repayment mortgage will be repaid as illustrated on Page 84, over a 20 year term.

In the tax year 2001 a first-time buyer will benefit from tax relief to the tune of £985 in the first year on a £100,000 mortgage (20% of £4,925), while other mortgage holders will benefit by £800 (20% of £4,000). This tax benefit will decrease each subsequent year as the amount of mortgage interest payable decreases.

Endowment mortgage

The other way a mortgage can be arranged is by the endowment method, which combines the home loan and a life assurance policy. Under this method the borrower pays the lender interest only for the entire term, while at the same time paying monthly premiums into a life assurance investment policy. (Since it is also a life assurance policy, you will not have to take out a separate mortgage protection policy.) If all goes well with investment markets, there will be sufficient growth to create an investment fund to pay off the original capital sum at the end of the 20 year term.

Unlike conventional annuity mortgages with which you repay both interest and capital each month, an endowment mortgage involves only the repayment of interest and this interest can qualify for full mortgage interest relief for the full duration of the loan. This was a major selling point of endowment mortgages in the early 1990s', but is of little merit now as mortgage interest relief has been clawed back significantly in recent years.

Repaying a £100,000 annuity mortgage

End of year	Annual repayments	Capital repaid	Loan outstanding at end of year	Interest paid	Interest * allowance for tax relief	
					First time home buyers	Other home buyers
£	£	£	£	£	£	£
1	7,908	2,983	97,017	4,925	4,925	4,000
2	7,908	3,136	93,881	4,772	4,772	4,000
3	7,908	3,296	90,585	4,612	4,612	4,000
4	7,908	3,464	87,121	4,444	4,444	4,000
5	7,908	3,642	83,479	4,266	4,266	4,000
6	7,908	3,828	79,651	4,080	4,000	4,000
7	7,908	4,025	75,626	3,883	3,883	3,883
8	7,908	4,230	71,396	3,678	3,678	3,678
9	7,908	4,446	66,950	3,461	3,461	3,461
10	7,908	4,674	62,276	3,234	3,234	3,234
11	7,908	4,913	57,363	2,995	2,995	2,995
12	7,908	5,164	52,199	2,744	2,744	2,744
13	7,908	5,429	46,770	2,479	2,479	2,479
14	7,908	5,706	41,064	2,202	2,202	2,202
15	7,908	5,998	35,066	1,910	1,902	1,902
16	7,908	6,305	28,701	1,603	1,603	1,603
17	7,908	6,628	22,133	1,280	1,280	1,280
18	7,908	6,967	15,166	941	941	941
19	7,908	7,323	7,843	585	585	585
20	7,908	7,843	0	65	65	65
Total	158,160	100,000		58,160	58,071	55,052

Assumptions:

- Interest Rate 5%

- Gross Repayments £659 p.m. or £7,908 p.a.

- Mortgage Interest relief is for a married couple in 2001

Pension mortgage

A pension mortgage is similar to an endowment one, in that only interest is paid on the loan during the term of the contract. In this case, the investment vehicle which is used to pay off the capital is the homeowner's personal pension plan. Under Revenue rules, a quarter of the final pension fund value can be paid out as a tax-free lump sum, and it is this sum which is used to repay the mortgage capital.

Pension mortgages, which attract mortgage interest relief on the loan and standard pension contribution relief, can be a very tax-efficient way to pay off a home loan. But they are only suitable for higher net worth, self-employed individuals with increasing incomes and the ability to repay the loan from other sources if the pension fund value is insufficient or unavailable to pay off the loan.

Variable or fixed rate?

Should you arrange your mortgage on a variable interest rate basis, or fix the interest for a period of years?

Nearly all new borrowers are offered a discounted fixed rate for the first year of their loan, which usually amounts to a saving of a couple of hundred pounds. In year two, you immediately revert to the variable rate of interest, which can go up and down over the term of the mortgage.

A fixed interest rate can provide considerable peace of mind and protect the borrower from the volatility of world money markets, but you can also suffer financially - as many people did after the 1992 currency crisis - if rates fall and yours is set at a higher level for a few more years. The cost of breaking a fixed rate mortgage can be very high: some banks charge nearly the entire interest balance that they could have expected to earn if you had seen out the contract.

If you do fix your interest rate make sure all terms and penalties are put in writing by the lender. Make sure they include a few "what if" scenarios - how much it would cost you if you break the contract with a year or two to go, for example.

Mortgage and home insurance

The monthly mortgage repayment is not the only one you will have to make: mortgage protection and buildings insurance are now compulsory in most cases and can cost up to 10% of your gross monthly mortgage repayments.

Mortgage protection insurance is a life assurance policy that covers the value of the mortgage and ensures that your debt to the bank or building society is paid off in the event of your death or that of your spouse. Rates are based on age and sex and the premiums can be paid monthly or annually. You are not obliged to purchase the policy from the lender and you should shop around for the best market rate, especially if you are a smoker.

An increasing number of new home owners are arranging serious illness cover as part of their mortgage protection policy in order that the loan can be paid off not only if they die but also in the event of a life-threatening illness. The cost is higher, but can be mitigated by arranging the policy on a decreasing term basis.

Example

John and Mary have a mortgage of £70,000 over 20 years. They are both age 29 and non-smokers. The monthly cost of a Conventional Mortgage Protection Plan and a Mortgage Protection Plan, which included Serious Illness Cover for John and Mary, will work out approximately as follows:

Plan type	Monthly cost	
	£	€
Conventional Mortgage Protection Plan	£10.00	€12.70
Mortgage Protection Plan plus Serious Illness Cover	£21.33	€27.08

Protect your mortgage repayments

If you are concerned about how your mortgage would be paid if you became ill or if you were made redundant, even for a short period of time, you may want to take out Mortgage Payment Protection cover. Available from all the major lenders, this insurance costs about £4.50 for every £100 cover required per month and pays out benefits if you become ill or disabled and are unable to work, or have been made redundant. You need to have been out of work for about 30 days before your first claim can be made and there is generally a 12 month payment limit per claim. Payment protection insurance like this is not cheap, and if you already have Permanent Health Insurance or serious illness cover, it may be unnecessary.

Protect the building

Building insurance is also compulsory if you take out a mortgage. Again, the lender wants to protect their share of the property in the event of a fire or other disaster. The premiums are based, not on the market value of the property, but on the cost of rebuilding. It is important that you have the property surveyed to ensure the rebuilding cost is correct and any increase in the cost of materials and labour are taken into account.

Most general insurance companies offer combined buildings and contents policies; some automatically provide contents cover worth up to half the value of the building cover. Engage an independent financial advisor to help you find the right policy for you and to help you make sure you have put a correct value on your fittings and personal belongings. Premium discounts may be available, which will depend on your age, whether the house is occupied during the daytime and if it is fitted with approved locks, fire and burglar alarms etc.

Local authority loans

Local authority loans are available to those on a single income who earned no more than £25,000 in the previous tax year. In the case of a two income household, two and a half times the principal income and once the second income must be less than £62,500. The maximum borrowing limit is £100,000 and the variable interest rate charged is approximately 6.42% but this includes mortgage protection cover.

Shared Ownership Schemes are also operated by local authorities and for many they offer the first step in purchasing a home of their choice. You need to raise a mortgage of between 40% and 75% of the value of the house, after which the local authority will then rent you the remaining share of the property for up to 25 years.

The maximum loan available under share ownership scheme is £60,000 while the maximum price you can pay for a new house under this arrangements is £150,000.

Say YES

Have a look at the following checklist and see if any of these areas in your finances could benefit from professional advice:

- Are you paying too much tax   Yes ○   No ○
- Do you – or do you plan to – work abroad?   Yes ○   No ○
- Children's Education – Will you plan for this?   Yes ○   No ○
- Redundancy/Early Retirement – Is this a likely option?   Yes ○   No ○
- Separation/Divorce – does this affect you?   Yes ○   No ○
- Buying a House – are you planning this?   Yes ○   No ○
- Your Pension – can your benefits be enhanced?   Yes ○   No ○
- Savings/Investments – Could they be more efficient?   Yes ○   No ○
- Your Livelihood/Health – Is it financially exposed?   Yes ○   No ○

Because We Can Help You!

If you tick even one "YES" to the questions above you'll find this Guide a very useful aid to helping you to get the most out of your finances.

If you'd like a consultation with one of our advisors to discuss your specific requirements or to seek advice about which options suit you best, please contact us to arrange a private consultation. We have a fixed private consultation fee of £50 (+ 21% VAT) for readers of this Guide. If you'd like to take advantage of this consultation offer:

Call Catherine McGuirk or Siobháin Usher
to arrange an appointment

Taxation Advice Bureau,   Tel: 01-6768633
Eagle House,   Fax: 01-6768641
Wentworth,
Eblana Villas   email: tab@eircom.ie
Dublin 2.   www.tab.ie

7

Getting the most out of your car

The cost of running a car is still a major item. Here is a handy formula that will help you to calculate, with a high degree of accuracy, what your car actually costs.

Each year the AA publishes a leaflet entitled "Motoring Costs" in which they divide motoring costs into two distinct categories:

• Standing Charges

• Operating Costs

A Standing Charge is any fixed annual cost which remains the same no matter how many miles you drive. An Operating Cost, on the other hand, is a cost which is directly related to the number of miles you travel, say for example, petrol.

Of course, your overall motoring costs depend to a large extent on the type of car you drive, your age, driving experience etc., but to make everything as straightforward as possible we have outlined below what the AA estimated were the average Standing Charges for a 1001 - 1250cc and for a 1751 - 2000cc car in May 2000.

Standing charges

Item	1001 - 1250cc		1751 - 2000cc	
	£	€	£	€
Car Tax	£160	€203	£323	€410
Insurance	£820	€1,041	£1,180	€1,498
Driving Licence	£4	€5	£4	€5
Depreciation	£1,250	€1,587	£1,812	€2,301
Interest Costs	£300	€381	£435	€552
Garage/Parking	£1,820	€2,311	£1,820	€2,311
AA Subscription	£59	€75	£59	€75
Total Standing Charges	£4,413	€5,603	£5,633	€7,152

Now that you have identified the Standing Charges above, we outline what the AA estimated were the Operating Costs in May 2000, expressed in pence per mile.

Operating costs (in pence)

Item	1001-1250cc		1751-2000cc	
	£	€	£	€
Petrol	8.410p	10.680c	11.836p	15.028c
Oil	0.153p	.194c	.242p	.307c
Tyres	1.302p	1.653c	2.102p	2.668c
Servicing	1.802p	2.288c	2.456p	3.118c
Repairs	5.032p	6.389c	6.724p	8.537c
Total Operating Cost per mile	16.699p	21.203c	23.360p	29.660c

By referring to these two tables you can see at a glance that if you own a 1001-1250cc car, drive 10,000 miles per annum, between Standing Charges and Operating Costs the AA estimates it will cost you an average of £6,083 p.a. or £116.98 p.w. at May 2000 prices. The corresponding figure for a 1751-2000cc car is £7,969 p.a. or £153.25 p.w.

Using your car for business purposes at work

If you use your car for business purposes one possible way of reducing your motoring costs is to charge your employer for the use of your car at work. Provided your employer agrees and provided you do not charge mileage rates in excess of the Civil Service Mileage Rates, these charges will be tax free in your hands.

The Civil Service Mileage rates effective in December 2000 were as follows:

Civil service mileage rates

Annual mileage	Under 1200 cc		1201 to 1500cc		1501cc and over	
	Rates per mile in pence					
	£	€	£	€	£	€
Up to 4,000	53.11p	67.44c	61.41p	77.97c	75.64p	96.04c
4,001 & Over	28.10p	35.68c	31.50p	40.00c	34.59p	43.92c

If you have a company car

The tax position relating to driving a company car is entirely different. Under the present Benefit In Kind (BIK) provisions many employees have reservations about the real benefits of driving a company car.

The general rule is that if your employer provides you with a company car and pays all the running expenses, you will be taxed at an amount equal to 30% of the original market value of the car, unless your annual business mileage exceeds 15,000 miles p.a.

If your business mileage exceeds 15,000 miles p.a. you will pay a reduced BIK as illustrated on page 92. In addition, if you pay some of the running cost of the car yourself BIK can be reduced further as follows:

% Reduction if:	2001
You pay for all the petrol used on private use	4.5%
You pay all insurance charges	3%
You pay all servicing charges	3%
You pay the road tax	1%

For example, if you pay for the petrol used on private mileage your BIK charge will be reduced from 30% to 25.5%. Vintage car enthusiasts are usually quick to spot that if the company car provided is a vintage car the "original market value" on which BIK is calculated will be extraordinarily low by today's standards.

Working away from place of work

Your BIK charge can be reduced by 20% if you spend 70% or more of your time away from your place of work and your annual business mileage exceeds 5,000 miles p.a. but does not exceed 15,000 miles p.a.

Company car/private car

Evaluating which is best for you in your particular circumstances can be a complex exercise and we suggest that you go about it as follows:

• First estimate your annual Standing Charges (A).

• Estimate your Operating Costs per mile (B).

• Estimate your total annual mileage (C).

• Calculate how much of your total annual mileage is business mileage.

From A, B and C above you can calculate your total annual cost. By simply applying the Civil Service mileage rate to your annual business mileage you can calculate the value of reimbursements your employer may pay you tax-free.

Taking a salary increase instead of a company car

Another consideration is salary in lieu of a company car. For example, if you do relatively low business mileage and are considering the option of giving up the company car in favour of a salary increase coupled with the ability to claim a small mileage allowance. The question you must ask yourself is "Will I lose money"? The following example will help you to answer this important question.

Example

Mary has a company car with an original market value of £15,000. She does 5,000 business miles a year and she pays tax at 44%. Her BIK will work out as follows with a company car.

	£	€
Original Market Value of Car	£15,000	€19,046
BIK @ 30%	£4,500	€5,714
Mary's Increased Tax Bill (£4,500 @ 44%)	£1,980	€2,514

The estimated cost of running Mary's car is £6,250 per annum

Mary has the option of giving up her company car, taking a salary increase of £2,900 and a mileage allowance of £3,350. (5,000 miles @ 67p per mile). Should she take it?

Mary's position

	£	€
Running Cost of Car	£6,250	€7,936
Salary Increase of £2,900	(£1,566)	(€2,212)
(Net of Tax @ 44% + Levies @ 2%)		
Mileage Allowance	(£3,350)	(€4,127)
Net Annual Cost of Car	£1,334	€1,597

The cost to Mary of the company car is £1,980 per annum i.e. her additional tax bill. If Mary provided her own car and she got an increase in salary of £2,900 & mileage allowance of £3,350, the net cost of running her car will work out at £1,334. A saving of £646 per annum.

HIBERNIAN

Norwich Union, CGU and Hibernian have merged to create one of the most powerful insurance, life and investment companies in the Irish marketplace.

With our combined strengths and resources to draw upon we'll be launching many new products over the coming months and years, and introducing innovations specifically designed to make doing business with us easier.

One thing that won't be changing, however, is our commitment to service excellence.

To find out more, contact your Financial Adviser.

Hibernian Life & Pensions, 60/63 Dawson Street, Dublin 2. Tel: 6178000 Fax: 6710803

8
Protecting your life-style

Everyone has something to protect – your wealth, your health, your life and those dearest to you. Insuring your own life against sudden serious illness or unexpected death relieves the financial burden on your dependants. Insuring your car, home and contents is yet another way for you to avoid financial disaster should anything unexpected ever happen to you.

The variety of insurance products available to you has increased considerably in recent years with the result that prices have now become very competitive. There are a number of different ways for you to arrange your insurance. You can either directly contact an insurance company of your choice or you can arrange insurance through your bank, building society or a service provider like a motor association. Alternatively you can contact an independent financial advisor who can offer you independent advice on the type of insurance protection that best suits your needs and your budgets.

Life assurance

The purpose of life insurance is to make sure that your dependants are financially secure in the event of your death. As a general rule, the younger you are, the better your health and the safer your lifestyle, the cheaper will be the cost of your insurance. You may not be able to obtain any life assurance cover at all if you are suffering from a serious illness. Alternatively, you could be offered insurance at a premium price – which, in insurance jargon, is called 'loading'. For example, a 50% loading could mean you pay 50% more than the average insured person of your age for the same amount of life cover.

Since women live longer than men, the cost of insurance cover for women is cheaper. Unfortunately, if you are a woman, this longevity will work against you at retirement age when you go seeking a pension.

How much cover do you need?

Ten times the size of your net, after-tax, salary is a standard gauge for the amount of life insurance cover you should have. A good rule of thumb when trying to decide your total level of cover - is to aim to provide a fund to adequately replace your income in the event of your premature death. This means that your income, the number and ages of your dependents, your assets and outstanding loan commitments etc. all have to be carefully considered. You may find that you don't need as much 'stand-alone' life cover as you might initially think if your employment benefits package includes a death-in-service benefit and a widow's/orphan's pension, or if your mortgage is covered by mortgage protection insurance. This is something that an independent financial advisor will be able to offer you invaluable advice about.

When you meet an independent financial advisor they will tell you that basic life assurance is arranged for a fixed number of years and comes in a number of forms:

Level term cover

This type of cover is relatively inexpensive. But it only pays out at death and has no underlying investment value. Quite simply, when you take out a term assurance plan, you agree to pay a specific or level premium over pre-agreed number of years. Every year, as you get older, your risk of death increases so your level premium is based on the average risk of death.

'Averaging' means that in the early years of your plan you'll pay too much in proportion to the actual risk of death involved, and this extra premium in the early years is used to "subsidise" the cost of your life assurance benefit in later years. If your plan is discontinued, or in the event of an early claim, before your pre-agreed number of years have elapsed, no surplus premium will be repaid.

Convertible term cover

This is slightly more expensive than Level Term Cover but it gives you the flexibility, without any further medical test or examination and regardless of any change in your health circumstances, to convert into another type of policy at any future date in your contract. This could include converting to a 'whole of life assurance plan' which could be a very valuable option for you to have because, regardless of any changes in your health, no unexpected 'loadings' are applied to your premium payable at conversion. Like all 'term' covers, this is a protection policy only and it will never acquire a cash value.

Decreasing term cover

This is a variation on the basic 'term' cover, which means that it is a protection policy only. Decreasing Term cover is often taken out as a mortgage protection policy where both the requirement and the amount of cover decreases as your mortgage is repaid and your need for protection recedes.

Guaranteed 'Whole of Life' cover

Effectively 'whole of life' is a term cover protection policy which guarantees to pay a specific sum of money whenever you die, provided, of course, that you continue to pay the premiums. Because of 'averaging' your premiums are relatively high at the outset, but they remain unchanged for the entire duration of your life. As you might expect, these policies do not have any residual or investment value but the cost is relatively cheap, particularly when you are young and healthy. They are very suitable if, for example, you are self-employed and don't have a pension plan but you want to provide long term financial protection to a dependent spouse or partner in the event of your death. They are also very useful if you have a handicapped child or relative who will need financial protection after your death.

Flexible unit linked life assurance

Unit linked Life Assurance policies are different – different from any of the life assurance policies we've discussed so far. Because, not only do these policies pay the sum assured on death, but they also acquire a cash value which means that you may get money in your hands if you decide to cancel or encash your policy after a number of years.

Because of its dual 'investment & protection' nature, this type of cover is more expensive than 'term' assurance. If the investment funds perform exactly in accordance with the Life Assurance Company's assumed growth rates, the sum assured will be maintained for the full agreed term. If the investment units over-perform, your life cover can be continued for a longer term at no extra premium. If the units under-perform your policy will "bomb out" unless you either increase your premiums or you are prepared to accept a reduction in the amount of your sum assured. In the early years your flexible Life Assurance policy will acquire a cash value as, described in the example below.

Guaranteed whole of life policies

Although the name sounds rather long and complicated, this policy is actually very straightforward. The 'whole of life' aspect means that your plan has a level premium payable from the time you take out the policy up to a specific age, normally 75 or 85. The 'guaranteed' aspect means that it will pay out the cash value of the plan or a guaranteed sum assured, whichever is the greater, whenever you die. So, in the event of your death, a minimum amount of money is always guaranteed. These plans normally acquire a cash value after approximately two years and, as illustrated in the example on page 99, the amount of cash can be quite substantial.

Note: There is a saying among Life Assurance professionals that 'a little life assurance can be a dangerous thing'. Effectively, what this saying means is that, all to often, the very fact that you know you have 'some kind' of a life assurance cover, lulls you into a false sense of security. The years slip by without you ever feeling the need to check and make sure that your 'fixed' level of protection is still sufficient for your 'changing' requirements. It's always good advice to discuss your changing requirements with an independent financial advisor on a regular basis.

Tax

Tax relief is no longer available on life assurance premiums. But take heed! If you're not careful about the way your policy is arranged at the outset, tax and other complications can arise in the event of a claim. Let's have a look at three important terms used in life assurance contracts.

Life Assured: The person on whose life the life assurance policy depends. For example you could assure your own life or you could have a joint life assurance with your spouse (highly recommended since the death of either spouse can cause considerable financial hardship for a family).

Monthly cost of a male, non-smoker, obtaining £250,000 life assurance cover

Age next birthday	25	35	45	55
A Decreasing Term over 20 Years	£11.80	£17.73	£47.43	£128.43
	€14.98	€22.51	€60.22	€163.07
B Level Term Over 20 Years	£19.19	£29.80	£71.98	£209.13
	€24.37	€37.84	€91.40	€265.54
C Convertible Term Over 20 Years	£20.81	£32.51	£78.91	£229.78
	€26.42	€41.28	€100.20	€291.76
D Flexible Life Cover Over 20 Years	£22.71	£47.67	£132.63	£355.80
	€28.84	€60.53	€168.41	€451.77
Projected Cash Value after; (Plan D)				
5 Years	£0	£673.00	£2,494.00	£6,165.00
	€0	€854.53	€3,166.73	€7,827.94
10 Years	£227.00	£2,092.00	£6,316.00	£15,503.00
	€288.23	€2,656.29	€8,019.67	€19,684.75
15 Years	£479.00	£2,521.00	£7,289.00	£18,103.00
	€608.20	€3,201.01	€9,255.12	€22,986.07

	25	35	45	55
E Guaranteed Whole of Life	£101.10	£162.19	£272.44	£471.64
	€128.37	€205.94	€345.93	€598.86
F Unit Linked Whole of Life (Premiums ceasing at age 85)	£100.51	£157.81	£269.50	£482.10
	€127.62	€200.38	€342.19	€612.14
Projected Cash Value after; (Plan F)				
10 Years	£10,238	£18,112	£28,546	£39,358
	€13,000	€22,998	€36,246	€49,974
20 Years	£30,664	£49,130	£69,481	£79,891
	€38,935	€62,382	€88,223	€101,441
30 Years	£62,422	£90,252	£109,253	£46,309
	€79,260	€114,596	€138,723	€58,800

Annual growth rate assumed: 7% p.a. (Plans D & F)

The Assured: (Grantee) The person, or party, entitled to receive the sum assured on the death of the life assured.

Insurance Interest: An insurable interest is necessary in every insurance contract. You have an unlimited insurable interest in your own life and that of your spouse. In other cases, you must normally substantiate your insurable interest before a plan can be commenced e.g. You could have an insurable interest in your business partner.

Naming Beneficiaries – inheritance tax

When you take out a life assurance policy you may wish to decide who the beneficiaries will be. If the policy is an "own life" plan, effectively you are both the "life assured" and "the assured". This means that the lump sum that is payable from the policy upon your death will form part of your estate and may be subject to inheritance tax. In the case of a joint-life policy, usually taken out by spouses, the death benefit is normally paid to the surviving spouse.

"Own Life" – benefit of making a Will

If your policy is arranged on an "own life" basis, your legal representatives, (i.e. your "executor" if you have made a Will) may be required to produce a grant of probate and proof of title before the life office can pay out the sum assured. However, if no Will exists, your policy benefits will be subject to the law of intestacy, with the results that the payments of the proceeds of your life assurance policy may not always be in accordance with your wishes.

"Life of Another" – encashment proceeds

If your life assurance policy is arranged on a "life of another" basis, then, when you die, that other person becomes the owner of the policy. And he or she may claim the encashment value of the policy from the Life Office by simply producing the policy document, together with your death certificate.

This is a very good idea for couples not legally married in the State, however you can loose control of the policy if your personal circumstances change.

Life assurance under trust

Setting up a life assurance policy under Trust is an increasingly popular way of making sure that your policy proceeds will not become part of your estate when you die. In addition, a Trust ensures:

- Quick and easy payment of the death benefit. The life office will pay the surviving trustee(s), usually your wife or children, on proof of death and the production of the policy document.

- By being a trustee of the policy yourself you can maintain a degree of control over the policy during your lifetime. The trust must be set up - by completing a standard trust form and nominating trustee(s) and the beneficiaries - before you commence the policy.

Income protection insurance

Unlike Life Assurance, which only pays out benefits on death, Disability or Permanent Health Insurance pays benefits if you become ill or injured and cannot work. Its aim is to replace your current income - up to retirement age if need be - and may also be included as part of your pension scheme.

If it is not provided as part of your pension scheme, you can purchase Permanent Health Insurance (or Income Continuance Insurance as it is also known) from a life assurance company.

How much does it cost?

The cost varies with age, sex, occupation and with the 'deferment period', which is explained in more detail below. Women on average suffer more ill health than men and consequently pay more for this type of insurance. Occupation is also a crucial factor in determining the cost of the risk involved and people who work in higher risk jobs (more likely to have an accident or illness and less likely to return to work than those in more sedentary jobs) normally have to pay more.

Deferment period

Most disability plans will not pay you any benefit until you have been out of work for at least four weeks - the deferment period. The longer the deferment period, which normally ranges from 4 to 13 weeks, the cheaper the premiums. At the outset of your plan you can decide on the length of the deferment period that best suits your budgets and financial protection requirements.

Hot and bothered?
Cool down, call Phone*assist*

Life's little illnesses and accidents can be very worrying. You've got lots of
questions and nowhere to turn.

Not any more. Now there's Phoneassist - an accident and illness advice
line with a qualified nurse waiting to give you the best advice possible,
whether it's information on illness or injuries, guidance on the best course
of action or even directions to thenearest 24 hour chemist, Phoneassist is
there to help - 7 days a week, 365 days a year. It's available as a free service
to all of our Lifestyle Protector and Life Options customers.

Phoneassist from Irish Life....going further to help.

Irish Life

To ensure that you don't actually end up financially better off claiming benefit (which could leave these plans open to abuse), many disability contracts put a limit on the amount of benefit payable and this limit applies regardless of your maximum level of benefit insured. Normally, you will not be able to receive in benefit more than 75% of your average annual earnings in the year prior to your disablement. Many plans also include the value of State Disability Benefits within this 75% rule.

Tax Relief – on income protection insurance

Disability or Permanent Health insurance premiums are eligible for tax relief at your highest rate of income tax. However, the amount of relief granted cannot exceed 10% of your total income. All Disability and Permanent Health Insurance benefits are taxed under PAYE.

Loan protection insurance

If you ever lose your job, become ill and are unable to work, any outstanding personal loans that you are committed to will still have to be repaid. This is why most lenders will offer you the option of **taking out Payment Protection Insurance** with any personal loans or mortgages that they advance to you.

This important protection option is normally only available to you at the time of taking out the loan or mortgage and it covers your monthly loan repayments if you ever become redundant, sick or disabled. Payment Protection Insurance usually costs only a few pounds extra per month and is included as part of your monthly loan repayments. Although it generally provides only 12 months of benefits per claim, the financial security and peace of mind that it brings can be very valuable and reassuring.

Optional Payment Protection Insurance should not be confused with compulsory Mortgage Protection Insurance. Mortgage Protection Insurance repays the mortgage in the event of death only.

If you already have adequate Permanent Health Insurance cover, you may feel that it is unnecessary for you to take out Payment Protection Insurance as well. After all, the whole purpose of PHI is to provide you with a replacement income so that you can meet your regular repayments and commitments. Keep in mind, however, that most PHI policies only pay benefits after an average of 26 weeks have elapsed, while many Payment Protection plans pay out benefits after just one month of redundancy, illness or disability.

Many newer generation Payment Protection policies offer you a serious illness option whereby your entire loan will be paid off if you contract any of the defined serious illnesses.

Serious illness insurance

Sold by all the leading life assurance companies, serious illness insurance is designed to alleviate the financial burdens of anyone who suffers a serious life threatening illness or condition. It does this by paying you a tax-free lump sum on official diagnosis of your serious illness. The average amount of cover provided is £100,000 and this lump sum can be used to meet your day-to-day living requirements, pay off your mortgage or even to meet the cost of health care.

The main illnesses and conditions include

Cancer, heart attack, stroke, kidney disease, multiple sclerosis, but most policies will also pay out for organ transplants, rare ailments like motor neurone disease and CJD, and in the rare chance that you contract HIV by accident or injury. The better policies also pay out benefits in the event of Permanent and Total Disability (PTD) (including loss of limbs, hearing or speech, Alzheimer's Disease, etc.), and offer cash benefit options if you are hospitalised.

Every insurer includes a slightly different list of conditions so it is always prudent for you to check these in advance with an independent financial advisor. The cost of cover varies with age and sex- older women pay the highest premiums since it is calculated that women suffer more illnesses. Although the lump sum benefit is tax-free, there is no tax relief available on serious illness policy premiums

Protecting your mortgage

Serious illness cover is becoming an increasingly popular part of mortgage protection life assurance policies, and both the level of cover and the premium payments can be arranged either on a level or decreasing premium basis.

In the latter case, your cover decreases in value with the decreasing value of your outstanding mortgage. The drawback to this, however, is that although your benefits will clear your outstanding mortgage, there will be no extra cash available to ease any other financial burdens you may face. By arranging your cover on a term basis, you will be guaranteed a lump sum (the size of the original mortgage) throughout the entire repayment duration of your loan.

Serious illness policies are often arranged by companies for key members of staff or directors. In this context they are known as "keyman" insurance and the benefits are paid, not to the individual but to the company or partners, to lessen any financial burden that they may face because of the absence of that key employee or director.

Health and medical insurance

Cutbacks in the public health service and long waiting lists for treatment have resulted in over a million people in Ireland opting to be covered by private medical insurance plans from the VHI, and, more recently, from BUPA Ireland. An additional incentive for taking out private medical insurance is that the annual premiums are tax deductible at the standard rate.

VHI now offers five basic plans (A - E), plus five enhanced plans, while BUPA Ireland has three plans, Essential, Essential Plus and BUPA Gold. In all cases, the cost of the various levels of cover depends on the hospital and type of accommodation (private or semi-private) that you choose. Because these health plans are "community rated", policyholders cannot be discriminated against, either on a cost or benefits level, because of their age. But, cover may be withheld for certain periods where pre-existing medical conditions exist.

Hospital cash benefit plan

Sold by non-profit, charitable-status, companies like The Hospital Saturday Fund (HSF) and Health Services Association (HSA), these schemes pay tax-free cash payments to members who need hospitalisation or a range of outpatient treatments.

Premiums, which can be a low as a few pounds a week, are age related, but they provide reduced benefits for dependents at no extra cost. Benefits are also paid for routine optical, dental and alternative medical treatments that are not covered by VHI and BUPA. Daily cash benefits are not paid for routine maternity in-patient stays, but new mothers are paid upon delivery a cash lump sum which can exceed the total benefit paid by health insurance plans like VHI and BUPA.

Hospital cash schemes are usually arranged on a group or company basis, but can also be purchased by individuals. There is no tax relief available on premiums.

Insuring your home and its contents

Your home and it contents are among your most valuable processions. Insuring them against fire, theft and other damage should be an important priority. If you have a mortgage you will have been required to take out compulsory buildings insurance, which varies in price depending on the value of your mortgage, the size, location and rebuilding cost of your property. Your lender requires this insurance, not for your benefit, but for theirs. You see, their major concern is to protect their financial interest vested in your property. You should take great care, therefore - especially once your mortgage is paid off - to ensure that your building and contents are properly valued and insured.

Proper valuation

Your rebuilding costs are not the same as the cost of your mortgage, or the market value of your property. If you have any doubt about the true value of your property you should arrange for an independent valuation or survey. Take care not to underinsure your building or contents because most home insurance policies include what is known as an "averaging" clause which determines that if you underinsure your property, for example, by 50%, the insurer is only obliged to pay you 50% the value of your claim.

Nowadays, the cost and the scope of benefits available in Home and Contents insurance policies vary widely. It pays to shop around to make sure that you get the best available value in terms of level of claim excesses, exclusions, discounts and risk cover. A good general insurance broker can help you assess the value of your buildings and possessions and carefully choose the right policy for your needs and budget.

If in doubt – seek out the best professional advice available

As we said at the outset of this chapter, you wealth, your health, your life and those nearest to you are important priorities when it comes to financial protection. Likewise, your home and its contents are among your most valuable processions. That's why it makes such good sense for you to seek out the best available independent professional advice before you make your final decision about what policies and protection arrangements suit your requirements best. Keep in mind that as you get older, get married, or your family commitments change, your protection requirements will change too. So you should get into the habit of regularly checking your existing arrangements to ensure that they are still adequate to meet your changing needs and, indeed, to ensure that you are not 'over protecting' yourself in any areas, for example, as your children grow up and become financially independent.

Keep everything in a secure available place

Always be prepared for the unexpected. Keep all your policy documents and financial papers in a secure available place so that they are readily accessible whenever they are needed. Some financial advisors offer safe-custody facilities which can be very useful. And example of this type of service is the free 'Sentinel' service provided by TAB, whereby tab professional advisors keep a watching brief on your financial arrangements and notify your dependants and beneficiaries of their entitlements and the whereabouts of policy documents etc., in the event of your unexpected death. For more details of this service, contact our web site at www.tab.ie or alternatively you may contact us at 01 - 6768633.

Three pension funds that are guaranteed winners.

Not everyone wants the same things from a pension, which is why Irish Life have designed a range of pension investment options to suit your client's needs.

For Security
Secured Performance Fund - the best guaranteed rate around

For Performance
Actively Managed Funds - our choice of actively managed funds now includes Fidelity Investments, the best in the world.

For Consistency
Consensus Fund - consistently performs above average
Whether your clients are looking for security or the maximum potential gain from their pension, rest assured that they'll be choosing a winner. So if you're looking for the best pension fund, look no further than Irish Life.

To find out more contact your Irish Life Account Manager or ring: **01 704 2000**

Irish Life

9

Making yourself pension-able!

Relative to our European neighbours, Ireland is still a young country. But there is no denying that the proportion of older to younger people is growing and that we are all living longer. The old standbys of pension provision - the State and the benevolent employer who provided a non-contributory pension for life, can no longer be relied upon to ensure a secure and prosperous old age.

Planning for your retirement therefore, is something that needs to be started before you reach middle age, after which, from the financial perspective, it may be too late to achieve the retirement income you expect. A properly funded pension - perhaps from a variety of sources - needs to be started as soon as a person starts working in order that there be sufficient time available for the fund to grow.

Once a person reaches their late 40s and early 50s it is important to keep track of your pension. For example, whether you should enhance it by making additional voluntary contributions. Also, fewer investment risks should be taken close to retirement .

Other financial issues like the level of life assurance you are carrying need to be addressed as well as the state of your mortgage and other debts. Housing and health insurance matters also need to be looked at, for example, you may want to consider making some provision for the long term care for both yourself and your spouse.

As retirement approaches, you shouldn't neglect the huge changes that will take place to your personal life when you leave your work. Do you have enough other interests to keep your mind and body occupied when you retire? Is there another job - on a paid or voluntary basis - that you'd like to do? What about continuing education, hobbies, travel?

An increasing number of people, who can afford to, ease themselves into retirement by scaling down their full-time jobs or careers a few years before they turn 60 or 65.

The Retirement Planning Council of Ireland is a non profit organisation that helps people prepare for their retirement well in advance. They hold regular courses and seminars, many of which are arranged through employers. In 1998 they published *The Retirement Book*, by Anne Dempsey, which explores the myriad of issues surrounding retirement.

The Retirement Planning Council of Ireland, may be contacted at:

27-29 Lwr Pembroke St., Dublin 2 Tel: (01) 661 3139.

Pensions

Unless you plan to work until the day you die, you need some kind of a pension income in your retirement. In this country, pension income comes in three basic forms:

- Social Welfare Pensions
- Occupational Pensions
- Personal Pension Plans

Social welfare pensions

Social Welfare Pensions fall under two main categories;

- Contributory Pensions.
- Non-Contributory Pensions.

Contributory pension

Your entitlement to a contributory pension is based on the amount and contribution class of PRSI you have paid during your working life.

Any other income you have will not affect your entitlement to a contributory pension.

Non-contributory pension

If you don't qualify for a contributory pension you may be entitled to a non-contributory pension. However, your entitlement to this type of pension is based on a means test and any income or assets you have may affect your entitlement to a non-contributory pension.

Retirement pension

A Retirement Pension is paid if you are insured for PRSI under classes A, E or H.

To qualify for a Retirement Pension you must:

• Be aged 65 or over.

• Be retired from insurable employment *.

• Satisfy the PRSI and retirement conditions.

* You earn less than £30 per week or if you are self-employed have earnings of less than £2,500.

Contributory conditions

The PRSI contribution conditions which must be met in order to qualify for a Retirement Pension are:

• You must have started paying contributions before you were 55 years of age.

and

• You must have at least 156 weeks of PRSI paid. Note 1

and

- A yearly average of at least 48 full rate contributions paid and/or credited from 1979 to the end of the tax year before you reach age 65 - this will entitle you to a maximum pension.

or

- For a minimum pension, you must have a yearly average of at least 24 weeks PRSI paid or credited from 1953 (or the year you first become insured - whichever is later) up to the end of the tax year before your 65th birthday. For a maximum pension, a yearly average of 48 weeks PRSI paid or credited in the relevant period is needed.

If you were insured in another member state of the EU, as well as in the Republic of Ireland, your full insurance record will be taken into account when deciding whether or not you are eligible for a Retirement Pension. Periods of insurance/residence in countries with which Ireland has a bilateral social security agreement may also be used to help you qualify for a Retirement Pension.

Periods of insurable employment can be combined to ascertain if you would be entitled to a Retirement Pension from each country.

Note: If you reach pension age from 6th April 2002, you must have 260 full rate employment contributions and from 6th April 2012 you must have 520 full rate contributions paid (of which at least 260 must be full rate employment contributions).

Retirement Condition

The retirement condition stipulates that at the age of 65 you must not enter into employment which is insurable under the Social Welfare Acts other than class J, i.e. people employed under a contract of service whose reckonable earnings are less than £30 per week, or £2,500 per year if self-employed. At the age of 66 you are once more free to take up any employment you choose. Basically, you must actually retire from full-time work at the age of 65 in order to qualify for a Retirement Pension.

Retirement Pension Elements

A Retirement Pension is payable in three distinct elements:

- A personal amount.

- An increase for a qualified adult.

- An increase for each dependant child.

If you qualify for a weekly social welfare payment, you will normally get extra amounts for a "qualified adult" and child dependants. A qualified adult is usually a spouse but can be the person you are living with as husband and wife. Your spouse/partner is regarded as your dependant if he/she is not getting a social welfare payment in his/her own right or has income of less than £60 per week and is not on a full-time FÁS non-craft training course. (For some short-term payments, not pensions, a spouse/partner can have income of up to £105 per week and still be regarded as partially dependant).

The maximum rates are set out below;

Retirement pension/old age contributory pension maximum weekly rates	Up to 5th April '01		From 6th April '01	
	£	€	£	€
Maximum personal rate	£96.00	€121.89	£106.00	€134.59
Increase for a qualified adult - under 66	£60.20	€76.44	£68.20	€86.60
Increase for a qualified adult - over 66	£64.60	€82.03	£79.60	€101.07
Increase per child - Full Rate	£15.20	€19.30	£15.20	€19.30
Increase per child - Half Rate	£7.60	€9.65	£7.60	€9.65
Living Alone Allowance for people age 66 or over	£6.00	€7.62	£6.00	€7.62
Extra allowance for people aged 80 or over	£5.00	€6.35	£5.00	€6.35

Note: The increase for dependants and Living Alone Allowance are paid in full, irrespective of what rate of Retirement or Old Age Contributory Pension you qualify for personally.

Contributory old age pension

The Contributory Old Age Pension is payable to insured people from the age of 66. Unlike the Retirement Pension, it is paid to you even if you are still working. It is payable in respect of PRSI class A, E, H and S.

The three main conditions which must be met in order to qualify for the Contributory Old Age Pension are:

- You must have become insured before the age of 56

  and

- You must have at least 156 weeks PRSI paid. From 6th April 2002 you must have 260 weeks full rate PRSI contributions paid and from 6th April 2012 you must have 520 weeks full rate PRSI paid (of which at least 260 must be full rate employment contributions.

  and

- For the minimum rate of pension, you must have a yearly average of at least 10 paid and/or credited contributions from 1953 (or the time you started insurable employment, if later) to the end of the last complete tax year before you reached 66. For the maximum pension, an average of 48 is needed.

- To qualify for the maximum rate of pension, a yearly average of at least 48 weeks PRSI paid or credited for the period from 5th April 1979 to the end of the tax year before you reach pension age is needed.

The rates of benefit for a Contributory Old Age Pension are the same as those listed for the Retirement Pension.

A special 50% Contributory Old Age Pension is paid to self employed (Class S) contributors who were aged over 56 when social insurance for the self employed was introduced in April 1988 and who have at least five years paid contributions since then.

Non-contributory old age pension

If you don't qualify for a Contributory Old Age Pension you may qualify for a non-contributory old age pension.

To claim a non-contributory old age pension you must:

- Be aged 66 or over

  - Be living in the State
  - Satisfy a means test.

The maximum rates are set our below.

Old age non-contributory pension/blind pension maximum weekly rates	Up To 5th April '01 £	€	From 6th April '01 £	€
Maximum Personal Rate	£85.50	€108.56	£95.50	€121.26
Increase for a qualified adult dependant	£51.70	€65.65	£60.70	€77.07
Increase per child dependant - Full Rate	£13.20	€16.76	£13.20	€16.76
Increase per child dependant - Half Rate	£6.60	€8.38	£6.60	€8.38
Living Alone Allowance	£6.00	€7.62	£6.00	€7.62
Extra allowance for people aged 80 or over	£5.00	€6.35	£5.00	€6.35
Blind Person's Pension Under 66	£77.50	€98.40	£85.50	€108.56
Blind Person's Pension between 66-80	£85.50	€108.56	£95.50	€121.26

Means test

When you make a claim for a non-contributory pension, a Social Welfare Inspector will normally investigate your entitlement to this pension in your own home and attempt to establish your weekly means. In assessing your means, a Social Welfare Inspector will take account of;

- Cash income.

- The value of any property personally used by you, such as a farm or shop. (Your home is excluded unless you are getting an income from it) *

- The value of any investments or capital held.

- The means of your spouse or other person cohabiting with you as husband and wife.

*   Rental income received from a person living with the pensioner is not counted, provided the pensioner is living alone except for that person.

From October 2000 you will get a **full** pension if you have savings or investments up to the amounts shown below and have no other means;

Pension	Savings	
	£	€
Old age (non-contributory)*		
Single person	£16,000	€20,316
Married/cohabiting couple	£32,000	€40,632
Widow's/widower's (non-contributory)	£16,000	€20,316

* **Note:** If you have dependent children, you can have extra savings and still get a pension.

If you are applying for or getting a non-contributory pension, you will still be entitled to **a minimum** pension even if you have the savings shown in the following table and have no other means;

Pension	Savings	
	£	€
Old age (non-contributory)*		
Single person	£44,999	€57,137
Married/cohabiting couple	£88,999	€113,005
Widow's/widower's (non-contributory) (over 66)	£44,999	€57,137

* **Note:** If you have dependent children, you can have extra savings and still get a pension.

Mixed insurance pro-rata pension

People who have paid Class B, C and D (public service rate) and who have a certain number of full-rate (A,E,H & N) PRSI contributions paid since 1953 may qualify for a Mixed Insurance Pro-Rata Retirement or Contributory Old Age Pension. The rate of pension is paid in proportion to your full-rate contributions. The increase for a qualified adult is also paid on a pro-rata basis.

Contributory widow(er)'s pension

The Contributory Widow(er)'s Pension is payable on the death of a spouse provided the PRSI contribution conditions are satisfied that:

- you are widowed

- you are divorced from your late spouse and have not remarried

- you are not cohabiting

  and

- You satisfy the PRSI contribution conditions

  or

- your late spouse was getting a Retirement Pension or an Old Age Contributory Pension which included an increase for you or would have but for the fact that you were getting a Carer's Allowance, Non-Contributory Old Age Pension or Blind Person's Pension in your own right.

The PRSI conditions may be based on either your own or your last spouse's PRSI record. However the two PRSI records cannot be combined. Whichever PRSI record is used must have;

- At least 156 PRSI contributions paid to the date pension age was reached or to the date your spouse died, if earlier

  and

- Either an average of 39 weeks PRSI contributions paid or credited over the three or five tax years (whichever is more beneficial) before reaching pension age (66 years) or before your spouse died (if earlier) for a maximum pension

or

- For a minimum pension, a yearly average of at least 24 weeks PRSI contributions paid or credited is needed since starting work up to the end of the tax year before reaching pension age (66 years) or the date your spouse dies if earlier. For a maximum pension, a yearly average of 48 weeks PRSI contributions paid or credited is needed.

With the exception of class J, K, M and P almost all PRSI contributions, including civil servants and public sector workers, are included for the Contributory Widow(er)'s Pension and Contributory Orphan's Allowance. Your entitlement to the Contributory Widow(er)'s Pension is not affected by any other income you may have.

Extra benefits

If you qualify for a full, or reduced pension, you may be entitled to Free Electricity/Gas Allowance, Free Television Licence, Free Telephone Rental Allowance, Fuel Allowance etc. Subject to certain conditions.

The maximum rates of contributory and non-contributory are set out below:

Contributory widow(er)'s pension maximum weekly rates	Up To 5th April '01		From 6th April '01	
	£	€	£	€
Maximum personal rate - under 66	£81.10	€102.98	£89.10	€113.13
Maximum personal rate - over 66	£89.10	€113.13	£102.00	€129.51
Child dependent	£17.00	€21.59	£17.00	€21.59
Living alone allowance				
Aged 66 or over	£6.00	€7.62	£6.00	€7.62
Aged 80 or over	£5.00	€6.35	£5.00	€6.35

Non-contributory widow(er)'s pension

If you are a widow(er) and have no dependant children, you may be entitled to claim a Non-Contributory Widow(er)'s Pension on the death of your spouse, provided you are not already entitled to a Contributory Widow(er)'s Pension and can satisfy the means test. See Page 115.

Non-contributory widow(er)'s pension maximum weekly rates	Up To 5th April '01 £	€	From 6th April '01 £	€
Maximum personal rate - under 66	£77.50	€98.40	£85.50	€108.56
Maximum personal rate - over 66	£85.50	€108.56	£95.50	€121.26
Living alone allowance				
Aged 66 or over	£6.00	€7.62	£6.00	€7.62
Aged 80 or over	£5.00	€6.35	£5.00	€6.35

One-parent family payment

One-Parent Family Payment is a payment for both men and women who, for a variety of reasons, are bringing up a child(ren) without the support of a partner.

A person who is unmarried, widowed, a prisoner's spouse, separated, divorced or whose marriage has been annulled and who is no longer living with their spouse is eligible to apply for this payment.

If you are getting the One Parent Family Payment you can earn up to £115.38 p.w. and still qualify for full payment. If you earn between £115.38 p.w. and £230.76 p.w. you may qualify for a reduced payment. If your earnings exceed £230.76 p.w. you can continue to receive the One Parent Family Payment for a year at half rate.

Contributory orphan's allowance

Where both parents have died, or one parent has died and the other has abandoned the child. This allowance is payable, provided that the PRSI contribution conditions are met.

These require that at least 26 weekly contributions have been paid at any time by the orphan's parent or stepparent, at the appropriate rate.

The PRSI contribution classes which cover the Contributory Orphan's Allowance are the same as those for the Contributory Widow(er)'s Pension.

The allowance is payable up to the age of 18, or 22 if the orphan is in full-time education. From May 2000 the weekly rate is £55.60 (£63.60 from 6th April 2001).

Non-contributory orphan's pension

The orphan's non-contributory pension is paid for a child or children if:

- Both parents are dead.

- One parent has died and the other is unknown.

- One parent is dead and the surviving parent has abandoned or failed to support the child.

- The child satisfies a means test.

- The child is living in the State.

A claim cannot be made for a child living with step-parents.

The allowance may be payable to the guardian of an orphan if the orphan does not already qualify for a Contributory Orphan's Allowance. The maximum rate of allowance payable from May 2000 is £55.60 per week (£63.60 from 6th April 2001), where the estimated weekly means of the orphan do not exceed £6. If the estimated weekly means of the orphan exceed £58.00 no benefit is payable. The allowance is payable up to the age of 18, or 22 if the orphan is in full-time education. However, the means test must be satisfied throughout the entire period.

Invalidity pension

An Invalidity Pension is payable instead of a Disability Benefit if you have been incapable of work for at least 12 months. In certain cases of serious incapacity a person who has been getting Disability Benefit for less than 12 months may also be considered for Invalidity Pension.

You must have paid PRSI at class A, E or H.

In order to claim Invalidity Pension you must have paid the appropriate PRSI contributions for at least 260 weeks and you must have had at least 48 weeks PRSI paid or credited in the last tax year before you apply.

The maximum rates are set our below.

Invalidity pension maximum weekly rates	Up To 5th April '01 £	Up To 5th April '01 €	From 6th April '01 £	From 6th April '01 €
Maximum personal rate				
- Under 65	£81.10	€102.98	£89.00	€113.01
- Age 65 or over	£96.00	€121.89	£106.00	€134.59
Increase for a qualified adult dependant - under 66	£53.30	€67.68	£60.30	€76.57
Increase for a qualified adult dependant - 66 or over	£58.00	€73.64	£73.00	€92.69
Increases for child dependants - Full Rate	£15.20	€19.30	£15.20	€19.30
Increases for child dependants - Half Rate	£7.60	€9.65	£7.60	€9.65
Living Alone Allowance for people aged 66 or over	£6.00	€7.62	£6.00	€7.62
Extra allowance for people aged 80 or over	£5.00	€6.35	£5.00	€6.35

Note: Increases for dependant child payable with the pensions dealt with in this section are paid for children living with you and dependant on you up to the age of 18 or 22, if they are in full time education.

The full rate for a dependant child is paid to you if you are entitled to an increase for adult dependant. If you do not qualify for payment for a qualified adult, the increase for child dependants is paid at half rate.

Why are Pensions so Value-ABLE?

If you were to retire today, your State pension would be **less than 30%** of the 'average industrial wage'. This means, with a State Pension alone, you may not be able to enjoy anything near to your current standard of living when you retire.

If you need more! ... the State is keen to help by offering you four very valuable tax advantages.

1.   Income Tax Relief on contributions paid

The first major advantage of a Private Pension Arrangement is income tax relief on contributions paid. For example, if the highest rate at which you pay tax is 42% (within the limits outlined later) you will receive back in the form of tax relief 42p out of every £1 you contribute - and, if the highest rate at which you pay tax is 20%, you will receive back 20p (within the limits outlined later) out of every £1 you contribute.

If your employer contributes to your pension your employer will also receive tax relief on any pension contributions he/she pays.

2.   A non-taxable benefit

Most benefits provided as a "perk" by employers - such as cars and preferential loans - will result in an increased tax liability for you. This does not apply to your employer's pension contributions.

3.   Tax-free investment growth

The contributions to pension are invested in a special fund, which is not subject to any tax on its investment profits. This is an important benefit, not available to other types of personal investments,and allows your pension fund to grow much more quickly.

4.   Tax-free cash on retirement

When you retire, you will have the option to take a cash sum from your pension plan - which will be totally tax-free. The maximum amount can be up to a quarter of the value of the fund or 1½ times your final salary.

There are two main types of Pension plan, **'Occupational Pension Plans'** and a **'Personal Pension Plans'**.

An Occupational Pension Plan is one which your employer - or Ltd. company - funds in the main. Many proprietory directors assume that they have a 'Personal Pension', when, in fact their pension plan is funded by a Ltd. company and, as such, is an Occupational Pension.

A 'Personal Pension Plan' on the other hand is funded entirely by you the policyholder, for example, if you are a sole trader, self-employed or in the absence of an Occupational Pension Plan provided by your employer - or Ltd. company -, you can decide to set up your own Personal Pension Plan.

Occupational Pensions

There is no legal obligation on an employer to provide a pension scheme for his/her employees, although many do. If an employer does set up a pension scheme, he/she is not obliged to include all employees in the scheme, but they cannot discriminate on the grounds of sex. Under Revenue Commissioner rules, and in order to claim tax relief, an employer is obliged to contribute at least 1/6th of the total cost of the pension and this is often cited as the reason why not all employers set up schemes.

The players

- The Employer: Sets up the occupational pension scheme and is usually responsible for the major share of the operating costs.

- The Members: Employees covered by the scheme and they must be given written particulars of all the essential features of the scheme.

- The Trustees: Individuals responsible for controlling the assets of the scheme, collecting and investing the contributions and for paying out the pension benefits in accordance with the scheme rules.

- The Administrator: The manager of the scheme.

- The Revenue Commissioners: Vet and approve each scheme.

- The Pensions Board: The statutory Government agency that supervises the registration, funding and operation of occupational pension schemes under the provisions of the Pensions Act 1990.

Defined benefit schemes

The majority of members of occupational pension schemes are in Defined Benefit Schemes. These are schemes where the employer guarantees to pay a pension that reflects your years of service and your final year's income. In ideal circumstances, where there is 40 years service, you will receive 2/3rds of final remuneration, the maximum allowed by the Revenue Commissioners. These pension schemes are known as defined benefit or final salary schemes and members are usually required to contribute about 5% of their income, a tiny proportion of the overall cost of funding a pension.

These were considered to be the best type of pension plan for many employees, particularly if you remained with the same employer until normal retirement. This is because of the certainty about the amount of pension income that you will receive on retirement.

Defined contribution schemes

The high cost of defined benefit schemes has put them out of favour with many employers. Many new pension schemes are now being set up are; Defined Contribution or Money Purchase Scheme under which both the employer and employee fund the pension. The employer makes no promises about the size of the actual pension that will be paid upon retirement; this will depend entirely upon;

- the amount of contributions paid

- the growth rates within pension fund

- annuity rates at the date of your retirement.

If you belong to a Defined Contribution Scheme and you wish to ensure you have an adequate pension income when you retire, you will need to take a more active role in monitoring the performance of your pension fund.

Defined Contribution Schemes do not offer the same level of security as Defined Benefit Schemes and this is particularly true in the event of ill health. Hence, many Defined Contribution Schemes will also include a Permanent Health Insurance (PHI) Plan as an integral part of the pension plan. This PHI contract will guarantee you a specific level of income in the event of a prolonged illness and can also ensure your pension contributions will continue to be paid for the duration of your illness, or up to normal retirement age.

Maximum pension benefits

The benefits that will be provided for you at retirement are contained in the rules of your own individual scheme. However, these benefits may not exceed the maximum approvable benefit limits set by the Revenue Commissioners. These maximum benefits may be summarised as follows:

Pension

The maximum pension is 1/60th of **final remuneration** for each year of service up to a maximum of 40 years. If you have more than five years service with your employer an "uplifted 60ths" scale may apply as follows:

Years of service at normal retirement age	Maximum pension as a fraction of your final remuneration
1-5	1/60th for each year
6	8/60ths
7	16/60ths
8	24/60ths
9	32/60ths
10 or more years	40/60ths

Note: Where the uplifted 60th scale is used, then your maximum pension will be deemed to be inclusive of any retained benefits under a previous Pension Plan or any paid up benefits under a Personal Pension Plan.

Final remuneration

Final remuneration may be defined as any one of the following:

* Remuneration for any one of the five years preceding the normal retirement date. "Remuneration" means basic pay for the year in question plus the average of any fluctuating emoluments over a suitable period, usually three years or more

  or

* The average of the total emoluments of any three or more consecutive years ending not earlier than 10 years before your normal retirement age

  or

126

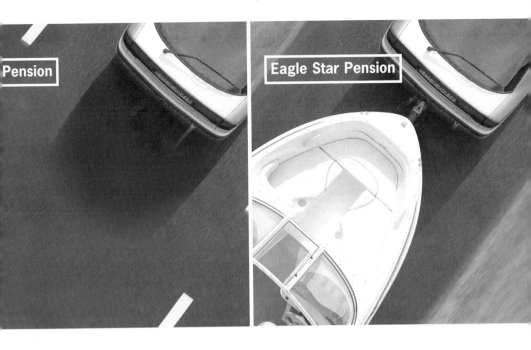

Pension

Eagle Star Pension

When you retire, a pension should let you do all the things you want to do. Of course, that depends on how well your pension fund performs. Which is why you should know, that out of all the unit-linked individual managed pension funds available, the three best performers over the last ten years have all been Eagle Star funds. In fact they have performed twice as well as the average of the other managed funds. So when choosing a pension, just remember - there are pensions ...and there are Eagle Star Pensions.

Talk to your broker or call Eagle Star,
Monday to Friday 9am-5pm, at 1850 202 102.

EAGLE STAR

A member of the **Z** *Zurich Financial Services Group*

www.eaglestarlife.ie

Irish Life	Canada Life	Standard Life	New Ireland	Lifetime	Friends First	Hibernian Life	Scottish Provident	Acorn Life	Eagle Star Perf.	Eagle Star Balanced	Eagle Star Dynamic
256%	292%	295%	296%	304%	304%	315%	325%	395%	609%	617%	678%

INDIVIDUAL MANAGED PENSION FUNDS TEN YEAR PERFORMANCE %

Source: MoneyMate. All figures and copy relate to individual pension managed growth and aggressively managed sectors. Returns based on offer/offer performance from 01/09/90 to 01/09/00 and do not relate to premiums paid into a policy. Unit values may be expected to fall as well as rise. Past performance is not always an indication of future returns which are dependent on future investment conditions.

Winner of the IBA/MoneyMate Best Managed Growth Pension Fund in 2000

- The rate of basic pay at the date of retirement, or on any date within the year ending on that date, plus the average of fluctuating emoluments over three or more consecutive years ending with the date of retirement.

Dynamising

In the case of the first two definitions each year's remuneration may be increased in line with the Consumer Price Index from the end of the relevant year up to your normal retirement date. This is referred to as 'dynamising' final remuneration.

Note: "Remuneration" includes all income and benefits which are assessable to income tax under PAYE, in the relevant employment e.g. BIK on a company car can be included as part of your final renumeration (certain restrictions apply to 20% Directors).

Cash lump sums

When you retire, usually between your 60th and 70th birthdays, you can convert part of your pension benefits into a tax-free lump sum. The maximum lump sum amount is usually worked out as a 3/80th fraction of your final salary for each year of service up to a maximum 40 years, or 1.5 times your final remuneration. If you have more than eight years service with your employer at normal retirement age, an uplifted scale may be used as follows to enhance your tax-free lump sum at retirement.

Years of service to normal retirement age	Maximum tax-free lump sum as a fraction of final remuneration
1-8	3/80ths for each year
9	30/80ths
10	36/80ths
11	42/80ths
12	48/80ths
13	54/80ths
14	63/80ths
15	72/80ths
16	81/80ths
17	90/80ths
18	99/80ths
19	108/80ths
20 or more	120/80ths

Where the uplifted scale is used as the allowable fraction it will be inclusive of any other retirement lump sum received or receivable in respect of service with any another employer.

Ill health

There is no specific definition of ill health in the Revenue pension guidelines, however incapacity is defined as follows:

"Physical or mental deterioration which is bad enough to prevent you from following your normal employment, or which very seriously impairs your earnings. It does not mean simply a decline in energy levels or ability."

Early retirement due to ill health

If you retire early due to ill health, the maximum pension you can receive will be the equivalent of the one you could have expected to receive had you worked until your normal retirement age.

Example

John commenced employment with his current employer at age 35. The pension scheme rules provide a retirement benefit of 1/60th for each year of service to normal retirement age, which is 65 years.

Now, five years later, John retires on grounds of ill health, after suffering a serious illness. His final remuneration prior to ill health was £30,000 per annum.

John's years of service to normal retirement age is 30 years, so, his maximum ill health retirement pension is:

30/60ths x £30,000 = £15,000 per annum.

In the case of early retirement due to ill health, your "final remuneration" will be calculated by a reference to the period preceding your actual retirement.

Early retirement not due to ill health

Where early retirement is taking place after age 50 other than due to ill health, then the maximum immediate pension is the greater of:

- 1/60ths of final salary remuneration for each year of actual service completed
  or

- The pension worked out by the following formula.

- N / NS x P
  N is actual number of years service to early retirement, NS is number of years of potential service to normal retirement age. P is maximum pension approvable if you had remained in service to your normal retirement age.

Example

John joined his employer at age 35. The scheme rules provide for a retirement pension of 1/60th of final remuneration for each year of service to age 65. John now aged 50 with a salary of £30,000 p.a., elects to take normal early retirement with his employer's consent.

N = 15, actual years service completed to age 50.
NS is 30, Potential Service to Normal Retirement Age.
P is 2/3rds - Maximum pension under Revenue guidelines.
So John's maximum early retirement pension is to be the greater of:
15/60ths x £30,000 = £7,500 per annum.

or

15/30 x 2/3rds x £30,000 = £10,000 per annum.

While the above outlines the maximum benefits which may be allowed by Revenue guidelines, it would be rare for most employers to provide this level of benefits on early retirement. Typically, the rules would provide for the calculation of benefits as outlined above. However, penalties for early retirement could then be applied to these calculations and your actual early retirement pension could be much less.

Tax-free lump sums on early retirement

On early retirement a tax-free lump sum may be taken within Revenue maximum limits. In the case of ill health retirement that maximum tax-free lump sum is similar to what you could have received if you had remained in service up to normal retirement age. This would normally give a maximum of 1.5 times final remuneration at the date of ill health retirement.

In the case of early retirement not due to ill health, the maximum tax-free lump sum is calculated as follows:

3/80ths of remuneration for each year of actual service or the sum calculated in accordance with the following formula;

N/NS x LS

N =   number of years service completed up to early retirement

NS =   The potential number of years that could have been completed by Normal Retirement.

LS =   The maximum approvable tax-free lump sum which could have be provided at normal retirement age.

In the example earlier John could get the greater of:

$$15 \times 3/80 \times £30,000 = £16,875$$

or

$$15/30 \times 120/80 \times £30,000 = £22,500$$

N = 15 John actual Service

NS = 30 Potential Service

LS = 120/80 Maximum allowed under Revenue guidelines.

Death-in-service benefits

A pension scheme will normally provide two benefits if you die in service before normal retirement age.

A tax free lump sum

The maximum tax free benefit is a lump sum of four times your remuneration at the date of death, together with a refund of any personal contributions to the scheme with "reasonable interest". This benefit would be payable to the trustees who, under the rules of the scheme, would have some discretion as to which of your dependants should receive the proceeds.

Pension benefits

Pensions may also be provided for your financial dependants. The maximum pension which could be paid to your spouse is 2/3rds of the maximum pension which you could have received if you had retired on grounds of ill health at the date of your death. Normally this would mean the maximum pension your spouse could receive would be 4/9ths of your remuneration at the date of your death.

Pensions may also be provided for other dependants subject to:

- The total pensions payable to all dependants not exceeding the maximum pension that you could have received if you had been retired on grounds of ill health on the date of death, and

- No one pension may exceed 2/3rds of the maximum pension payable to you.

This effectively means that if the maximum spouse's pension is to be 4/9ths of your final remuneration, the children's pensions could be provided for up to 2/9ths of your final remuneration.

Death after retirement

Many pension schemes will provide a guaranteed period of pension payments after your retirement whether you live or die. This guaranteed period can be up to 10 years. If the guaranteed period is five years or less on death after retirement then the remaining instalments may be paid at the Trustees' discretion in a lump sum to your dependants. If the guarantee is more than five years the outstanding instalments will be paid in pension form to your beneficiaries.

Spouses and dependants pensions may be provided in addition to this guarantee.

The maximum spouse's pension that may be provided is 2/3rds of the maximum pension that could have been provided for you at retirement.

A pension may also be provided for dependants provided:

- The total of the spouses and dependants pension does not exceed the maximum pension which you could have received at retirement.

- No one pension may exceed 2/3rds of the maximum pension that could have been provided for you.

The term "maximum pension" is defined as the maximum pension at normal retirement age, increased in line with the Consumer Price Index from the date of retirement up to the date of death.

Pension increases

Generally speaking, a pension may be increased in line with the rise in the Consumer Price Index each year. Alternatively, increases at a compound rate of 3% per annum compound may be promised and paid, regardless of the Consumer Price Index. However, if your pension at retirement was less than the maximum Revenue approvable pension at retirement age, this pension may be increased at a faster rate than the increase in the Consumer Price Index until it reaches the level of the maximum approvable pension.

Preserved pension benefits

Section 28 of the Pensions Act gives you a statutory right to a 'preserved benefit' if you leave employment any time before normal retirement age provided:

- You have completed at least five years service as a member of the pension scheme

  and

- At least two years of this service was completed after 1st January 1991.

In the case of a **defined contribution** scheme the preserved benefits are the benefit secured by contributions, paid by your employers and yourself, on or after 1st January 1991.

In the case of a defined **benefit scheme** the preserved benefit is calculated in accordance with the following formula:

> T/N x Pension expectation, based on scheme rules, where
> T = scheme service for retirement benefits after 1st January 1991, and
> N = total potential scheme service

Example

Mary joined company at age 18. She joined the pension scheme for retirement benefits at age 25. Her pension expectation under the scheme is 2/3rds x final remuneration at age 65.

At 1st January 1991 Mary is 35, she leaves service at age 45 and her remuneration is £20,000 p.a.

Calculation of "Preserved Benefit"

Final pension expectation	£	€
2/3rds x £ 20,000	£13,333 p.a.	€16,929
T (Service After 1/1/91)	10 years	
N (Total Potential Scheme Service)	40 years	
Preserve Pension Benefits = 10/40 x £13,333 p.a.	£3,333 p.a. at age 65	€4,232

The preserved benefit under a defined benefit scheme must be 'revalued', at the end of each calendar year from 1st January 1996 onwards, by the lesser of 4% p.a. or the 'increase in the CPI'. For 1996 the revaluation factor was 1.6%; for 1997 it was 1.5%; for 1998 it was 2.4% and for 1999 it was 1.6%.

As an alternative to maintaining the preserved benefit with your old employer, you may elect, within two years of leaving service, to have the value of the preserved benefit transferred to either:

• The pension scheme of a new employer

or

• to a 'Buy out Bond'.

The trustees of the old scheme also have the right to transfer the value of your preserved benefits to a "Buy out Bond", with or without your consent, after the end of the same two-year period, if the transfer value is less than the specific amount - currently this is £3,000.

Vested rights

Prior to the introduction of the 1990 Pensions Act you had no legal right to retain the pension benefits accrued to you if you left your employment.

However, many pension schemes did and still do allow employees to retain accrued pension benefits. Prior to 1st January 1991, these rights were known as **"Vested Rights"**.

Example

In the example earlier if Mary had vested rights on leaving her old employer, her retained pension benefits would work out as follows:

Final pension expectation	£	€
2/3rds x £ 20,000	£13,333 p.a.	€16,929
T (Service after 25th Birthday)	20 years	
N (Total Potential Scheme Service)	40 years	
Preserve Pension Benefits = 20/40 x £13,333 p.a.	£6,667 p.a. at age 65	€8,465

Refund of personal contributions

Many contributory pension schemes will allow you take a refund of your personal pension contributions, with or without interest, when you leave employment with less than five years qualifying service.

These refunds will normally be subject to tax at 25%.

If you are entitled to Statutory Preserved Benefits in respect of employment service after 1st January 1991, then no cash refund may be taken in respect of employment after 1st January 1991.

If you paid contributions before 1st January 1991 you may be entitled to a refund of these contributions, with or without interest, if you leave your employment.

Check the rules of your individual scheme carefully before you decide to take any cash refund, particularly if your scheme gives you fully "Vested Rights". This is because if you take a refund of your own contributions when you leave, your employer will also get back his/her contributions over this same period and you cannot retain any rights to these pension benefits in respect of that employment. This could have major implications for your long term retirement income.

Pensionable salary

Many Defined Benefit Schemes do not give the maximum Revenue approvable pension benefits and many integrate your Social Welfare retirement pension benefit entitlements with the employer's pension scheme.

You don't need to phone a friend...

Which of these leading With-Profit pension providers comes out ahead on performance over 10, 15 and 20 years?

- Standard Life
- Norwich Union
- Friends First
- Scottish Provident

The correct answer is: Standard Life.

Yes, Standard Life comes out ahead* of its three major competitors, for net yields to maturity over 10, 15 and 20 years. This is why you should consider Standard Life for your Personal Pension investments. For more reasons why, please contact your financial adviser or a Standard Life office near you or email: marketing@standardlife.ie

* *According to The Irish Times 2000 Personal Pension Survey, based on 10, 15 and 20 year net yields to maturity. Figures for Standard Life over 15 and 20 years are based on traditional With Profit products, which have been replaced by unitised products currently sold. Past performance is not necessarily a guide to future results.*

STANDARD LIFE

Typically, the objective is that the benefits from your employer's pension scheme and your Social Welfare pension at normal retirement age will amount to 2/3rds of your final remuneration.

This objective is met by defining your 'pensionable salary' as actual salary less a deduction to allow for Social Welfare benefits. Typically, this deduction would be 1.5 times the PRSI retirement pension for a single person in the case of a N/60ths pension scheme.

Example

	£	€
Retirement Pension (May '00) for a single person £96 per week	£4,992 p.a.	€6,339 p.a.
SW deduction for pensionable salary (£4,992 x 1.5)	£7,488	€9,508
John's Final Salary	£31,000 p.a.	€39,362 p.a.
John's Pensionable Salary (£31,000 less £7,488)	£23,512 p.a.	€29,854 p.a.
Expected Retirement Benefit 2/3rds x £23,512 p.a.	£15,674 p.a.	€19,902 p.a.
Expected Social Welfare Retirement Pension	£4,992 p.a.	€6,339 p.a.
Total Expected Pension (Scheme plus Social Welfare)	£20,667 p.a.	€26,242 p.a.

Giving yourself a better pension- AVCs

Not all employers provide the maximum pension benefits allowed by the Revenue Commissioners. If this is the case in your scheme, you may, depending on the rules of your scheme, top up your pension benefits at your own expense by paying what is known as an **Additional Voluntary Contribution**, or AVCs.

An AVC is a private pension arrangement into which you can contribute up to 15% of your salary in any one tax year (this 15% includes any other contributions you may be making to the main scheme) and claim full tax relief. The Revenue have two preconditions; one, your topped-up benefits may not exceed the maximum benefits permissible under their rules and two, your total contributions may not exceed five times your employer's pension contribution.

Reasons for commencing an AVC

Since many private sector pension schemes fail to provide the maximum benefits allowable, it would be a very good idea for you to check the position of your own scheme. If you don't have a member's handbook, get one and examine the rules.

- The maximum pension a person can receive is the equivalent of 2/3rds of final remuneration after 10 years service. Yet your scheme may only set out 1/60th of your final pay per year of service. If you work for 25 years, your final pension from the company would only be 25/60ths, well short of the allowable maximum of 40/60ths. This makes you a good candidate for an AVC.

- Your pension scheme may not make provision for a spouse's pension if you die in retirement.

- Your retirement pension may not be indexed, to take account of cost of living rises. The Revenue Commissioners will allow an AVC to top-up increases in your pension benefits in retirement.

- Your pension scheme may not provide for death-in-service benefits, the maximum of which is a lump sum payment the equivalent of four times your final remuneration.

- Your pension scheme may not take into account non-salary benefits like a company car,annual bonus, overtime etc.

- Your pension scheme may not allow you to retire early on full benefit and may even penalise you.

- Under your pension scheme Social Welfare entitlement may be deducted from the maximum 2/3rds of your final remuneration you are allowed to receive. If so, you should consider topping up to the amount that equals 2/3rds of your final remuneration.

Employer approval

You will need your employer's approval to join or set up an AVC. If your scheme already makes provisions for AVCs, simply contact your employer and join. If it doesn't, make a case for one or for permission to source one yourself outside in the market place.

Legally, this type of individual AVC plan is treated as an asset of the main scheme, but it can only be used to provide pension benefit for you or your dependants.

Tax

If your AVC contributions are deducted at source, full relief from both PAYE and PRSI will be granted automatically. If you pay by direct debit, and this usually happens if your AVC is provided by an outside independent pension company, you claim the income tax relief direct from your Inspector of Taxes by way of an allowance. This way you get PAYE relief. However, no PRSI relief can generally be obtained when you pay AVC contributions by direct debit.

Leaving your job and AVCs

The same rules will apply to AVCs as apply to ordinary contributions so, if you leave your job while making contributions to an AVC, depending on the rules of your main scheme and your length of service, you may be entitled to reclaim some or all of your contributions back, less 25% tax. See Page 135.

Pensions as a saving mechanism

Providing a pension for your retirement can be a costly exercise, particularly if your retirement plan is commenced later in life. This point is emphasised so often that many older employees are discouraged from ever commencing a pension plan. This is unfortunate as a pension plan can be used as a very effective way of accumulating a tax-free lump sum on retirement.

Example

Let us assume:

- You are aged 58 and you have worked with your current employer for the past 14 years and you are not a member of your employer's pension scheme.

- Your gross earnings are £35,000 p.a. and you pay tax at 44%.

- You wish to accumulate a lump sum on retirement and can afford to contribute say £200 p.m. after tax to a plan starting in the 2001 tax year.

Let us look at two options:
1.   You save £200 in a building society - average interest rate 3% p.a.
2.   You pay £370 p.m. into a pension scheme.

See page 140 showing how these two options compare.

139

Under Option 2 you have approximately twice as much money working for you at a similar cost to yourself and this is reflected in your fund at retirement age (65) which is based on Eagle Star's Autometric SuperCapp Pension Plan and assumes an annual growth rate of 5.5% p.a. As you will have had 20 years service with your employer at normal retirement, one and a half times your final salary may be taken in a cash tax-free lump sum. If you had less than 20 years service with your employer at normal retirement, a smaller tax-free lump sum would be available in cash and the balance of the fund could be taken in the form of a pension.

Savings & Pensions				
		Option 1 £		Option 2 £
Gross Remuneration		£35,000		£30,000
Less: Pension Contribution		NIL		£4,500
Total Income (A)		£35,000		£25,500
Tax @ 22%	£28,000	£6,160	£25,500	£5,610
Tax @ 44%	£7,000	£3,080		-
		£9,240		£5,610
Less: Tax Credits				
Personal Allowance				
9,400 @ 22%		(£2,068)		(£2,068)
PAYE Allowance				
1,000 @ 22%		(£220)		(£220)
PRSI & Levies		£1,658		£1,424
Saving Plan		£2,400		Nil
Outgoings (B)		£11,011		£4,746
Disposable Income (A-B)		£23,989		£20,754
Estimated Funds @ Age 65		£18,941		£38,789

Maximum funding rates

Maximum funding rates for occupational pension schemes are the estimated contributions required to produce a fund to pay you the maximum Revenue approvable pension benefits at normal retirement age. This maximum rate will be inclusive of your contributions and your employer contributions. The following chart illustrates the potential cost of providing maximum pension benefits within Revenue guidelines, assuming you commenced paying contributions to a pension fund at one of the appropriate ages.

Age at Entry	30	35	40	45	50	55	60
Percentage of salary required to fund each pension element	%	%	%	%	%	%	%
Member's pension at normal retirement	12.87	15.56	19.30	24.86	33.93	51.29	97.68
Escalation of member's pension @ 5% p.a. in retirement	5.85	7.08	8.78	11.31	15.44	23.34	44.45
Spouse's pension after member's death in retirement	2.73	3.30	4.10	5.28	7.20	10.89	20.74
Escalation of spouse's pension at 5% p.a.	3.74	4.53	5.62	7.24	9.88	14.93	28.44
Death in service	2.23	2.63	3.16	3.85	4.73	5.84	7.01
Widow's pension after member's death in service	2.20	2.60	3.10	3.70	4.50	5.40	46.40
Escalation of widow's Pension @ 5% p.a.	.98	1.16	1.38	1.65	1.99	2.37	2.71
Income in disability escalating @ 5% p.a.	1.58	1.82	2.11	2.46	2.85	3.16	2.99
Pension premium protection in disability	.57	.78	1.12	1.66	2.59	4.23	7.31
Total as a % of gross salary	32.75	39.46	48.67	62.01	83.11	121.45	257.73

Source - Irish Life

Hanock annuity

Occasionally, an employer may wish to provide to a pension for a retiring employee where no pension provision already exists.

In this situation, a Hanock Annuity can be bought. Hanock Annuity can provide the similar retirement package to a conventional pension plan.

A Hanock Annuity has two significant advantages:

- The cost of purchasing the Hanock Annuity is treated as a business expense for the employer and so reduces the employer's taxable profits in the relevant year;

- The cost of purchasing the Hanock Annuity is not treated as a benefit in kind from an employee's point of view.

Retirement income

At retirement if you are in a defined benefit scheme the pension you receive will be directly related to your final salary and your length of service (See Page 126). However if you are in a defined contribution scheme you will have a number of different options to consider at retirement, which will usually include a combination of the following;

- A tax free lump sum.
- A Pension or Retirement Annuity
- Investment in an Approved Retirement Fund (ARF).

Tax Fee Lump Sum

All pension plans allow you to take a certain portion of your benefits at retirement in a cash lump sum. This lump sum is tax free while your annual pension or amounts paid from an approved retirement fund (see page 149) will be taxable. This makes taking the tax free lump sum an attractive option.

As an employee or company director, how much you can get tax free depends on;

- your length of service with the employer (see page 126)
- your shareholding in the company (see page 149)
- Additional Voluntary Contributions you have paid (see page 137)

Note: If you are a member of a defined benefit company pension plan, the tax free lump sum is usually paid for by reducing your pre-set pension by a fixed formula. Depending on financial conditions at the time of your retirement, the relative generosity of this formula may change, so check out the details in advance.

Retirement Annuities and Pensions

A Retirement Annuity is a financial product sold by a life assurance company; it is the technical name for a pension. It operates by you paying all or part of your retirement fund to the life assurance company and in return the life assurance company guarantees to pay you an annuity or pension for the rest of your life and/or the life of your financial dependents starting after your death.

How big will your pension be!

The factors that usually decide the size of your pension are:

- The **amount of money** in your retirement fund
- Your **age** at retirement. The older you are at retirement the higher your pension will be relative to the fund.
- **Extra Benefits** – pension indexation, dependant pensions and guarantees can all be included in your pension from the outset, however these extra benefits will result in a lower initial pension payable to you.
- **Interest rates** – the higher the level of interest rate at your retirement the higher your pension will be.

Buying a pension

The process of buying a pension is usually carried out by a financial adviser – either your own if you have a personal pension plan or the trustees if you have a company pension plan.

Most pension plans invest in company shares, property and other investments that change in value on a daily basis. As a result, the value of your pension fund in the weeks before your retirement can also change on a daily basis. This means that the final value of your pension fund is usually not used when obtaining a retirement annuity quotation before retirement.

Instead, a rate is quoted that when multiplied by the value of your pension fund on the date of your retirement gives you the yearly amount of your pension. This rate is known as the "annuity rate" e.g. if your pension plan had a value of £ 100,000 and the annuity rate quoted was 10% then your pension would be £ 10,000 p.a.

The simplest form of pension is a level single life pension i.e. a pension for the rest of your life at a fixed annual rate.

Retirement age

The older you are at retirement the higher your pension is likely to be. This is because your retirement fund has more time to grow before your retirement and is more likely to pay out benefits over a shorter period.

Example

A £ 100,000 retirement fund would currently buy the following single life level pension at the relevant retirement ages:

Retirement age	Male		Female	
	£	€	£	€
50	£6,578	€8,352	£6,391	€8,115
55	£7,084	€8,995	£6,785	€8,615
60	£7,809	€9,915	£7,340	€9,320
65	£8,838	€11,222	£8,136	€10,331
70	£10,254	€13,020	£9,290	€11,796
75	£12,100	€15,364	£10,921	€13,867

Average post retirement interest rate assumed is 5.82 %

Ill Health At Retirement

In general, annuity terms quotes by insurance companies are offered to everyone regardless of the state of their health. The disadvantage of this is that people in poor health at retirement and who are unlikely to live for a long time should deserve better annuity rates.

One insurance company, Hibernian, does currently offer better annuity terms to people who are in poor health at retirement. The improved terms they offer will depend on the individual circumstances.

Pension indexation

Your retirement is likely to extend over 20 years or more. Over that time, rising prices can significantly reduce your standard of living if you are on a fixed income.

As an example, the following table shows the higher prices of some common consumer good over 20 years from now assuming different levels of price inflation:

Consumer goods	Cost today	Cost in 20 years' time with yearly inflation of		
		2.5% (each year)	5.0% (each year)	7.5% (each year)
Daily newspaper	£0.85	£1.39	£2.26	£3.61
Pint of beer	£2.85	£4.67	£7.56	£12.11
Litre of milk	£0.69	£1.13	£1.83	£2.93

Pension Increases

There are two different ways your pension may be increased during your retirement to protect your standard of living against inflation, the first option increases your pension by a fixed rate each year. The typical levels of annual increase chosen are 3% or 5% p.a.

Future pension increases are paid for by starting your initial pension at a lower level of benefit. This means your pension gives you a more steady standard of living throughout your retirement. The following table shows a typical reduction in your initial level pension benefits if a 3% or 5% yearly pension increases are chosen at retirement.

Yearly pension increase rate	Reduction in a level pension paid at retirement.
3%	28%
5%	44%

The fixed rate method of pension increase is the traditional way to guard against the effects of future inflation. However, it has one major flaw. If inflation turns out to be higher than expected in future years then choosing a relatively low fixed increase rate may not be enough to ensure your pension gives you a steady standard of living in your retirement.

With this in mind some life assurance companies have now introduced new options for the Irish annuity market. These new options can directly link annual increases of your pension to the rate of inflation. This protects you against an unexpectedly high level of inflation in future years. The chosen measurement for inflation is normally the Consumer Price Index.

Provision for dependents

At retirement you can also buy a pension for people who are financially dependent on you. A spouse is the most common type of dependent but elderly family relatives and children (particularly handicapped children) may also qualify as dependants. To protect them, you may choose to have a pension paid to them for the rest of their lives, starting after your death.

Cost of a dependant's pension

A dependant's pension is paid for by reducing the level of your single life pension. The reduction needed to pay for a typical spouse's pension is as follows:

Level of spouse's pension	Reduction in your own pension
Half of your pension	13%
Two-thirds of your pension	17%

However, if your dependant is significantly younger than you, the reduction needed in your own single life pension may be much larger.

Guarantees

One guarantee normally included with many pensions is a guaranteed payment period, this means your pension is guaranteed to be paid for a fixed number of years from the start. Its purpose is to ensure your dependants get a minimum financial return, even if you die shortly after retirement.

The Revenue Commissioners allow you to choose a guaranteed payment period from 0 up to 10 years. A guaranteed payment is paid for by a reduction in the pension paid to you or your dependents. The following table shows the reduction you will suffer in pension for a typical retirement annuity with a payment period guaranteed for 5 and 10 years :

Guaranteed Period	Percentage decrease in pension
5 years	1 %
10 years	3 %

The small decreases in the pension benefits reflect the low risk of people dying in the early years of their retirement.

Interest Rates

Long term interest rates can have a major impact on the level of your pension benefits at retirement. Below we illustrate what a £100,000 fund would buy in pension benefits at age 60 assuming the long term interest rates illustrated below were available on long term cash deposits or government stocks at the date of your retirement.

Long term interest rate	Male			Female		
	Annuity rate	Pension payable		Annuity rate	Pension payable	
%	%	£	€	%	£	€
5.65	8.780	£7,719	€9,801	7.251	£7,221	€9,169
6.65	9.500	£8,452	€10,732	7.961	£7,931	€10,070
8.65	10.960	£9,952	€12,636	9.420	£9,390	€11,923

If you are in a defined benefit scheme you do not have to worry about interest rates at retirement as your pension will be directly related to your final salary, your employer carries the interest rate risk.

Why have annuity rates fallen?

The major factor here is interest rates. These have fallen substantially over the last few years largely because of EMU. There is also an expectation in the market place that this is not a short term adjustment but that we have entered a "new-world" where low interest rates are the norm. Low interest rates mean the life assurance company can earn less on its fixed interest investments so less money is available to provide pension income for you.

However, interest rates are not the whole answer. At the same time as interest rates have been decreasing, pensioners have been seeing much improved mortality levels. Medical capabilities have improved substantially which means people are living longer. This means pensions will need to be paid over longer periods - this also reduces the initial level of pension payable at retirement. A rough estimate is, that the cost of purchasing an annuity will increase by between ½% and 1% each year over the foreseeable future just to pay for these improvements in mortality rates.

That's Asset Management on the ball

Canada Life launched its own asset
management team in Autumn 1998.
Since then, it has proved to be one of the
top performing management teams in
Ireland. Canada Life/Setanta's investment
funds have shown impressive returns in
recent surveys as a result.

Setanta has achieved these returns
through an innovative and original
approach. This is based on a world-wide
view of investments and disciplined
teamwork.

The Setanta managed Focus 15 Fund
is the No.1 performing unit linked
investment fund*, delivering 28.4% growth.

This unique fund is now available in the
pensions market.

To find out more about the range of
Canada Life/Setanta investment funds,
talk to your Broker, Canada Life Financial
Adviser, or call us on (01) 210 2000.

Canada Life

Canada Life House, Temple Road,
Blackrock, Co. Dublin
www.canadalife.ie

* Source Moneymate, offer to offer performance, since launch,
22nd Nov 1999 to 22nd Nov 2000. Past performance is not
necessarily a guide to future performance, as unit prices can
fall as well as rise.

Approved Retirement Funds (ARF's)

Up until 1999 pension legislation allowed you use your retirement fund (excluding you tax free lumpsum) for one purpose only - that was buy a retirement annuity or pension from a life assurance company on the date of your retirement. Because of fallen interest rates retirement annuities had become highly controversial as many retirees objected to having to commit these funds to buy a pension at retirement when the prices were not particularly attractive. The compulsory nature pension annuities was addressed by the Minister in the 1999 Budget when he introduced Approved Retirement Funds (ARF's) for the first time.

An ARF's or Approved Retirement Funds are defined in the 1999 Finance Act as funds "which are managed by a Qualifying Fund Manager and which complies with the conditions of Section 784B".

If you are a Proprietary Director, or self-employed or an employee who is not in an occupational pension scheme or if you have made additional voluntary contributions to an occupational pension plan, ARF's give you three new valuable options at retirement.

- The option to take up to 25% of your accumulated pension fund in a tax-free Lump Sum.

- An option to place 75% of your accumulated pension fund in an ARF.

- The option to take the 75% of your accumulated fund in cash (less tax and subject to certain conditions). See Page 151.

Proprietary director

For ARF's a Proprietary Director is one who controls more than 5% of the voting rights in a company or in a company's parent company. Shares, which are held by the director's spouse or minor children, are taken into account as are shares held by trustees of a settlement to which a director or a director's spouse has transferred shares.

Tax free lump sum option

If you have a Personal Pension Plan, you can take a lump sum of up to 25% of your accumulated fund at retirement, tax-free.

If you are a Propriety Director in an Occupational Pension Plan you have a choice of two different options:

- You have a right to take the normal lump sum in accordance with your Occupational Pension Scheme Rules. This typically amounts to a maximum of 150% of final remuneration with 20 years service. However, if you choose this option your cannot avail of the new ARF rules.

- Alternatively you can decide to opt for a tax-free lump sum of up to 25% of your accumulated fund and avail of the new ARF rules.

ARF options

An ARF enables you to control your pension fund assets at retirement and to direct future investment strategy through a Qualified Fund Manager. A Qualifying Fund Manager (QFM) can be one of the following:

- Bank
- Building Society
- Credit Union
- Post Office Savings Bank
- Life Assurance Company
- Certain bodies which are authorised to raise funds from the public for collective investment, such as unit trusts, UCITS, authorised investment companies etc.
- An authorised members of the Irish Stock Exchange or member firms, which carry on business in the State or a Stock Exchange of another EU member State, who have notified Revenue of their intention to act as a QFM.
- Other persons approved by the Minister for Finance.

Who can avail of ARF's?

- Personal Pension Policyholders, at any time prior to the benefits of their pension funds becoming payable. In normal circumstances this is between age 60 and 75, but it can occur earlier due to ill health.
- Proprietary Directors who are members of an Occupational Pension Scheme can avail of an ARF at any time before their pension becomes payable. A Proprietary Director can also choose voluntary early retirement from age 50 onwards.

- Directors and employees who have made additional voluntary contributions to an occupational pension scheme.

No other individual may avail of an ARF e.g. it is not possible for your personal representative to set up an ARF for your dependents after your death. Neither is it possible for you to pay funds directly into an ARF – it must come from an approved pension arrangement or another ARF.

Setting up your ARF

First you choose a Qualifying Fund Manger, then the funds to be transferred must be certified by the Institution holding your pension funds prior to your retirement e.g. your pension provider, trustees or an employer pension scheme, or it can be another Approved Retirement Fund. The Certificate will state your name and identify you as the beneficial owner of the relevant pension funds.

In addition to this certificate a Declaration must be completed by you indicating your name, address and tax number. This Declaration declares that your pension investment funds are derived solely from a Personal Pension Plan or Occupational Pension Scheme, AVC's or from another ARF. It will also indicate that the funds are not part of an Approved Minimum Retirement Fund.

What is an approved minimum retirement fund? (AMRF)

An Approved Minimum Retirement Fund (AMRF) is a special kind of ARF. Its purpose is to address the criticism that the new rules could allow a spendthrift to dissipate their retirement benefits too quickly. Have a look at the table on page 152 and you'll see immediately how AMRF's come into the equation when your 'specified income' on retirement does not exceed £10,000 pa.

Features of an AMRF

The maximum amount that can be invested in an AMRF is £50,000. In certain circumstances the amount actually invested may be lower or nil.

An AMRF is similar to an ARF but is subject to special restrictions.

The initial investment cannot be accessed prior to the earlier of death or age of 75.

AT A GLANCE ! - YOUR NEW CHOICES AT RETIREMENT

Your Accumulated Pension Fund

1 First, you can take up to 25% of this fund tax free
* See Page 149 under "Tax Free Lump Sum"

2 Next you must establish - does your "specified income" exceed £ 10,000 p.a.?

3

IF YOUR "SPECIFIED INCOME" DOES NOT EXCEED £ 10,000 P.A

3

IF YOUR "SPECIFIED INCOME" EXCEEDS £ 10,000 P.A.

The First £ 50,000 of your Pension Funds

And with any Surplus over £ 50,000

Must be invested in an AMRF

See Approved Minimum Retirement Fund Page 151

Or used to buy a pension annuity

You can opt to buy a Pension Annuity

Alternatively, you may decide to withdraw the total fund less tax

Inve an

See Ap Retire Fun Page

Only surplus accumulated in your AMRF may be withdrawn before you are 75 years of age. These withdrawals will be taxable.

4

After age 75 any withdrawals made from the overall fund and will be taxable.

Any withdr made wil taxable

While an AMRF can be transferred between fund managers, the legislation specifically requires that when this happens the total amount must be transferred. Profits and gains can be withdrawn from an AMRF before you reach the age of 75 but they cannot be transferred to another AMRF independent of the initial investment.

The AMRF automatically converts into an ARF on death, or the attainment of age 75.

Specified income

The legislation makes it quite clear that an AMRF is a fall-back position for individuals who are otherwise not well provided for in terms of retirement income, so if you have "specified income" of £10,000 or more available to you at retirement age there is no requirement on you to effect an AMRF.

"Specified Income" is defined as a pension or an annuity which is payable to you for life. This can include any ordinary pension annuity or Social Welfare Pensions and Foreign Pensions.

Timing your retirement under the new rules is important from the point of view of specified income e.g. if you retire a month before your Social Welfare pension becomes payable, it will not count as specified income.

It is possible for you to increase your specified income by purchasing a pension annuity under the traditional pension rules. Once this annuity is in payment it will become specified income.

Remember, under the new rules you must have the full £10,000 specified income to avoid creating an AMRF e.g. a specified income of £9,000 will still require you to create the full AMRF of £50,000 at retirement.

ARF investments

- Within an ARF you can – through your QFM - invest in bank or building society deposits, life assurance products, or other forms of investment, such as stocks and shares, property etc.

- You can make withdrawals from your ARF at any time, subject to the terms of the investment option you choose.

- You may also use your ARF to buy a pension annuity at any time.

Multiple ARF's

The new legislation clearly envisages that you may have more than one ARF.

Personal pensions

In the context of Personal Pensions this can arise through simply having a range of different policies and there is no requirement on you to exercise all your encashment options at the same time. This can allow you flexibility to extract tax-free cash from your different Pension Plans on a phased basis over a number of years. For Example if you had 10 policies each worth £15,000, you could encash one policy each year between ages 60 and 70 taking 25% of each policy tax-free. This would reduce the effective tax rate from 22% to 16.5% for standard rate taxpayers and from 44% to 33% for higher rate taxpayers.

New rules and old rules

It is possible for proprietary directors to have a number of benefits accumulated over the years with various employers. Some of these benefits may relate to periods when you were a Proprietary Director and some may not. Where benefits are held separately it would appear that the new rules will be applied separately to each benefit and some will qualify under these new rules and some may not.

If on the other hand as a Proprietary Director you amalgamate all your benefits into a scheme in respect of which you are Proprietary Director it would appear that all the benefits would qualify under the new rules, even if some of the transfer values were in respect of employments in which you did not satisfy the criteria of a Proprietary Director.

Annual statement

A QFM must provide an annual statement to the beneficial owner of each ARF. This statement must be issued within three months of the end of the year of assessment (by 6th July each year).

Drawing on an Approved Retirement Fund or an Approved Minimum Retirement Fund

You can draw on an Approved Retirement Fund in part or total at any time. However, you can only withdraw from the accumulated investment profits of an Approved Minimum Retirement Fund before age 75. Any withdrawal from an Approved Retirement Fund or Approved Minimum Retirement Fund is taxable.

ARF income options

If you take a regular income from an Approved Retirement Fund, unlike a traditional pension, this income is not guaranteed for life. The main advantage of an Approved Retirement Fund is that it helps you retain flexibility and control over your pension fund investments after retirement.

With a traditional pension you are converting your pension fund into a guaranteed income for your own life and that of your chosen financial dependants. It does not matter if the returns from investment markets are poor, or if you or your dependants live for a very long time because all the relevant pensions are guaranteed by the life assurance company.

The chart on page 156 compares the relative advantages of using an Approved Retirement Fund and a Traditional Pension Arrangement to providing a regular future income for you and your family. The table shows the yearly potential incomes from a pension fund of £ 100,000 and assumes you retire at age 60.

Traditional pension

This section shows a single life Inflation Protected Pension. It will guarantee to pay this amount for life, no matter how long you live and the payment will increase by 3% each year. This traditional pension is based on male rates - rates for women will be lower. However, unlike the Approved Retirement Fund, there is no cash-in value once the pension has commenced.

Traditional Pension			Approved Retirement Fund			
Increasing at 3% a year			ARF growing at 4% p.a.		ARF growing at 7% p.a.	
Age	Cash-in value	Annual income before tax	Cash in value before tax	Annual income before tax	Cash-in value before tax	Annual income before tax
	£	£	£	£	£	£
60	0	6,160	92,833	6,160	95,635	6,160
61	0	6,345	88,954	6,345	94,609	6,345
62	0	6,535	84,776	6,535	93,329	6,535
63	0	6,731	75,464	6,731	91,773	6,731
64	0	6,933	70,301	7,141	89,920	6,933
65	0	7,141	64,778	7,355	87,747	7,141
66	0	7,355	58,880	7,576	85,229	7,355
67	0	7,576	52,589	7,803	82,339	7,576
68	0	7,808	45,888	8,037	79,049	7,803
69	0	8,037	38,759	8,279	75,329	8,037
70	0	8,279	31,181	8,527	71,147	8,279
71	0	8,527	23,136	8,783	66,469	8,527
72	0	8,783	23,136	9,046	61,260	8,783
73	0	9,046	14,603	9,318	55,479	9,046
74	0	9,318	5,559	5,635	49,088	9,318
75	0	9,597	0	0	42,041	9,597
76	0	9,885	0	0	34,293	9,885
77	0	10,182	0	0	25,795	10,182
78	0	10,487	0	0	16,494	10,487
79	0	10,802	0	0	6,335	10,802
80	0	11,126	0	0	0	6,335

Source – Irish Life

ARF income

In the Approved Retirement Fund section, the growth rates we illustrate are those recommended by the Society of Actuaries in Ireland. Actual return could be higher or lower than those illustrated. It is obvious from this chart if your Approved Retirement fund only grows at 4% p.a. and your withdrawals are the equivalent of a traditional pension, your ARF fund will "bomb out" at age 74. On the other hand if the ARF fund grew at 7% p.a. it would bomb out at age 80 - the key to ARF investments is to select a fund that will give both security and high growth rates long term.

Tax

ARF Taxes fall under two main headings; **Taxes during your retirement** and **taxes on death**.

Taxes during your retirement

All withdrawals from ARF funds first accepted on or after 6th April 2000 will be subject to PAYE (see Page 364 for taxes on ARF funds first accepted before 6th April 2000).

Taxes on death

ARF Funds Left To	Tax Due
Surviving Spouse – cash transferred into another ARF.	• No tax on transfer to a surviving spouse's ARF. • All subsequent withdrawals by the spouse will be liable to Income Tax under PAYE. • Exempt from Inheritance Tax.
ARF - cash directly to a surviving spouse.	• The full amount is treated as income of the deceased spouse in year of death and taxed accordingly. • Exempt from Inheritance Tax.
Children over 21 at date of parent's death.	• Standard rate tax on amount inherited, deducted at source. • Exempt from Inheritance Tax.
Children under 21 at date of parents' death.	• No income tax liability. • Amount is subject to Inheritance Tax.
Others.	• The full amount is treated as income of the deceased in year of death and tax accordingly. • Balance subject to Inheritance Tax.

A quick reference guide to traditional and new retirement options.

Benefits being taken from	Traditional retirement options	New retirement options
Personal pension plan	25% of benefit can be taken as tax-free lump sum. • Balance taken in pension.	25% of benefit can be taken as tax-free lump sum. Balance* can be; • Invested in an ARF, or • Taken as **taxable** lump sum, or • Taken in pension.
Occupational pension scheme for proprietary director.	• Tax-free lump sum of up to 150% x final remuneration, for 20 years or more service • Balance taken in pension.	25% of benefit can be taken as tax-free lump sum, regardless of service. Balance* can be: • Taken as **taxable** lump sum, or • Invested in an ARF, or • Taken in pension.
AVC's	• Take, in conjunction with main scheme tax free lump sum up to an overall maximum of 150% of final remuneration, for 20 years or more service. • Balance must be taken in pension.	• Take, in conjunction with main scheme, as tax free lump sum up to an overall maximum of 150% of final remuneration, for 20 years or more service. • Balance* can be: • Taken as **taxable** lump sum, or • Invested in an ARF, or • Taken in pension.

* subject to £ 50,000 being invested in an AMRF or converted into a guaranteed income for life, if you do not, at that time, have specified income for life of at least £ 10,000 a year.

Personal pensions

Personal pension plans are of interest mostly to employees who are not in an occupational pension scheme and to the self-employed. They are savings plans designed to yield a fund on retirement and financial protection in respect of early death or disability. They are particularly attractive because, up to certain limits depending on your age, all contributions to personal pension plans are fully tax-deductible and profits realised by a life assurance company on the investments within these plans are not liable to any tax. The Revenue Commissioners have laid down a number of rules governing Personal Pension Plans:

- A personal pension is usually paid after the age of 60 and before age 75. However, it is not necessary to stop working before you can commence receiving a pension.

- A pension may also become payable before the age of 60 if you become, as the rule states, "permanently incapable through infirmity of mind or body of carrying on his own occupation or any occupation of a similar nature for which they are trained or fitted".

- 25% of the total accumulated fund may be taken as a tax-free cash lump sum, on retirement.

- A pension may be provided, for a spouse or dependants, provided the total amount paid after your death does not exceed your own pension entitlements.

- You can retain ownership of the fund by transferring it to an ARF (Approved Retirement Fund). See page 149

Starting a plan

The main aim of a personal pension plan is to enable you to build up a large cash fund in a tax efficient manner for retirement. This cash fund will normally come from the contributions you make to the fund during your working life and the investment profits earned by these contribution within the fund over the years. So, the size of your cash fund at retirement will be decided by four main factors:

- Starting Early.

- Investment Strategy.

- Growth Rates.

- Tax Reliefs.

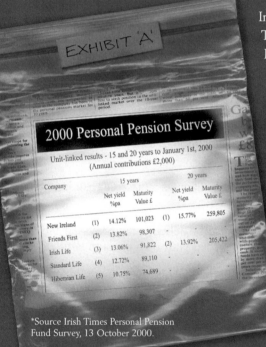

Starting early

The importance of starting early is illustrated in the following example.

John, Joanne, Mary and Pat started paying a contribution of £1,000 p.a. to a personal pension plan 10, 15, 20 and 25 years before their 60th birthdays. Each pay tax at the high rate (42%) and each fund grows at 8.25% p.a. net of all charges. If all four assumptions work as planned, at retirement each pension fund will have the following values:

John's	£17,255
Joanne's	£32,406
Mary's	£56,784
Pat's	£91,844

If we analysis these retirement funds we will see that they are made up of three segments.

☐ Growth generated within each fund.
■ The net contributions paid into the fund (i.e. premiums paid less tax relief claimed).
▨ Tax relief @ 42%.

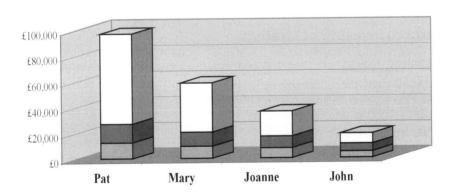

Have a look at the chart above and you'll quickly see that the segment with the greatest potential for future value is the growth generated within the funds itself. See how much growth is generated within Pat's fund over 25 years as opposed to what John's contributions have achieved over 10 years. Quite simply, the earlier you start your pension plan, the greater the potential for large fund values at retirement.

Investment strategy

A good fund manager will make your money work hard for you within the parameters set by the individual pension fund you choose. You set these parameters initially when you complete the proposal form by deciding into which type of fund you wish your contributions invested.

Different types of pension funds will carry different levels of investment risk and hence give different levels of return. Investment risks are normally measured by investment strategy and investment strategy can be classified under four headings:

- Cautious.

- Measured.

- Active.

- Aggressive.

Cautious investment strategy

This strategy will lead to investments in assets with many similarities to cash and short term government stock. It will suit you if you are due to retire soon or if you have a low risk threshold.

Measured investment strategy

A measured strategy will invest in equities, property and EU government stocks etc. It may also offer some level of underlying guarantee with potential to give higher than average returns over a chosen period.

Active investment strategy

An active investment strategy will invest in equities, property and government stocks etc. with a greater emphasis on equities and will probably have no underlying guarantee.

Aggressive investment strategy

The most risky of all with potential to give the highest returns over the long term. An aggressive investment strategy will probably be totally equity based, and is suitable during your early years of your working life or if you have a high tolerance to risk.

The importance of growth

Now that we've seen how starting early can have an enormous effect on the actual value of your pension fund, there is one other important influential factor which must be taken into consideration. This is the type of investment strategy (and risk) that you are prepared to take with your money.

Let us assume that you invest £1,000 p.a. over 25 years in a personal pension plan.

Fund A grows at 5.25% p.a. net of all charges - a cautious low-risk investment strategy.

Fund B grows at 8.25% p.a. net of all charges - a measured medium -risk investment strategy.

Fund C grows at 11.25% p.a. net of all charges - an aggressive high-risk investment strategy.

Each fund, assuming that nothing unexpected happens to your investment, will mature approximately as follows:

Fund A	£ 58,769
Fund B	£ 91,844
Fund C	£146,549

At first glance Fund C looks the most effective. To achieve these high returns, however, this fund will be heavily based in equities, - the most volatile investments of all. The much lower returns generated by Fund A reflect the fact that your money will be predominantly invested in Cash Deposits and Gilts and hence is very secure.

As a prudent investor you will adapt an investment strategy to suit your individual circumstances at different times. For example, in the early years you may be prepared to adopt an aggressive strategy while in the years coming up to your retirement you'll opt for a more caution option, one that will protect the gains that you have already made.

Tax relief

From 6th April 2001 the maximum contributions on which relief can be claimed are as follows;

163

	% of net relevant earnings
Under 30 years of age	15%
30 to 39 years of age	20%
40 to 49 years of age	25%
50 years of age and over	30%

Relevant Earnings

Relevant earnings consist of income from non-pensionable employment or from self-employment. A husband and wife have separate relevant earnings which cannot be aggregated for pension purposes. PHI benefits are considered relevant earning for pension purposes.

Net relevant earnings

These consist of relevant earning less capital allowances, trading losses and certain other charges e.g. covenants and mortgage interest for which you can claim tax relief.

Back dating tax relief

Personal contributions paid between 5th April and the following 31st January may be offset against your taxable income in the preceding tax year, provided you elect to do so.

Example

John is under 30 and a 44% taxpayer. In December 2000 he pays an initial pension contribution of £10,000 to a Personal Pension Plan. John's net relevant earnings are as follows:

| 2000/01 | £35,000 |
| 1999/00 | £32,000 |

John can claim relief up to 15% of his net relevant earnings in the current tax year (2000/01). Under the backdating provisions he can claim up to 15% of his net relevant earnings in the preceding tax year (1999/00) provided he paid the relevant contributions before 31st January 2001 and he elects to have the relevant part of this £10,000 contribution offset against his 1999/00 income. His position will work out as follows:

Tax year	Net relevant earnings	Maximum contributions 15%	Tax relief 44%	Net cost
	£	£	£	£
2000/01	£35,000	£5,250	£2,310	£2,940
1999/00	£32,000	£4,750	£2,090	£2,660

As we pointed out earlier two of the major attractions of pension plans are tax relief available on the contributions you pay and the tax concession granted to the pension providers on investment returns.

If you are a higher rate taxpayer, the aggregate benefit of these two reliefs can effectively treble your fund over a period of 25 years.

Death before retirement

Excluding life assurance cover, most personal pension plans will provide for the payment of a lump sum to your estate if you die before claiming a pension. This lump sum is payable to your personal legal representatives and will be distributed according to the terms of your Will if you have made one, or according to the terms of the Succession Act if you have not.

Early retirement due to ill health

Normally, you may not draw on your pension accumulated under any of these plans until you reach 60. Legislation does, however, provide for early retirement if you become "permanently incapable through infirmity of mind or body, of carrying on your own occupation or any occupation of a similar nature for which you are trained or fitted".

Retiring

You can normally retire at any time between the ages of 60 and 75 years. However, you are not obliged to retire before you take your pension. At retirement age or on early retirement due to ill health, your choices will normally include the option to take up to a maximum of 25% of your accumulated fund as a tax-free lump sum and to use the balance to purchase an annuity or to transfer it to an ARF/AMRF. See Page 149.

Contribution dilemma for the self employed

One of the many peculiarities, not to mention injustices, of our taxation system is that the self-employed and people in non-pensionable employment still get well and truly clobbered by Revenue rules when planning their pensions compared to the very favourable tax position enjoyed by employees in pensionable employment.

While the Minister improved the position dramatically in 1999 there still remains a major dilemma.

Perhaps the best way to explain the dilemma that the self-employed, and people in non-pensionable employment, can find themselves in when it comes to providing for their own pension is to compare their strictly regulated contribution position with that of their employee pension plan counterparts.

The rules allow the self-employed and people in non-pensionable employment to contribute a fixed percentage of their net relevant earnings to a personal pension plan with full tax-relief.

Employers, on the other hand, may contribute whatever contributions are necessary to build up a pension fund, which will provide their employees with a pension of 2/3rds final pensionable salary, plus a widow's and dependent's pension, plus the annual escalation in the value of these pensions to offset the increases in the cost of living during their retirement.

To illustrate this point, let us take a look at Eric in non-pensionable employment wishing to retire at age 65, embarking on a personal pension plan now. The maximum percentage of net relevant earnings, which he may contribute to a personal pension plan and get full tax relief with effect from 5th April 1999, are as follows:

Age	Maximum pension contributions as % of net relevant earnings
Under 30 years	15%
30 to 39	20%
40 to 49	25%
50 years & over	30%

Let us assume that Eric now starts making these maximum annual contributions to his personal pension plan. The chart below illustrates his *average* yearly contributions as a percentage of his net relevant earnings, between the date of commencement and retirement age 65.

Eric's age when he commenced the plan	Eric's average annual contribution as % of his net rental earnings
25	24.375
30	25.710
35	26.670
40	28.000
45	28.750
50	30.000
55	30.000
60	30.000

Up to 5% of Eric's Net Relevant Earnings can be allocated to purchase a life assurance cover, and because life assurance cover is just about essential for everyone in this category, the reality is that it leaves a smaller amount for pension contributions. Because of this stringent 'pension contributions ceiling' self-employed and people in new pensionable employment must take great care to start their pension scheme early. Otherwise their pension income could end up as only a tiny fraction of their final income.

It is not always easy for self-employed people to have the money or foresight, at a time when they are setting up in business to make the maximum contributions allowed at that time to a pension plan. But if they don't the financial consequences can be very punitive.

If Eric was an employee, Eric's employer could make the pension contributions illustrated below and get full tax relief on these payments, assuming Eric had no existing pension provision and that he will have 10 years pensionable service with his employer at normal retirement (65).

Eric's age when contributions commenced	Maximum annual contributions as % of Eric's salary
30	32.75
40	48.67
45	83.11
60	257.73

Pension contributions above are illustrated as a percentage of Eric's pensionable salary and it is assumed that they commenced at one of the relevant ages.

To cap it all, if Eric's employer fails to make these maximum payments, Eric himself may contribute up to 15% of his salary to finance any shortfall in benefits not provided by his employer. And yes! these costs can be offset against Eric's personal taxable income.

Women fare even better within an employer's pension schemes, as they tend to live longer and retire earlier than men and thus require a larger pension fund at normal retirement age to provide maximum pension benefits.

As you can see, the financial difference between these two examples is quite extraordinary. So what should a person in self-employment, or non-pensionable employment, do to aspire towards securing some of the additional financial well being that members of occupational pensions plans can receive?

The basic advice is to start making pension contributions as early as possible, preferably in your early twenties.

If you're a late starter, as so many are, you should talk to a good financial advisor about additional investment opportunities that will help to supplement your retirement income.

Another possibility is for you to become an employee with the aim of building up to 10 years of pensionable service before retiring. Your employer (who may of course, be your own company) could then provide all your pension benefits in a tax efficient manner.

Life assurance and pensions

Should you die before reaching the age of 75, or retirement, most plans can provide for the payment of an additional lump sum by way of life assurance cover. This sum is normally tax-free.

If you include this facility in your pension, the main advantage is that the full cost of the life assurance chosen can be offset against your taxable income, provided that this premium does not exceed 5% of your net relevant earning and that, overall, the contributions to your personal pension plan remain within the 15% or 30% limit outlined earlier.

Disability insurance

Another feature which can be built onto most personal pension plans is Disability Insurance and for self-employed people this can be very useful.

In the event of your becoming disabled, or for any other reason are too ill to work, disability insurance could provide monthly payments of up to 75% of your income prior to disablement up to normal retirement age or for the duration of your illness, if this is shorter. Payments normally commence after a period has elapsed from the date of your disability. This period could be 13, 26, or 52 weeks, depending on the particular plan you choose.

The full cost of Disability Insurance can be offset against your taxable income, provided it does not exceed 10% of your total income.

Comment: Disability Insurance is well worth considering.

Tax

Social welfare pensions

Social Welfare pensions are liable to Income Tax; however, no tax is deducted at source. If your Social Welfare pension is your only source of income you may be exempt from tax altogether as your income will be below the relevant exemption limit. (See page 198).

If you are in receipt of other income on which you pay PAYE e.g. a pension from your former employer the Revenue will reduce your tax free allowance by the amount of your Social Welfare pension. This means that you will pay more tax on your employer's pension and this compensates for the fact that no tax is deducted from your Social Welfare pension.

If you pay income tax under the self assessment, Preliminary Tax will be payable on your Social Welfare pension in the normal way.

Other Irish pension income

Other Irish pensions are liable to income tax under Schedule E, similar way to your salary. Tax is deducted at source under the PAYE.

UK pension

A UK Pension, other than a government pension received in Ireland by an Irish resident, is taxed in Ireland only. A UK pension paid by a government or a local authority to an Irish resident UK citizen in respect of services rendered in the discharge of government functions will be taxable only in the UK. For example, a UK citizen resident in Ireland who receives a pension from the UK Government is liable only to UK tax on this pension.

Foreign pensions

Foreign pensions received in Ireland by an Irish resident will normally be taxed in the country of residence only.

10

Social welfare benefits at a glance

Pay-related social insurance

The main PRSI legislation comprises the Social Welfare (Consolidation) Act, 1993 together with subsequent amendments. The subject is a wide one and here we outline:

- How much you pay.

- Your benefit entitlements.

Contribution years

The contribution year for PRSI purposes is the same as the tax year, beginning 6th April and ending the following 5th April. Contribution years are normally referred to as tax years.

*Note:*The tax year will change to a calendar year with effect from 1st January 2002.

Benefit years

The benefit year begins on the first Monday in January each year. Your entitlement to short-term PRSI benefits is normally based on your paid and/or credited contributions in the tax year ending the previous 5th of April.

So, if you cease to pay PRSI contributions, your entitlement to benefits will normally last for the remainder of that calendar year and the following calendar year.

PRSI contributions are calculated as a percentage of your gross pay, less any payments you may make to an approved pension scheme which are deducted at source by the employer and approved by the Revenue Commissioners. PRSI contribution costs are normally shared by the employee and employer. For the majority of employees, PRSI contributions are collected through the PAYE tax system.

The following chart shows how the Class A1 rate, which is the PRSI Class most employees pay, is calculated in the 2001 tax year.

	Employee		Employer	
	Rate %	Ceiling in £	Rate %	Ceiling in £
Health Levy	2.00	£28,250		
Pension	1.53	£28,250	3.48	No ceiling
Occupational Injury	Nil	Nil	0.50	No ceiling
Redundancy	Nil	Nil	0.40	No ceiling
Others -unemployment, disability, maternity, dental or optical benefit etc.	2.47	£28,250	7.62	No ceiling
Total	6.00		12.00	

Health levies are not payable for employees earning less than £226 per week.

The employers contributions for employees earning less than £280 per week is 8.50%. From the 6th April 2001, people paying the full rate of PRSI will have a weekly exemption from Social Insurance on the first £100 of their income.

Those paying the modified PRSI will have a weekly exemption of £20 per week.

Claiming social insurance benefits

Normally, to claim a social insurance benefit it is necessary to have a minimum number of PRSI contributions. PRSI contributions are normally classified as follows:

• PRSI Paid

  and

• PRSI Credits.

172

PRSI contributions are payable each week during which you are working in insurable employment. There is no charge for PRSI credits but for many benefits they can be as valuable as PRSI contributions paid.

First PRSI paid

When you become insured for the first time under the Social Welfare Acts you are automatically given PRSI credits for the earlier part of that tax year, in addition to credits for the previous two tax years. For example, if you commenced employment for the first time on the 5th of October you would be entitled to credits from the 6th of April to the 4th of October plus the two previous tax years. These credits can help you qualify for Disability Unemployment, an Adoptive Benefit as soon as you have worked and paid PRSI contributions for 39 weeks.

Credits after you have become insured

If you stop paying PRSI contributions, PRSI credits are normally awarded for the weeks you receive Disability Benefit, Unemployment Benefit, Maternity Benefit, Invalidity Pension, Retirement Pension or Injury Benefit. Similarly, credits may be awarded for the weeks in which you received Unemployment Assistance, if you are eligible for credits. (If you have never worked you wouldn't get credits with Unemployment Assistance).

A break in PRSI

If two consecutive tax years have elapsed without contributions having been paid or credited, no additional PRSI credits can be awarded until a further 26 PRSI contributions have been paid.

Voluntary contributions

A person who ceases to be insured under Pay-Related Social Insurance can, if under 66 years of age, opt to continue insurance on a voluntary basis for limited benefits, provided 156 PRSI contributions have been paid and you apply within 12 months of the end of the tax year during which you had paid PRSI or had a PRSI credit. There are two rates of voluntary contributions:

• The high rate of voluntary contribution applies if you were compulsorily insured at the higher rates of PRSI. Voluntary contributions at this rate normally provide the PRSI pension benefits.

Social welfare benefits at a glance

PRSI classes and benefit entitlements

	A	B	C	D	E	H	J	M	P	S	See Page
Adoptive Benefit	*	-	-	-	*	*	-	-	-	*	179
Bereavement Grant	*	*	-	*	*	*	-	-	-	*	187
Carer's Benefit	*	*	*	*	*	*	-	-	-	-	183
Disability Benefit	*	-	-	-	*	*	-	-	*	-	184
Invalidity Pension	*	-	-	-	*	*	-	-	-	-	120
Maternity Benefit	*	-	-	-	*	*	-	-	-	*	177
Occupational Injuries Benefit	*	*	-	*	-	-	*	*	-	-	185
Old Age Contributory Pension	*	-	-	-	*	*	-	-	-	*	114
Orphan's Contributory Allowance	*	*	*	*	*	*	-	-	-	*	119
Redundancy	*	-	-	-	-	-	-	-	-	-	181
Retirement Pension	*	-	-	-	*	*	-	-	-	-	111
Treatment Benefit - Dental, Optical, Hearing Aids & Contact Lenses	*	-	-	-	*	*	-	-	*	-	175
Umemployment Benefit	*	-	-	-	-	*	-	-	*	-	179
Widow's/Widower's Contributory Pension	*	*	*	*	*	*	-	-	-	*	117
Working in the EU											
- Unemployment Benefit	*	-	-	-	-	*	-	*	-	-	189
- Health Services	*	*	*	*	-	*	*	*	-	*	189

- The reduced rate of voluntary contribution applies to certain Public Servants insured at the lower rates. Voluntary contributions at this level normally provide for Contributory Widow(er)'s Pension and Orphan's Contributory Allowance.

Remember, Social Insurance contributions are not a tax but their effect is very similar as you pay contributions out of your gross income. However, it should also be pointed out that benefits are not means-tested and you are entitled to them as a right once you satisfy the necessary contribution conditions.

PRSI benefit entitlements

Summarised on page 174 are:
The main benefit entitlements applicable to the relevant PRSI Classes.

- The page reference to where you will find the necessary back-up information in this guide.

Treatment benefits

Treatment Benefit covers Dental Benefit, Optical Benefit, Contact Lenses and Hearing Aids.

Dental benefit

Dental Benefit is available to persons who are paying PRSI at classes A, E, H and P and their dependent spouse.

Dental benefit covers a number of different items of dental treatment some of which are free, while for others you must pay part of the cost:

- Dental examination, diagnosis, scaling and polishing, including mild gum treatment are free. For other treatment the Department of Social, Community and Family Affairs will pay a set amount and you pay the balance.

- You can also have dentures fitted, repaired or replaced. The Department of Social, Community and Family Affairs will give a fixed amount towards the cost and you must pay the balance.

Optical benefit

Optical Benefit is available to persons who are paying PRSI Classes, A, E, H and P and their dependent spouses. Optical Benefit covers a number of different items of optical treatment: sight test, advice from a doctor, optician or an ophthalmic surgeon are normally free.

Glasses with a certain kind of frame are also free. If you desire more expensive frames the Department will pay a fixed amount towards the cost and you pay the balance. Repairs to your glasses may also be free depending on the nature of the actual repairs.

You can only claim Optical Benefit directly from a doctor, an optician or an ophthalmic surgeon, who is on the approved panel of The Department of Social, Community and Family Affairs.

Contact lenses

If you get contact lenses instead of glasses, the Department of Social, Community and Family Affairs will pay a fixed amount i.e. the same amount as is paid for glasses, and you must pay the balance. If, however, you need contact lenses for medical reasons the Department will pay up to half the cost subject to a maximum of £225, provided you have a doctor's recommendation.

Hearing aids

Hearing Aid Benefit is available to PRSI Classes, A, E, H and P and their dependent spouses.

Before you make a claim for hearing aids, it is normally necessary to have a letter of recommendation from your doctor and to satisfy the contribution conditions.

You should then be entitled to a refund of 50% of the cost from Social Insurance up to a maximum of £225, provided you get your hearing aid from an approved supplier.

The Department of Social, Community and Family Affairs will normally pay half the cost of repairs.

PRSI Conditions for Treatment Benefit (Dental and Optical Benefit, Hearing Aids and Contact Lenses)

176

Age	Contributions required
Under 21 years	39 weeks PRSI paid since starting work.
Between 21 and 24 years	39 weeks PRSI paid and 39 weeks PRSI paid or credited in the governing tax year, of which a minimum of 13 weeks must be paid contributions. The 13 weeks paid can be in any one of the last four tax years or in the current tax year - see below.
Between 25 and 65 years	260 weeks PRSI paid and 39 weeks PRSI paid or credited in the governing tax year, of which a minimum of 13 weeks must be paid contributions - see below.
Over 66 years	260 weeks PRSI paid and 39 weeks PRSI paid or credited in either of the last two years before reaching age 66, of which a minimum of 13 weeks must be paid contributions.

Note: The 13 weeks paid contributions can be in the relevant tax year on which the claim is based, in one of the two previous tax years or in any tax year after the relevant tax year.

If you are eligible for Treatment Benefit at age 60 or 66, you and your dependent spouse will be eligible for as long as you both live. If your spouse was entitled to Treatment Benefit at the time of death and you were dependent on them at the time, you may retain entitlement for as long as you remain a widow(er).

Maternity benefit

Maternity Benefit is payable to women in current employment or self employed insured at PRSI Classes, A, E, H and S.

Maternity Benefit is not payable on your spouse's insurance. It is payable only where the mother is an insured person and satisfies the PRSI conditions on her own insurance record.

Who can qualify

You will qualify for Maternity Benefit if you are an employee and you;

- are in employment which is covered by the Maternity Protection Act 1994 immediately before the first day of your maternity leave (the last day of insurable employment may be within 10 weeks of the expected date of birth of the baby);

- are or have been self-employed;

  and

- satisfy the PRSI contribution conditions.

Contribution conditions

- You must have at least 39 weeks PRSI paid since you first started work and at least 39 weeks PRSI paid or credited in the relevant tax year before the year in which your maternity leave starts.

  or

- 39 weeks PRSI paid in the 12 months immediately before the first day of your maternity leave.

For claims made in	The relevant tax years are
1999	1997/98
2000	1998/99

If you are self-employed you must have

- 52 weeks PRSI contributions paid at Class S in the last relevant tax year before the year in which your claim is made

  or

- 52 weeks PRSI contributions paid at Class S in the second last relevant tax year before the year in which your claim is made

The allowance is payable for a continuous period of 14 weeks. Of this 14 weeks, you must take at least 4 weeks (up to a maximum of 10 weeks) before your baby is due. Otherwise, you may lose benefit.

From May 2000 the weekly rate of payment is 70%, based on a weekly average of gross earnings in the relevant tax year, up to a limit of £12,840 p.a. or £172.80 per week maximum or a minimum of £90.70 per week from May 2000.

Budget 2001 change: From 6th April 2001 the minimum rate of Maternity Benefit is £98.70 and the maximum rate is £183. The number of weeks of payment is also being extended from 14 to 18 weeks.

Adoptive benefit

Adoptive Benefit is payable for 14 weeks to adoptive parents paying PRSI at class A,E, H and S who satisfies the contribution conditions. The rate of payment and the PRSI contribution conditions are the same as those applying to Maternity Benefit (see above).

Budget 2001 change: The number of weeks of payment is extended from 14 to 18 weeks.

Unemployment benefit

Unemployment Benefit is available to PRSI Classes A, H and P.

Unemployment Benefit is paid weekly and to qualify you must:

- Be unemployed.
- Be capable of work.
- Be available for and genuinely looking for full-time work.
- Be under age 66.
- Have suffered a substantial loss of employment and earnings.
- Satisfy the PRSI conditions.

PRSI conditions

You must have at least 39 weeks PRSI paid and at least 39 weeks PRSI paid or credited in the relevant tax year. The relevant tax year is the last complete tax year before the year you claim. Unemployment Benefit is normally paid from the fourth day after you claim. However, if you had lodged a claim for Disability or

Is your family working and finding it hard to make ends meet?

Did you know that Family Income Supplement is based on

net pay?

SW 22

Family Income Supplement

FIS

" an option for families on low income..."

Department of Social Welfare

It could benefit your family to enquire about the scheme at your Social Welfare Local Office or the FIS section in Longford Tel: 01 874 8444 or 043 45211 or Information Service at 01 8748444

Unemployment Benefit or Maternity Benefit in the previous 13 weeks, payment may be made from your first day of unemployment.

Age conditions

If you are under age 18, Unemployment Benefit can be paid for up to 156 days (6 months).

If you are 18 or over and under age 65, Unemployment Benefit can be paid for up to 390 days (15 months).

If you are aged between 65 and 66 when your Unemployment Benefit ends, you may continue to receive it up to age 66, provided you have at least 156 weeks PRSI paid.

Note: People paying class "P" PRSI are entitled to unemployment benefit for up to 13 weeks in each calendar year.

Redundancy Payments

If you receive a redundancy payment in excess of £15,000, you may be disqualified from receiving Unemployment Benefit for up to nine weeks. This disqualification does not apply if you are aged 55 years or more.

How to claim

"Sign-on" for Unemployment Benefit at your nearest Social Welfare office on the first day of your unemployment and bring your P45 (if you have it) with you, together with two forms of identification. One of these should be your Birth Certificate or Passport.

Once your claim is in payment, you can nominate a post office where you wish to be paid.

Short-time/night work

If you work on systematic short-time, you can get Unemployment Benefit for the days you do not work. However, the total number of days at work and on benefit cannot be more than five in any week.

Re-qualifying for benefit

If you have exhausted your Unemployment Benefit, you may re-qualify after working and paying PRSI for 13 weeks. Any weeks you work after you have drawn 6 months benefit, count towards the 13 weeks needed to requalify. At age 65 you do not need the 13 weeks paid to requalify.

Unemployment Benefit is made up of a personal rate plus extra amounts for your dependants.

Tax

Unemployment Benefit is taxed at your relevant rate of tax. However, the first £10 per week of your Unemployment Benefit together with additional payments for child dependants is exempt from tax. Also, if you receive Unemployment Benefit for short time working, e.g. if you work a three day week, any Unemployment Benefit received for other days is exempt from income tax.

Reduced benefits

If you are getting a Widow's/Widower's Pension or One-Parent Family Payment from the Department of Social, Community and Family Affairs, half the personal rate of benefit is payable. This also applies if you are receiving a social security widow's pension from another EU country. No increases are payable for child dependents.

Disqualifications

Unemployment Benefit is not paid in the following circumstances, if you are:

- Out of work because of a trade dispute.
- Absent from the State (unless you are going to another EU country to look for work).
- Imprisoned.
- Convicted of an offence in relation to Unemployment Benefit (you can be disqualified for three months).

You can be disqualified from payment for up to nine weeks if you:

- Lose your job through your own misconduct.
- Leave your job of your own will and without good reason.

- Refuse an offer of suitable work.

- Refuse to do a FÁS course without good reason.

- Do not avail of any reasonable opportunity of getting suitable work.

Back to work allowance

This scheme allows the unemployed or those receiving the One Parent Family Payment, Blind Person's Pension or Disability Allowance for 12 months to take up employment or self-employment and retain a percentage of their social welfare payment and secondary benefits (subject to certain conditions). You will be paid 75% of your existing Social Welfare payment the first year, 50% for the second year and 25% for the third year, along with your earnings. Any newly created jobs are eligible under this sector. Self-employed participants will continue to get their full Social Welfare payment for the first year, then 75%, 50% and 25% respectively over the next three years, other support is also available e.g. training and advertising costs.

Carer's Benefit

Carer's Benefit is payable to PRSI classes A,B,C,D,E and H. It is payable to people who leave work in order to care for a person(s) in need of full-time care and attention.

Who can qualify

You will qualify if you - the Carer;

- are age 16 or over and under age 65/66

- live with the person(s) you are looking after or in close proximity

- have been employed for the previous three-month period

- satisfy the PRSI contribution conditions

- give up employment to care for a person(s) on a full-time basis (this employment must have been for a minimum of 19 hours per week or 38 hours per fortnight)

- are not employed or self-employed outside the home (you may work up to 10 hours per week.

- are living in the State

- are not living in a hospital, convalescent home or other similar institution

  and

- the person(s) you are caring for is/are;

    - so disabled as to need full-time care and attention (medical certification is required)

    - not normally living in a hospital, home or other similar institution

PRSI conditions

For a first claim you must have;

- 156 contributions paid since entry into insurable employment

  and

- (a) 39 contributions paid in the relevant tax year

  or

  (b) 39 contributions paid in the 12 month period before the commencement of the Carer's Benefit

  or

  (c) 26 contributions paid in the relevant tax year and 26 contributions paid in the relevant tax year prior to that

Disability benefit

Disability Benefit is available to PRSI classes A, E, H and P.

It is payable if:

- You are under 66.

- Are unfit to work due to illness.

- Satisfy the PRSI conditions.

PRSI conditions:

- 39 weeks PRSI paid

  and

- 39 weeks PRSI paid or credited in the relevant tax year, of which 13 must be paid contributions.

If you do not have 13 paid contributions in the relevant tax year, the following years may be used to satisfy this condition:

- either of the two most previous tax years.

- the most recent complete contribution year;

  or

- the current contribution tax year.

The relevant contribution year in the last complete contribution year before the benefit year in which the Disability Benefit claim is made. The benefit year begins on the first Monday of January in each calendar year and ends on the Saturday immediately before the first Monday in the next calendar year.

Tax

Disability Benefit is taxed at your relevant rate of tax. However, additional payments for child dependants are exempt from income tax. In the 2001 tax year, six weeks (36 days) is exempt from tax.

Occupational injuries benefit

Occupational Injury Benefit is available to PRSI Classes, A, D, J and M. People in employment insurable at PRSI contribution class B may qualify for limited benefit.

The Occupational Injuries Scheme provides social insurance cover for accidents at work and certain diseases contracted due to the work you do. It includes the following:

Injury benefit

This consists of a weekly payment during a period of incapacity for work as a result of an injury received or a disease contracted due to the work you do. It is payable for a maximum of 26 weeks. If you are still unable to work after 26 weeks you may be entitled to Disability Benefit (see page 184).

Disablement benefit

This is a payment in the form of a weekly or monthly pension or, in some instances, a lump sum. It is paid to persons who suffer the loss of physical or mental faculty as a result of an injury at work or a disease contracted at work.

Unemployability supplement

If you are receiving Disablement Benefit and you are not entitled to Disability Benefit, you may qualify for Unemployability Supplement. You must be permanently incapable of work in order to claim this payment.

Survivors benefits (death benefits)

These consist of Widow(er)'s Pension, Orphan's Pension, Dependent Parent's Pension and Funeral Grant.

Medical care

Any medical expenses incurred as a result of an injury at work or a disease developed due to the nature of your work may be claimed under the occupational injuries scheme provided:

• The expenses cannot be met under the Health Acts by your Regional Health Board,

  and

• They are reasonable and necessary.

Employees covered

With very few exceptions, all employees over 16 are covered under this scheme, regardless of the level of their earnings or their age. Permanent civil servants have limited cover only. Among those not covered by the scheme are members of the Defence Forces and the Garda Síochána.

Note: If your accident does not immediately result in disablement or incapacity but you think that it might in the future, you should apply to the Department of Social, Community and Family Affairs for a declaration that the accident was an occupational one. In this way you will be safeguarding your right to benefit in the event of a future claim.

Early retirement due to ill health

This scheme applies if you are a Public Servant paying PRSI at Classes B,C and D and have to give up work because of ill health. It basically gives you PRSI credits to keep your insurance record up-to-date and protects your Contributory Widow's/Widower's Pension and Orphan's Contributory Allowance.

To apply for these credited contributions, you should complete the application form CR35.

Bereavement grant

A small death grant is available to PRSI classes A, B, C, D, E, M and S. The grant, based on PRSI contributions, is payable on the death of:

- an insured person.

- the wife or husband of an insured person.

- the widow or widower of a deceased insured person.

- a contributory pensioner (or spouse of a contributory pensioner).

- a child under age 18, or under 22 if in full-time education (where either parent or the person that the child normally lives with satisfies the PRSI contribution conditions).

- the qualified adult of a contributory pensioner, including those who would be a qualified adult but are getting another Social Welfare payments, e.g. Carer's Allowance.

- a qualified child.

- an orphan or a person to whom an orphan's (contributory) allowance is payable.

When an adult dies, a death grant may be paid based on the PRSI record of the deceased or the spouse of the deceased.

When a child dies, a death grant may be paid based on the PRSI record of either parent or on the record of the person the child normally lives with.

PRSI conditions

The PRSI record used must have enough contributions to satisfy the following conditions:

- 156 contribution weeks paid since entry into insurable employment

or

- at least 26 PRSI contributions paid since entry into insurable employment

and

- 39 PRSI contributions paid or credited in the relevant tax year

or

- a yearly average of 39 PRSI contributions paid or credited over the 3 or 5 tax years before the death occurred or pension age was reached (age 66 at present)

  or

- a yearly average of 26 weeks PRSI contributions paid or credited since 1979 (or since starting work if later) and the end of the tax year before the death occurred or pension age was reached (age 66 at present)

  or

- a yearly average of 26 weeks PRSI contributions paid or credited since 1st October 1970 (or since starting work if later) and the end of the tax year before the death occurred or pension age was reached (age 66 at present)

The relevant tax year is the last complete tax year before the year in which the death occurs or pension age was reached.

Claim forms are available from most Post Offices or from your local Department of Social, Community and Family Affairs office. From 2nd February 2000 the amount of the Bereavement Grant is £ 500 and for a widow(er) with dependant children it is £1,000.

Funeral grant

If the death was due to an accident at work or occupational disease, a higher Funeral Grant under the Occupational Injuries Scheme may be payable instead of a Death Grant.

Working in the EU

As Ireland is a member of the EU, you are legally entitled to look for work in any Member State without a work permit. Each Member State has a national placement service, similar to FÁS. If you wish to seek work in any of the EU countries, you can apply through a FÁS employment services office for a job in the country of your choice. Details of your application will be circulated abroad through the SEDOC system free of charge and if any suitable vacancies arise, you will be notified.

If you qualify for Unemployment Benefit here and have been registered and in receipt of benefit for at least four weeks, you may have your Unemployment Benefit transferred to another EU country for up to 78 days provided you look for and register for work in that country within seven days. You must register for work within seven days from the date you last claimed Unemployment Benefit in Ireland for your unemployment payments to be continuous.

Form E301

This is required to claim Unemployment Benefit. It gives details of your social insurance and employment record and is available from EU Records Section, Social Welfare Services Office, Floor 1, O'Connell Bridge House, D'Olier Street, Dublin 2. Phone (01)8748444. You should also bring your birth certificate as it may be required in certain circumstances.

Health services

EU Regulations also apply to your Health Service entitlements. In the UK you are entitled to a Medical Card and the UK Health Services, as soon as you have an address in the UK and register with a doctor. If you are on a temporary stay in any other EU country you will be entitled to the same Health Services as the nationals of that country. Form E111 is normally required to claim these Health Benefits in all EU countries, excluding the UK.

PRSI/EU documents
• **Form E104** is required if you are claiming Sickness or Maternity Benefit.

- **Form E301** is required if you are claiming Unemployment Benefit.

- **Form E111** is required to claim Health Service Benefits in EU countries excluding the UK.

Forms **E104** and **E301** are available from ;
      International Records Section,
      Social Welfare Service Officer,
      Floor 1,
      O'Connell Bridge House
      D'Olier St.,
      Dublin 2.

while Form **E111** is available from your local Health Board.

Taxation of social welfare payments

Non-taxable

The following payments are not liable to Income Tax:-

- Unemployment Assistance

- Maternity Benefit

- Family Income Supplement

- Back to Work Allowance

- Health & Safety Benefits

- Supplementary Welfare Allowance

Taxable

The following payments are taxable:-

- Retirement Pension

- Contributory Old Age Pension

- Widow's/Widower's Contributory Pension

- Contributory Orphan's Allowance

- Invalidity Pension

- Widow's/Widower's Non-Contributory Pension

- Deserted Wife's Benefit

- Contributory Orphan's Allowance

- Disability Benefit

- Unemployment Benefit

- Occupational Injuries Benefit

- One-Parent Family Payment

- Carer's Allowance

Taxation of unemployment benefit

The first £10 per week of Unemployment Benefit, together with additional payments for child dependants paid with Unemployment Benefit, is exempt from tax. Also, if you receive Unemployment Benefit for short time working, e.g. if you work a three day week, any Unemployment Benefit for other days is exempt from income tax.

Taxation of disability benefit

For the 2000/01 tax year the first six weeks payment (36 days) of disability benefit and payments for child dependants will be ignored for tax purposes. Any increases for child dependents are exempt from tax.

Note: Non-Contributory Old Age Pension, Non-Contributory Widow's/Widower's Pension, Non-Contributory Orphan's Pension, Carer's Allowance, Blind Person's Pension together with social assistance allowance for deserted wives, prisoner's wives and lone parents are also liable to tax. However, as these payments are subject to a means test it would be unlikely that a person in receipt of one of these payments would be liable to tax.

Notice to Employers

Revenue issued an important notice to all employers recently relating to the

- *PAYE Tax Credit System* from 6 April 2001 and

- *the introduction of a calendar Tax Year from 1 January 2002.*

Any employer who has not received a copy of the notice can access the information on our website at www.revenue.ie or request a copy from our 24 hour Forms and Leaflets service at (01) 8780100.

Revenue

Website http://www.revenue.ie

11

Making the income tax system work for you

The day to day control of the tax system is exercised by the Revenue Commissioners, who operate under the guidance of the Minister for Finance. The country is divided into tax districts to which Tax Inspectors are appointed. Tax Inspectors have responsibility for issuing annual tax returns and agreeing annual tax liabilities.

If you disagree with your Tax Inspector's computation of your tax liability, you may appeal it under certain circumstances to the Appeal Commissioners.

Tax agreed between individuals and their Tax Inspector or tax assessed by a Tax Inspector and not appealed within the appropriate time limits is collected by the Office of the Collector General.

Annual returns

PAYE taxpayers are obliged to make a return when requested to do so by their Tax Inspector. Individuals liable to self assessment and proprietary company directors are obliged to make a Return of Income on or before the 31st January for the tax year ending the previous 5th April, whether they are requested to do so or not. If you miss the due date you are subject to a surcharge. This surcharge applies to the full tax payable for the year, regardless of PAYE or any other tax already paid. If your tax return is submitted before the 31st of March, the surcharge is 5%, subject to a maximum of £10,000. Where it is submitted after that date, the surcharge is 10%, subject to a maximum of £50,000.

If you are in doubt about what should be included on your returns, your obligations will be fulfilled if you draw your Inspector's attention to the matter in question. This provision will not apply if the Inspector or the Appeal

Commissioners believe that the doubt was not genuine and you were trying to avoid or evade paying the tax.

Assessments

In general, tax assessments will not be raised until after your return of income has been received. The assessment will be based on the amounts included in your return. If you default on making a return or if the Inspector is dissatisfied with your return, they may raise an assessment.

Where the Inspector is satisfied that the correct tax has been paid for any tax year, they may elect not to raise an assessment for that year. However, you will be notified in writing of this decision. A time limit of six years has been set for raising assessments where a full return of income has been made.

Appeals

If you disagree with your Tax Inspector's computation of your tax liability, you may appeal it under certain circumstances to the Appeal Commissioners, but an appeal will not be allowed against an assessment made by reference to your own figures or figures agreed by you.

Where an estimated assessment is made in the absence of your return, an appeal will only be allowed after your return has been submitted and the tax due on the basis of that return has been paid. The grounds for appeal and what is being appealed against must be stated in the notice of appeal.

Tax credits

From 6th April 2001 a full credit system will be introduced. This system will replace the existing Tax Free Allowance based system. See Chapter 12 "PAYE made easy" for more details.

Change in the tax year

From 1st January 2002 the tax year will change to the calendar year. The year to 31st December 2002 will be the first full tax year under the new system. Because of this changeover the 2002 tax year will be preceded by a short transitional tax "year" which will run from 6th April 2001 to 31st December 2001. During this short tax "year" PAYE taxpayers will pay tax on the actual income earned in the period from 6th April 2001 to 31st December 2001. Self employed taxpayers will be assessed on 74% (270 days ÷365 days) of their profits from their trade or profession for the 12 months period ending 31st December 2001.

Income tax allowance, tax credit and tax bands will also only be allowed at 74% of the annual amounts for the short tax "year".

Classification of income

Income is classified under a number of headings. These headings are known as schedules and the income falling under each is as follows:

Schedule C:

Those who have deducted income tax from certain payments are assessed under this schedule e.g. Banks.

Schedule D:

Case I: Profits from a trade.

Case II: Profits from a profession.

Case III: Interest not taxed at source and all foreign income.

Case IV: Taxed interest income not falling under any other case or schedule.

Case V: Rental income from properties in Ireland.

Schedule E:

Income from offices or employments together with pensions, benefits-in-kind and certain lump sum payments arising from an office or employment.

Schedule F:

Dividends and other distributions from Irish-resident companies.

Tax allowances / Credits

	1999/00		2000/01	2001 full year	2001 9 months
	@ Standard Rate 24%	@Marginal Rate 46%	@Standard Rate 22%	@Standard Rate 20%	@Standard Rate 20%
Single Person	4,200		4,700	5,500	4,070
Married Couple	8,400		9,400	11,000	8,140
Widowed Person					
With dependent children	4,200	500	4,700	5,500	4,070
Without dependant children	4,200	500	5,700	6,500	4,810
Widowed Person (in year of bereavement)	8,400		9,400	11,000	8,140
One-Parent Family					
Widowed Person (Except in Year of Bereavement)	1,050	2,650	4,700	5,500	4,070
Other Person (Deserted, Separated or Unmarried)	1,050	3,150	4,700	5,500	4,070
Widowed Parent Allowance					
First Year After Bereavement		5,000	10,000	10,000	7,400
Second Year After Bereavement		4,000	8,000	8,000	5,920
Third Year After Bereavement		3,000	6,000	6,000	4,440
Fourth Year After Bereavement		2,000	4,000	4,000	2,960
Fifth Year After Bereavement		1,000	2,000	2,000	1,480
Home Carer's Allowance		-	3,000	3,000	2,220
PAYE Allowance		1,000	1,000	2,000	1,480
Age Allowance					
Single/Widowed		400	800	800	592
Married		800	1,600	1,600	1,184
Incapacitated Child Allowance (Income Limit)		800 (2,100)	1,600 (2,100)	1,600 (2,100)	1,184 (1,554)
Dependent Relative Allowance (Income Limit)		110 (5,152)	220 (5,564)	220 (6,032)	163 (4,464)
Blind Allowance					
One spouse blind		1,500	3,000	3,000	2,220
Both spouses blind		3,000	6,000	6,000	4,440
Additional Allowance for Guide Dog		650	650	650	481

Computation of your income tax liability

Income tax is payable on your taxable income, i.e. your total assessable income for a tax year, less deductions for any allowances, non standard rate allowances (not tax credits) to which you may be entitled.

Tax bands and rates

2000/01	2001 (12 months)	2001 (9 months)
Single/Widow(er)	**Single/Widow(er)**	**Single/Widow(er)**
First £ 17,000 @ 22%	First £ 20,000 @ 20%	First £ 14,800 @ 20%
Balance @ 44%	Balance @ 42%	Balance @ 42%
One Parent Family	**One Parent Family**	**One Parent Family**
First £ 20,150 @ 22%	First £ 23,150 @ 20%	First £ 17,131 @ 20%
Balance @ 44 %	Balance @ 42 %	Balance @ 42 %
Married Couple - Both Spouses Working	**Married Couple - Both Spouses Working**	**Married Couple -Both Spouses Working**
First £ 34,000 @ 22%	First £ 40,000 @ 20%	First £ 29,600 @ 20%
Balance @ 44%	Balance @ 42%	Balance @ 42%
Married Couple - Only One Spouse Working	**Married Couple - Only One Spouse Working**	**Married Couple -Only One Spouse Working**
First £ 28,000 @ 22%	First £ 29,000 @ 20%	First £ 21,460 @ 20%
Balance @ 44%	Balance @ 42%	Balance @ 42%

Individualisation

In the December 1999 Budget the Minister for Finance introduced the concept of individualisation with effect from 6th April 2000.

Prior to the introduction of individualisation the married rate tax band was double that of a single person. This applied regardless of whether one or both spouses worked. However, from 6th April 2000 the standard rate tax band for a married couple, where both spouses have income, was increased by the lower of ;

- £11,000, or

- the income of the lower earning spouse.

The maximum standard rate band available to either spouse is £29,000.

Income exemptions limits

A person whose income does not exceed the following limits, is completely exempt from income tax.

	1999/00	2000/01	2001 Full year	2001 9 months
	£	£	£	£
Single/Widowed Person	£4,100	£4,100	£4,100	£3,034
Married	£8,200	£8,200	£8,200	£6,068
Person 65 years:				
- Single / Widow(er)	£6,500	£7,500	£8,500	£6,290
- Married	£13,000	£15,000	£17,000	£12,580
Additional allowance per child	£450	£450	£450	£333
Additional allowance for third and subsequent children	£650	£650	£650	£481

Marginal relief

Marginal relief is available for those whose total income exceeds the above exemptions limits on the previous page and is less than twice the relevant limit. It restricts the tax payable to 40% of the difference between your income and the appropriate exemption limit.

Example

Sean is a married man aged 70, his total income for 2000/01 is £15,000. His tax liability would normally work out as follows:

	£	€
Total Income	£18,000	€22,855
Taxable	£18,000	€22,855
18,000 @ 22%	£3,960	€5,028
Less: Tax Credits		
Personal £9,400 @ 22%	(£2,068)	(€2,626)
Age £1,600 @ 22%	(£352)	€447
Tax @ 22%	£1,540	€1,955

However, marginal relief will restrict Sean's overall tax liability to £800. (£18,000 - £15,000 = £5,000 x 40% = £1,200)

Increased exemption/dependent children

If you have dependent children, the general exemption limit can be increased, by £450 for the first and second child and £650 for the third and subsequent qualifying children.

Personal allowances & tax credits 2000/2001

Single allowance

This allowance is granted to the following

- Individuals who are single

- Married couples who opt for single/separate assessment - both partners receive a single allowance

- Separated couples who have not opted for joint assessment.

From 6th April 1999 tax relief for this allowance is granted by way of a tax credit at the standard rate of tax only.

Married allowance

This allowance, which is double the single allowance is granted to married couples who;

- Are assessed to tax under joint assessment
  (See Marriage Matters on Page 289)

  or

- Are living apart but one partner is maintaining the other and is not entitled to claim tax relief on the maintenance paid (for more details on this see The Breakdown of Separation and Divorce on Page 299).

From 6th April 1999 this allowance is granted by way of a tax credit at the standard rate of tax only.

Single parent allowance

This allowance is granted to a parent or guardian, of a qualifying child who is not entitled to the married person's allowance. However, it is not available to an unmarried couple who are living together as man and wife.

- For a single/widowed person, the allowance is £4,700 for 2000/01.

From April 2000 this allowance is granted by way of a tax credit at the standard rate of tax only.

Qualifying child

To qualify a child must:

- Have been born in the tax year

  or

- Be under the age of 16 years at the commencement of the tax year

  or

- If over 16 years of age be receiving full-time education at any college, school or other educational establishment, or be permanently incapacitated by reason of mental or physical infirmity and if over 21 years of age, be so incapacitated before reaching that age.

If the dependent child's income exceeds £720 p.a. the One Parent Family Allowance is reduced pound for pound for any income the dependent child has in excess of £720 p.a.

Widowed parent allowance

An additional allowance is granted to widowed parents for the five tax years following the year of bereavement. The allowance is £10,000 in year one, £8,000 in year two, £6,000 in year three, £4,000 in year four and £2,000 in year five.

From 6th April 2000 this allowance is granted by way of a tax credit at the standard rate of tax.

Home Carer's Allowance

The Home Carer's allowance of up to £3,000 by way of a tax credit at the standard rate of income tax (22% for 2000/01) was introduced from 6th April 2000. The allowance may be claimed by a married couple where one spouse cares for one or more dependent people. If the Home Carer has income in their own right of less than £4,000 per annum the full home carer's allowance may still be claimed. If you have income between £4,000 and £5,000 per annum you may claim a reduced allowance. Only one allowance is due irrespective of the number of persons being cared for.

In order to qualify for the allowance the following conditions apply

- The married couple must be jointly assessed to tax - it does not apply where married couples are taxed as single persons.

- The Home Carer must care for one or more dependent persons. A dependent person is:

    (a)   a child for whom social Welfare Child Benefit is payable

    or

    (b)   a person aged 65 years or over;

    or

(c)   a person who is permanently incapacitated by reasons of mental or physical infirmity.

A dependent person does not include a spouse.

• The dependent person(s) must normally **reside** with the married couple for the tax year.

You can also claim the carers allowance for a dependent relative who is cared for outside the home provided they live in a neighbouring residence or within two kilometers of the carer

If your income exceeds £5,000 in a year you can still claim the Home Carers Allowance provided. The allowance was granted for the immediately preceding tax year.

A married couple cannot claim both the Home Carer's Allowance and the increased standard rate tax for dual income couples (see page 197). However, they can claim whichever of the two is more beneficial. In practice, the tax office will grant the more beneficial treatment.

Incapacitated child allowance

Where a child is:

• Under 16 years of age during the tax year

   or

• 16 years or over and had become permanently incapacitated while under 16 years of age, the allowance is £1,600 p.a. or the amount spent on the maintenance of the child aged over 16 years, if this amount is less than £1,600.

The allowances are reduced by £1 for every £1 by which the child's income exceeds £2,100.

From 6th April 2000 this allowance is granted by way of a tax credit at the standard rate of tax only.

Age allowance

An allowance is available if you or your spouse are over 65 years of age in the relevant tax year. In the case of a married couple the deduction for 2000/2001 is £1,600 and for a single or widowed person it is £800.

From 6th April 2000 this allowance is granted by way of a tax credit at the standard rate of tax only.

Dependent relative allowance

This allowance is granted to claimants who prove that they maintain at their own expense any person who is:

- A relative of themselves or their spouse, who is incapacitated by old age or infirmity from maintaining themselves.

- Their or their spouse's widowed mother, whether incapacitated or not .

- A son or daughter who resides with them and whose services they depend on by reason of old age or infirmity.

The allowance of £220 p.a., which has remained unchanged for a number of years, is reduced by the amount by which the income of the person whom the claim is made for exceeds the maximum rate of old age contributory pension payable to a single person (£5,564 in 2000/01). The allowance is not very significant in itself but it is necessary to avail of this relief before you can claim other allowable expenses for a dependent relative e.g. medical expenses (no longer necessary after 6th April 2001). If two or more people help maintain the relative the allowance is divided between them in proportion to the amounts contributed by each.

From 6th April 2000 this allowance is granted by way of a tax credit at the standard rate of tax only.

Employed person taking care of incapacitated individual

This allowance of £8,500 in 2000/01 and £10,000 in 2001 is claimable where you employ a person to take care of a family member who is totally incapacitated, owing to old age or infirmity.

The following points are noteworthy:

- "Totally incapacitated" has not been defined.

- Employment is necessary.

- An allowance may not be claimed under this section along with an allowance for an incapacitated child allowance or dependent relative allowance in respect of the employed person.

From 6th April 2000 this allowance is granted by way of a tax credit at the marginal rate.

Blind person's allowance

An allowance of £3,000 is available during the tax year if you are blind. If both you and your spouse are blind, an allowance of £6,000 may be claimed.

A blind person for the purpose of this relief is a person "whose central visual acuity does not exceed 6/60 in the better eye with correcting lenses, or whose central visual acuity exceeds 6/60 in the better eye or in both eyes but is accompanied by a limitation in the field of vision that is such that the widest diameter of the visual field subtends an angle no greater than 20 degrees".

From 6th April 2000 this allowance is granted by way of a tax credit at the standard rate of tax only.

Mortgage interest relief

Interest payments are divided into two categories:

- Loans on Main Residence.

- Other Loans.

Loans on main residence

Mortgage interest relief is available by way of a tax credit at the standard rate of tax in respect of interest on money borrowed for the purchase, repair, development or improvement of your sole or main residence situated here in Ireland or in the U.K. Alternatively, this relief may be claimed for interest paid on a loan to purchase a residence for a former or separated spouse or a dependent relative if this accommodation is provided by you rent-free. Your dependent relative must be one in respect of whom you claim the Dependent Relative Allowance of £220 - i.e. their income must not exceed £5,564 p.a. (2000/01).

From 6th April 2000 first time mortgage holders, for the first five years can claim 100% tax relief on the interest paid within the following limits ;

£5,000 for a married couple, who are jointly assessed for tax
£5,000 for a widow(er)
£2,500 for a single person

Other buyers can claim 100% tax relief on interest paid within the following limits;

£4,000 for a married couple who are jointly assessed or a widowed person.
£2,000 for a single person.

Budget 2001 change: From 1st January 2002, the relief will be granted at source by the mortgage provider and will be netted off the monthly mortgage repayment.

Example

John and Mary are 44% tax-payers and will pay mortgage interest of £6,500 in the 2000/01 tax year. Their mortgage interest relief will work out as follows:
A.   Assumes that John and Mary have claimed mortgage interest relief for the first time less than five years ago.
B.   Assumes that John and Mary have claimed mortgage interest relief for the first time more than five years ago.

	2000/01	
	Less than 5 years mortgage holders £	More than 5 years mortgage holders £
Mortgage Interest paid	£6,500	£6,500
Maximum interest allowed for tax purposes	£5,000	£4,000
Tax relief @ 22%	£1,100	£880

Bridging loan interest

Additional Relief is available on Bridging Loan Interest. A bridging loan is a loan to finance the disposal of your sole or main residence and the acquisition of another residence for use as a sole or main residence. The position on bridging loan interest is as follows:

- It is subject to the same restrictions as mortgage interest. However, both reliefs may be claimed for the relevant period.

- The additional allowance is for a period of 12 months only from the date on which the loan was granted. If the bridging period falls partly into one tax year and partly into another, the allowance is apportioned on a time basis according to the number of months falling into the respective years.

- No tax relief is granted for bridging loan interest which exceeds the limit of 12 months.

If after the end of the 12 month period the old home is still unsold, interest will continue to be allowed in the normal way if it is occupied as the sole or main residence. If the old residence is unoccupied, no interest deduction is allowed after the end of the 12 month period. If the owners, having failed to sell their former residence, rent out the property, the interest paid will not qualify as bridging loan interest.

Example

In 2000/01 John Smith, a married man, paid:
Mortgage interest of £5,400. On 1st July 2000 Mr. Smith obtained bridging finance from a bank as he was unable to sell his previous home. The bridging loan was repaid in full on 31st December 2000. The interest paid on the bridging loan amounted to £3,000. John's interest allowance for 2000/01 is as follows:

- Mortgage interest will be restricted to £4,000.

- As the bridging loan was for a period of 6 months the maximum amount of interest allowable will be restricted to; £3,000 x 6/12 = £1,500.

	Interest paid		Interest allowable	
	£	€	£	€
Mortgage Interest	£5,400	€6,857	£4,000	€5,079
Bridging Loan Interest	£3,000	€3,809	£1,500	€1,905
	£8,400	€10,666	£5,500	€6,984

Other loans

There are no restrictions on the amount of interest on which tax relief may be claimed in the following circumstances.

- Interest paid out for business purposes under Case I and II of Schedule D.

- Interest on money borrowed to pay death duties.

- Interest on money borrowed to acquire an interest in a company or partnership or in granting a loan to a company or partnership.

Payments made under Deeds of Covenant

Tax relief on covenants is available only in the following circumstances;

- Covenant to people over 65;

- Covenant to permanently incapacitated individuals.

Note: Payments by a parent to a son or daughter under 18 will not qualify for tax relief.

If you pay tax at 44% (42% after 6th April 2001) you may reduce your tax liability and increase the disposable income of the covenantee. In addition, if the covenantee pays tax at a lower rate or is exempt from tax, a tax advantage may be gained.

Example

John has an annual income of £32,000 and he pays tax at 44%.
In 2000/01 he wishes to supplement his widowed mother's (aged 76) income by £1,900 p.a. His mother's income is a pension of £5,000 p.a.
John can do this in one of two ways:

- Hand over £1,900 to his mother each year.

  or

- Complete a Deed of Covenant for £2,436 - it gets a little complicated here! He deducts tax at the standard rate (22%) from this gross amount and pays the balance of £1,900 to his mother.

We illustrate both positions below. When all the paperwork is completed, under a Deed of Covenant John will be better off by £536 p.a. and his widowed mother is better off by £536 p.a.

If you have any difficulty with the paperwork, contact us and we will send you our Covenant Kit (cost £20).

A note of caution; if John's mother's pension is a non-contributory pensioner, the covenant income will be taken into account for means-test purposes and may affect the amount of pension she will receive.

John's Position   2000/01

		Without Covenant		With Covenant	
		£	€	£	€
A	Total Income	£32,000	€40,632	£32,000	€40,632
B	Less:Deed of Covenant	-	-	(£2,436)	€3,093
	Taxable	£32,000	€40,632	£29,564	€37,539
	Tax Payable				
	£28,000 @ 22%	£6,160	€7,822	£6,160	€7,822
	£ 4,000/£1,564 @ 44%	£1,760	€2,235	£688	€874
		£7,920	€10,056	£6,848	€8,695
	Tax on Covenant £2,436 @ 22%	N/A	N/A	£536	€681
	Total Tax	£7,920	€10,056	£7,384	€9,376
	Less: Tax Credits				
	Personal £9,400 @ 22%	(£2,068)	(€2,626)	(£2,068)	€2,626
	PAYE £1,000 @ 22%	(£220)	(€279)	(£220)	(€279)
C	Net Tax Payable	£5,632	€7,151	£5,096	€6,471
D	Direct Payment to Mother	£1,900	€2,413	£1,900	€2,413
	Net Income	£24,468	€31,068	£25,004	€31,749
		A - (C+D)		A-(C+D)	

John's Mother's position   **2000/01**

		Without Covenant		With Covenant	
		£	€	£	€
A	Deed of Covenant	Nil	*Nil*	£2,436	*€3,093*
B	Pension	£5,000	*€6,349*	£5,000	*€6,349*
	Total Income	£5,000	*€6,349*	£7,436	*€9,442*
	Taxable Income (Income Under Exemption Limit)	Nil	*Nil*	Nil	*Nil*
	Tax Payable	Nil	*Nil*	Nil	*Nil*
C	Tax Refund Due (tax paid by John)	Nil	*Nil*	£536	*€681*
D	Payment from John	£1,900	*€2,413*	£1,900	*€2,413*
	Disposable Income	£6,900	*€8,761*	£7,436	*€9,442*
		(B+D)		(B+C+D)	

Retirement annuity pension contributions

Income tax relief is available for premiums paid to an approved personal pension scheme, to provide income in your retirement between the ages of 60 and 75 on non-pensionable earnings.

Relief is restricted as a percentage of net relevant earnings as follows;

Under 30	15%
Aged 30 but less than 40	20%
Aged 40 but less than 50	25%
Aged 50 and over	30%

PAYE allowance

The PAYE allowance is £1,000 for 2000/01 (£2,000 for 2001). However, if in the tax year your PAYE earnings are less than £1,000, the allowance will be reduced to the amount of your PAYE earnings. If you are married and both spouses pay PAYE, each is entitled to a PAYE allowance of £1,000.

The following PAYE income does not qualify for a PAYE allowance:

*   Income paid to a proprietary director or a spouse of a proprietary director.

*   Income paid by an individual or a partner to their spouse.

A proprietary director is a director who controls, either directly or indirectly, 15% or more of the share capital of the company.

The PAYE allowance is available to children of proprietary directors and the self employed, provided they work full-time in their parent's business and their salary exceeds £3,600 p.a.

From 6th April 1999 tax relief for this allowance is granted by way of a tax credit at the standard rate of tax only.

Medical insurance

Tax Relief is available on the amount of the subscription paid to the VHI/BUPA. Tax Relief is granted on the full amount paid in the preceding tax year at the standard rate of tax.

Budget 2001 change: From 6th April 2001 tax relief on medical insurance will be granted at source.

Example

£700 was paid in year ended 5th April 2000 to the VHI. A deduction of £700 will be allowed against the assessable income of 2000/01.

Medical expenses

Relief is also available for health expenses incurred in the provision of health care in respect of yourself, your spouse and your dependants. Health expenses include the following:

- Services of a Practitioner

- Drugs and Medicines

- Hearing Aids

- Physiotherapy or similar treatment

- Wheelchair/Wheelchair Lift

- Orthopaedic Bed/Chair

- Home Nursing and Special Nursing

- Kidney Patients Expenses

- Child Oncology Patients (certain items of expenditure)

- In Vitro Fertilisation

- Glucometer Machine for a Diabetic

- Coeliacs
  Cost of gluten free food for coeliacs. As this condition is generally ongoing, a letter, instead of prescriptions, from a doctor stating that the taxpayer is a coeliac sufferer is acceptable. Receipts from supermarkets in addition to receipts from a chemist are acceptable.

Dental treatment will qualify for tax relief as follows;

- Crowns which are permanently cemented to the existing tooth tissue. Crowns which form part of a bridge do not qualify for relief.

- Veneers/Rembrant Type Etched Fillings.

- Tip Replacing where a large part of the tooth needs to be replaced and the replacement is made outside the mouth.

- Gold Posts which are inserted in the nerve canal of a tooth to hold a crown.

- Gold Inlays which are smaller versions of a gold crown. Relief will only be available if they were fabricated outside the mouth.

- Endodontics - Root canal treatment: This involves the filling of the nerve canal and not the filling of teeth.

- Periodontal Treatment which includes, Root planing, Curettage and Debridement, Gum Flaps and Chrome Cobalt Splint.

- Bridgework consisting of an enamel retained bridge or a tooth supported bridge.

- Orthodontic Treatment which involves the provision of braces and other similar treatments.

- Surgical Extraction of Impacted Wisdom Teeth when undertaken in a hospital. In order to obtain tax relief certification from the hospital will be required.

Nursing Care and, in certain circumstances, maintenance paid to a nursing home, for a dependent relative for whom you receive a dependent relative allowance, may qualify for income tax relief.

To qualify, the nursing home must be approved by the relevant health authority and provide regular nursing services and the dependent relative must be in need of and avail of these nursing services.

Budget 2001 change: From 6th April 2001 tax relief will be available for qualifying medical expenses incurred on behalf of an independent relative regardless of their level of income. It will no longer be necessary to claim the dependent relative allowance to claim this relief.

Exclusions

Health Care specifically excludes expenses relating to

- Routine maternity care.

- Routine ophthalmic treatment.

- Routine dental treatment.

Routine maternity care

This means maternity care received by a woman while she is a patient in a hospital. Also, the first 14 days spent in a hospital in respect of a pregnancy is deemed to be routine care. The 14 days need not be consecutive.

Budget 2001 change: From 6th April 2001 tax relief will be available on expenses incurred from routine maternity care.

Routine ophthalmic treatment

This means sight testing and advice as to the use of spectacles or contact lenses and the provision and repairing of spectacles or contact lenses.

Routine dental treatment

This means the extraction, scaling and filling of teeth, bridgework and the provision and repairing of artificial teeth and dentures. The first £100 for an individual and £200 for a family is excluded from any claim made.

Relief for any Income Tax year is given by repayment i.e. a refund after the relevant 5th April. A condition for eligibility is that your return of income has been made for the year and all tax paid as due.

Medical expenses incurred, which are not in respect of routine health care or not covered by medical insurance, should be claimed on Form **Med 1**.

A claim for relief for the cost of dental treatment other than routine dental treatment must be accompanied by a certificate (Form Med 2 Dental) signed by a qualified practitioner.

Guide dog

A standard £650 per annum is allowed as medical expenses where a blind person maintains a trained guide dog and is the registered owner with the Irish Guide Dog Association.

Permanent health insurance

Permanent Health Insurance protects your income against accidents or illness for up to 75% of your normal earnings. After a specific period has expired, the benefits are paid for the duration of your incapacity or to a specific age, whichever is the earlier. Income tax relief may be claimed on the contributions made to a Permanent Health Insurance scheme.

Budget 2001 change: With effect from 6th April 2001 contributions to permanent health benefits by PAYE tax payers will move to a "Net Pay" basis i.e. the contribution will be deducted from your gross salary prior to the application of tax and PRSI.

The amount of relief granted cannot exceed 10% of your total income for the year of assessment in which the premiums are paid. All receipts from a PHI plan are taxable, regardless of whether or not the relief is claimed on premiums paid.

Rent relief for private rented accommodation

A taxpayer who is, or whose spouse is, aged 55 years or under may claim relief in respect of rent payable for private rented accommodation at the standard rate of tax (£750 for a single person, £1,500 for a married couple, £1,125 for a widowed person). If you are over 55 and paying rent for private rental accommodation, the relief is £2,000 for a single person, £3,000 for a widowed person and £4,000 for a married couple, at the standard rate of tax.

Budget 2001 change: From 6th April 2001 rent relief for a single person under 55 is increased to £1,000 and £2,000 for a widowed or married person. If you are single and over 55 the amount is increased to £2,000 and £4,000 for a widowed or married person.

Long term unemployed

From 6th April 1998 an additional allowance is available to any person who has been long term unemployed and who is returning to work.

	Year 1 £	Year 2 £	Year 3 £
Additional Personal Allowance	£3,000	£2,000	£1,000
Child Tax Allowance	£1,000	£666	£334

You can opt to claim the allowances in the tax year you commence work, or if you prefer, you can commence your claim in the year of assessment following your return to work.

Note: Long Term unemployed means that you have been continuously unemployed and in receipt of Unemployment Benefit, Unemployment Assistance or Lone Parents Allowance for the 12 months prior to taking up employment.

People with disabilities who have been in receipt of Disability Allowance or Blind Persons Payment for at least 12 months can also claim this allowance from 1st January 1999.

Fees paid to private colleges

Tax relief is available at the standard rate of tax on college fees paid for yourself or a dependent relative. The following courses apply;

Tuition fees paid for certain full time and part time undergraduate courses of at least 2 years duration. The maximum amount of fees on which you can claim tax relief is £2,000.

Tuition fees paid for certain training courses in the area of Information Technology and Foreign Languages. The relief applies to fees between £250 to £1,000.

From 5th April 2000 tax relief is also available on certain postgraduate courses.

Donation/gifts

Tax relief is available in respect of donations/gifts made to certain approved bodies/charities as follows:

- Donations made to an "approved body" to teach "approved subjects". The minimum deduction is £100 and the maximum deduction is £10,000.

- Gifts for education in the Arts - minimum deduction £100, maximum £10,000.

- Gifts to, or for the benefit of, designated schools. Relief is granted at the standard rate on aggregate gifts of a minimum of £250 and a maximum of £1,000 in a single year of assessment.

- Gifts made to third level institutes. Minimum donation £ 250.

- Donations to designated charities - An individual is not entitled to claim tax relief on donations made to charities. However, if an individual makes a donation to a designated Third World Charity, the payment will be treated as having been made net of tax. The charity can then reclaim the tax from the revenue. The minimum donation is £200 and the maximum is £750.

- Donation of heritage items.

- Donation for gifts or money to the state which are used for any purpose or towards the cost of which public moneys are provided.

- Donation of over £1,000 made to the Scientific and Technological Education (Investment) Fund.

Relief for investment in corporate trades (BES)

The maximum BES allowance you may claim in any tax year is £25,000. The minimum allowance is £200. A married couple can obtain a total allowance of £50,000 in a single tax year, if each has income of £25,000 in their own right.

Where amounts in excess of £25,000 are invested in any tax year, or if the tax deduction is greater than the total income, the excess can be carried forward to future years.

Relief for investment in the Film Industry /Section 35

Special tax incentives were introduced in 1987 for investment in the film industry - known as Section 35 investments. In order for a film to qualify as a "Section 35 investment", the film must be given a certificate by the Minister for the Arts, Culture, the Gaeltacht and the Islands and it is also necessary that a certain amount of the production work be carried out in Ireland.

Tax relief is available at your highest rate of tax on 80% of your investment up to a maximum investment of £25,000 per annum. A married couple can claim tax relief on 80% of their investment up to a maximum investment of £50,000 provided each has sufficient income.

Seafarer allowance

A new allowance of £5,000 is available for seafarers. This allowance can be offset against the seafaring employment. It is conditional on the seafarer being at sea on a voyage for a least 169 days in a tax year. This allowance does not apply in any year where the individual claims the Foreign Earnings Deduction. The 169 days is being reduced to 161 days.

Budget 2001 change: The number of days abroad for the purpose of this allowance is being reduced from 169 days to 161.

Service Charges

Tax relief is available on service charges paid to local authorities. The maximum amount on which you can claim tax relief is £150.

12

PAYE made easy

The Pay As You Earn (PAYE) system applies to you if you have income from employment or pension directly assessed.

PAYE ensures that the excess of your weekly or monthly pay over your tax credits is taxed by your employer at the appropriate rate.

Tax Credits

Prior to the introduction of tax credits, tax allowances were granted at your marginal rate of tax, therefore if you paid tax at the higher rate you could claim tax relief at your highest rate of tax. However, with the introduction of tax credits most allowances are allowed at the standard rate of tax only, regardless of whether you are a higher rate tax payer or not. This means that tax allowances benefit each individual by the same amount.

Tax credit system - from 6th April 2001

From 6th April 2001 a "full tax credit system" will be put in place. This new system will replace the existing Tax Free Allowance based system. As a result of this change Tax Tables and Table Allowances will no longer feature in the PAYE system.

From 6th April 2001 tax will be calculated at the appropriate tax rates on gross pay and this tax will then be reduced by any tax credits due, in order to arrive at the net tax payable.

As the 2001 tax year will be a short "year" the standard rate band and tax credits will be granted at 74% of the annual amount.

217

Before the start of the new tax year, around February or March, your tax office will issue a Notification of Determination of Tax Credits. This notice replaces the existing certification of tax free allowances.

The Notification of Determination of tax credit and standard rate cut off point will show the following information;

• Standard rate cut off point

• Tax credit due to you

• Your rate(s) of tax

Standard rate cut off point

This is the amount of income you can earn at the standard rate. The amount will depend on whether you are married, single or widowed. Also if you have any allowances which are allowed at the higher rate of tax e.g. pension contribution, this will increase your "standard rate cut off point".

	Standard rate band 2001			
	Full year		**Short year**	
	£	€	£	€
Single person	£20,000	€25,395	£14,800	€18,792
Married couple (one spouse working)	£29,000	€36,822	£21,460	€27,249
Married couple (both spouse working - maximum)	£40,000	€50,790	£29,600	€37,584
One parent family	£23,150	€29,394	£17,131	€21,752

The tax credits and standard rate cut off point will vary depending on the circumstances of each individual.

Income tax is calculated for each pay period by applying the information supplied by the notification against the gross pay as follows;

The standard rate of tax (20% in 2001) is applied to your gross pay up to the standard rate cut off point for that week or month. Any balance of income over that amount in the pay period is taxed at the higher rate (42% in 2001). This gives

218

the gross tax payable. The gross tax payable is reduced by a tax credit as per the notification sent by your tax office, to arrive at the net tax payable.

Example

John who is married has gross earnings of £50,000, his wife Mary has no income. For 2001 a Notice of Determination of tax credits issues showing;

Standard rate cut off point of £21,460 per annum or £564.74 per week (only 38 weeks in short tax year)	• Based on a standard rate band of £29,000 for a married couple - one spouse working. (74% of full amount to take into account short tax year)
Standard rate of tax is 20% Higher rate of tax is 42%	• Based on standard rate of tax of 20% and a higher rate of 42%
Tax credits of £1,924 per annum or £50.63 per week (74% of full amount)	• Personal £11,000 @ 20% = £2,200 • PAYE Credit £ 1,480 @ 20% = £400 £2,600

John's income tax would be calculated as follows for the first week

Gross Pay	£961.54	(£50,000/52)
Tax on £564.74 @ 20%	£112.95	(Standard rate up to a maximum of £564.74 which is the standard rate cut off point for John as advised by his tax office).
Tax on £396.80 @ 42%	£166.66	(Higher rate of tax on excess of income over the standard rate cut off point).
Total Tax	£279.61	Total of higher and standard rate tax.
Less: Tax Credits	(£50.63)	Tax credit as advised by the tax office.
Total Tax due for this week	£228.98	Total tax less tax credit.

Coded Income/Benefit in Kind

If you receive any benefits from your employer e.g. company car, the amount of your tax credits are reduced by the amount of the Benefit in Kind at the standard rate of income tax and the standard rate tax band is reduced by the amount of that income.

Example

John receives a company car from his employer. The amount of the Benefit in Kind is calculated at £5,000. John's standard rate tax credit will be reduced by £5,000 @ 20%. His standard rate tax band will also be reduced by £5,000 in order to arrive at the standard rate cut off point.

Non Standard rated relief's

If you have deductions from income tax which qualify for tax relief at the higher rate of income tax, your tax credits will be increased by the amount of the relief at the standard rate of income tax and the standard rate tax band will also be increased by the amount of the relief in order to arrive at the standard rate cut off point.

Example

Paul is married and has a gross income of £50,000. His wife, Mary has no employment income. Paul's personal and PAYE tax credits amount to £2,600 (£13,000 at 20%). He has a standard rate tax band of £29,000 and his rates of tax are 20% and 42%. Paul also pay's £2,000 into a personal pension scheme. Tax relief on which is allowed at the higher rate of tax. Paul's tax credit will increase by £400 (£2,000 @ 20%) . His standard rate tax band will also increase by £2,000 in order to arrive at the standard rate cut off point.

Example

Mary, who is married has an income of £50,000 per annum. Her husband has no employment income. She also has a benefit in kind of £2,000 the tax of which is collected through the PAYE system. Mary also pays £1,000 into a personal pension scheme. Her standard rate cut off point is £29,000 (rate band for a married couple one spouse working). Her rate of tax is 20% and 42%.

Calculation of Mary's tax credits		Full year		Short year (74%) of full year	
		£	€	£	€
Married	£11,000 @ 20%	£2,200	€2,793	£1,628	€2,068
PAYE	£2,000 @ 20%	£400	€508	£296	€376
Total		£2,600	€3,301	£1,924	€2,443
Increased by Pension	£1,000 @ 20%	£200	€254	£148	€188
Reduced by Benefit in Kind	£2,000 @ 20%	(£400)	(€508)	(£296)	€376
Net Tax credits		£2,400	€3,047	£1,176	€1,493

Calculation of Mary's standard rate cut off point	Full year		Short year (74%) of full year	
	£	€	£	€
Standard rate band (married couple one spouse working)	£29,000	€36,822	£21,460	€27,249
Increased by pension	£1,000	€1,270	£740	€940
Reduced by Benefit in Kind	(£2,000)	€2,539	(£1,480)	€1,879
Standard Rate cut off point	£28,000	€35,553	£20,720	€26,309

Summary

Existing tax free allowance	New tax credit system
Gross pay is reduced by the TFA as advised by the tax office in order to arrive at the taxable pay.	Gross pay is taxed at the appropriate tax rate(s) to give the gross tax.
The taxable pay is taxed at the appropriate tax rate as advised by the tax office to give the tax payable.	The tax office will advise you of the standard rate cut off point for each pay period. The standard rate of tax is applied to pay up to that limit. Any balance of pay over that amount in any pay period is taxed at the higher rate.
The appropriate rate of tax is determined by reference to the estimated income and the inclusion of a table allowance to spread tax deductions evenly through out the tax year.	The gross tax is reduced by a tax credit as advised by the Tax Office to arrive at the tax payable.

PAYE emergency tax

The emergency tax operates when:

(a)   Your employer has not received a Notification of Determination of tax credits and standard rate cut off point for you for the current year or your Form P45 for the current or previous tax year.
       or
(b)   You have given your employer a completed form P45 with "E"written on it.

For the year 2001 the PAYE emergency tax-free allowance for the initial period of employment and the rates at which tax will be deductible are set out below.

If paid weekly:

	2001	
	Tax credit	**Rate**
	£	**%**
First Week	£106	20%
Second Week	£106	20%
Third Week	£106	20%
Fourth Week	£106	20%
Next 4 weeks	£Nil	20%
Each Subsequent Week	£Nil	42%

Tax refund during unemployment

Any refund due to you when you become unemployed will be made by the Revenue Commissioners on application by you to the Inspector of Taxes on Form **P50** accompanied by Parts **2** and **3** of Form **P45.**

PAYE refund after the year end

The tax year ends on 5th April and sometime after this date your employer will give you a form **P60** which is a certificate of your gross pay and tax deducted in the previous tax year. You have a legal right to this document.

If there are any additional allowances or deductions not claimed during this year, these should be documented and forwarded with your annual return and P60 to your Inspector of Taxes requesting a refund.

The Inspector will in due course send you a balancing statement (Form **P21**). If a repayment is due a cheque will be attached.

Example

An employee's pay is £346 per week. Tax credits for the year are £1,500 (£29 per week). Tax rate is 20%.

Position at	Cumulative taxable pay £	Cumulative tax £	Cumulative tax credits £	Cumulative net tax
Week 10	£3,460	£692	£290	£402

Following a claim, your Tax Inspector issues you with a new Notice of Determination of tax credits and standard rate cut off point in week 11 for £1,900 or £37 per week. With effect from 6th April your position at week 11 is as follows:

Position at	Cumulative taxable pay £	Cumulative tax £	Cumulative tax credits £	Cumulative net tax £
Week 11	£3,806	£761	£407	£354

Since tax of £402 already been deducted you will be given a tax refund by your employer of £48.

Note: Where the Week1/Month 1, Emergency or Temporary basis applies, no refund of tax may be made by the employer as cumulative tax-free allowances or cumulative pay are not taken into account.

Allowable deductions incurred for your employment

For expenses to be allowable for tax purposes they must be incurred for your employment and must be "wholly, exclusively and necessary" for the purpose of performing the duties of your employment. This rule is very strictly interpreted.

Motor and travelling expenses

A mileage allowance agreed between you and your employer for the use of your car for business purposes is not taxable provided it does not exceed the civil service mileage rate. However, you are not entitled to claim the cost of getting to or from work but only expenses incurred in the actual performance of your occupation.

Flat rate expenses

Special flat rate allowances are allowed to certain categories of workers such as teachers, nurses, journalists and building workers for expenses. The amounts are agreed from time to time between trade unions and professional bodies and the Revenue Commissioners.

Round sum expenses

If you get round sum expenses from your employer they will be regarded as part of your salary and taxed accordingly, unless you can demonstrate that the expenses were incurred "wholly, exclusively and necessarily" in the performance of your duties. If your expenses actually exceed the sums reimbursed, you are entitled to an expense allowance for the excess.

Employee tax-effective benefits

Here we list benefits which may be paid to you tax-free or tax efficiently by your employer:

1. If an employee is working away from normal base, **daily and overnight allowances** to cover the cost of lunch, evening meal, bed & breakfast etc. may be paid in accordance with a scale agreed between an employer and employee and approved by the Inspector of Taxes. Certain conditions must be fulfilled in order to qualify for these tax free payments. Daily allowances can range from £8 to £21 per day while an overnight allowance can be up to £72 per day.

2. **Canteen meals and refreshments,** provided these are available to all employees or luncheon vouchers up to 15p per working day.

3. **Rent-free or low rent accommodation** provided this is necessitated by the job.

4. **Non-cash personal gifts** for reasons not connected with work but including retirement presents.

5. Share in an employer's **Revenue-approved profit sharing scheme** (subject to certain limits). See Page 235.

6. **Staff entertainment** and outgoings at a reasonable cost.

7. **Pool transport** to place of work.

8. **Sporting and club facilities** provided by the employer to all employees. Sporting and club facilities paid by the employer for individual employees can give rise to Benefit In Kind charges.

9. **Inducement payments** before employment (in certain circumstances).

10. **Mileage allowance** agreed between the employer and employee for the use of the employee's car for business purposes. The rate cannot exceed the Civil Service Mileage Rate.

11. **Scholarship** income and bursaries.

12. **Lump sum payment** on retirement or removal from an employment within certain limits. See Page 245.

13. Payments under the **Redundancy Payment** Act 1967. See page 246.

14. Payments made on account of **injury or disability.**

15. **Working clothes**, overalls and tools provided by the employer.

16. Certain **marriage gratuities**.

17. Remuneration to Irish employees who are **working permanently abroad** (certain conditions to be met). See page 259.

18. Employer's contributions to a statutory or **Revenue-approved pension scheme**. See page 124.

19. Cost to the employer of providing **life assurance** cover of up to eight times the employee's salary.

20. Cost of providing sick pay/**permanent health insurance.**

21. Cost of providing contributions to V.H.I./BUPA (higher rate tax payers will suffer BIK penalties)

22.   From 6th April 1999 **Monthly/Annual Bus/Rail Travel Passes** provided by employers to their employees.

23.   From 6th April 1999 **Childcare Facilities** provided by employers on a free or subsided basis, provided;

-    The childcare facility is either provided on the employer's premises,
      or
-    The employer provides the childcare facility jointly with other participants, for example, with other employers, on premises made jointly available by one of the employers in the joint scheme. However, the employer must be wholly or partly responsible for both financing and managing the childcare facility provided for employees.

24.   **Staff Suggestion Schemes**
       Staff suggestion schemes, which improve efficiency and productivity in your place of employment, may be rewarded by your employer, usually by way of a tax free lump sum payment, provided certain conditions are met.

       The maximum amount that an employee can receive is the lower of 10% of the expected net financial benefit during the first full year of implementation of the suggestion or 10% of the employee's gross salary.

       If the award is made to a group, the tax free amount to the group is the lower of 10% of the expected net financial benefit during the first year of implementation of the suggestion.

       or

       £10,000

       but

       the amount paid to individual group members cannot exceed 10% of their gross salary.

There is also an overriding limit of £5,000 per employee per annum. Any amounts exceeding these limits are subject to income tax in the normal manner.

25. Strictly, the cost of relocating your home is a personal expense, however , if it is a requirement of your job to move home and certain procedures are followed, your employer may compensate you for these costs without attracting tax.

The types of expenses covered are:

- Auctioneer's fees, solicitor's fees and stamp duty arising from moving home.

- Furniture removal costs.

- Storage charges.

- Insurance of furniture and items in transits.

- Cleaning stored furniture.

- Travelling expenses on removal.

- Temporary subsistence allowance while looking for new accommodation.

Requirements

- Prior approval is obtained from the tax office before the payment is made.

- The cost must be borne directly by the employer in respect of actual expenses incurred by you.

- The expenses are reasonable.

- The payments are properly controlled.

Receipts must be provided (apart from temporary subsistence), and Revenue must be satisfied that moving home is necessary.

13

Employee benefits & shares

Company cars

If your employer provides you with a company car, you are liable to income tax on this benefit.

The amount liable to tax is 30% of the original market value of the car. The Original Market Value is usually the list price of the car less a cash discount. This cash discount would not normally exceed 10%. However, if you pay towards some of the running costs of the car, the 30% can be reduced as illustrated below.

	2000/01 %	2001 %
All petrol for private use paid by employee	4.5	4.5
All insurance charges paid by employee	3.0	3.0
All servicing charges paid by employee	3.0	3.0
All road tax charges paid by employee	1.0	1.0

Contribution by employee

If you contribute to the cost of the running of the car, your BIK for the year will be reduced by the amount contributed.

If your business mileage exceeds 15,000 a year, your BIK is reduced according to the table below.

Business mileage not exceeding	% B.I.K. payable 2000/01	% B.I.K. payable 2001
15,000	100	100
16,000	97.5	97.5
17,000	95	95
18,000	90	90
19,000	85	85
20,000	80	80
21,000	75	75
22,000	70	70
23,000	65	65
24,000	60	60
25,000	55	55
26,000	50	50
27,000	45	45
28,000	40	40
29,000	35	35
30,000	30	30
Over 30,000	25	25

If you have a company car and your private mileage does not exceed 5,000 miles p.a. the Revenue Commissioners may require you to verify this by actual daily meter readings over a period of three months.

20% reduction in BIK

Your BIK charge can be reduced by 20%, provided all of the following conditions are met:

- You spend 70% or more of your time away from your place of work.

- Your annual business mileage exceeds 5,000 miles p.a. but does not exceed 15,000 miles p.a.

- You work an average of at least 20 hours per week.

- You keep a log book, detailing the mileage, nature and location of business and amount of time spent away from your employer's business premises. This log must be available for inspection by your Inspector of Taxes, if requested.

Working abroad

If you work abroad during the year the Benefit in Kind on your company car may be reduced provided you work aboard for at least 30 days in the year. However, this reduction may not apply if the car is available to your spouse or other family members.

Car available for less than a full year

If a car is only available for part of the tax year, e.g. when you first get the car or the year you leave employment with the company, the BIK is reduced by the number of months the car is not available to you.

Also if the car is only available to you for a portion of the year, the business mileage will be "annualised" in order to calculate the percentage reduction for business mileage.

The annualised business mileage is calculated using the following formula

$$A \times \frac{B}{C}$$

A = Actual Business Mileage

B = 12 (Months)

C = Number of months which company car is available to you.

Example

John receives a company car on 6th December 2000. The original market value (OMV) of the car is £20,000 and the company pays all the running expenses. His business mileage for the period from 6th December 2000 to 5th April 2001 is 7,500 miles.

This BIK will be calculated as follows for 2000/01

OMV of Car	30%
£20,000 x 30% x 4/12	2,000

The BIK of £2,000 is reduced depending on John's business mileage. However, because John only had a company car for four months of the year his business mileage must be annualised in order to calculate the percentage reduction for business mileage.

		£	€
Business mileage for 4 months		7,500	
Annualised business mileage	7,500 x 12/4	22,500	
Business mileage of 22,500 means John's BIK is charged @ 65%			
BIK for 2000/01 = £ 2,000 x 65%		£1,300	€1,651

Reimburshing running costs

Where the company provides a car for a director or employee and pays all the motoring expenses, the Benefit-In-Kind charge may be minimised by re-imburshing to the company for some of the running costs of the car. This can be more favourable than the company providing a car and paying all the expenses.

Car pools

Cars included in car pools are treated as not being available for an employee's private use and no tax liability arises on the provision of a car from a car pool provided all of the following conditions are met:

- The car is made available to, and actually used by, more than one employee and in the case of each of them it is made available to them by reason of their employment, but is not ordinarily used by any one of the employees to the exclusion of the others.

- Private use by each employee is incidental to other use.

- The car is not normally kept overnight at, or in the vicinity of, any of the employees' homes.

Company van

If an employee has the use of a company van for private use Benefit In Kind is calculated as follows:

$$\frac{A \ \text{x} \ \text{Annual Private Mileage}}{\text{Total Annual Mileage}}$$

Where A is the cost of van x 12.5% plus total running expenses.

Example

Sean is provided with a company van, which he also uses for private use. His annual mileage is 25,000 of which 7,000 is private mileage. The cost of the van is £10,000 and the running expenses are £5,400 p.a. Sean's BIK is calculated as follows:

$$\frac{*£6,075 \ \text{x} \ 7,000}{25,000} = £1,701$$

* (Cost x 12½% + £5,400 running costs)

Preferential loans

A preferential loan is a loan made to an employee by his employer (directly or indirectly) on which he pays no interest or interest at a rate lower than the specified rate.

- The Benefit in Kind for tax purposes is the difference between the interest paid (if any) and interest calculated at the specified rate. However, the amount of interest assessed to tax will qualify for mortgage interest relief as "deemed interest" subject to the normal limits.

For the tax year 2000/01 the specified rate for a loan used to purchase, repair or improve your main residence is 4%. For other loans the specified rate is 10%.

Budget 2001 change: From 6th April 2001 the specified rate of 4% is increased to 6% and the 10% is increased to 12%.

Example

John is married and joined the bank in January 1994. In April 1994, he was granted a preferential house purchase loan of £60,000 @ 3% p.a. He pays tax at 44%, his position is as follows for 2000/01:

	2000/01	
	£	€
Preferential House Purchase Loan	£60,000	€76,184
Interest Paid £60,000 @ 3%	£1,800	€2,286
Benefit-In-Kind (BIK)		
£60,000 @ 4%	£2,400	€3,047
Less: Interest Paid	£1,800	€2,286
Benefit in Kind	£600	€762
Interest Relief for Tax Purposes		
Interest Paid	£1,800	€2,286
Deemed Interest Paid	£600	€762
	£2,400	€3,047

As Mortgage Interest Relief is given at the standard rate, the allowances on John's TFA Certificate will, therefore, include a Benefit-in-Kind of £600 and £1,200 @ 44%.

Example

Jim has a non-qualifying loan from his employer of £20,000 at an interest rate of 3% p.a.

Benefit In Kind (BIK)	£	€
Loan £20,000 @ 10%	£2,000	€2,539
Interest £20,000 @ 3%	£600	€762
Benefit In Kind	£1,400	€1,778

Accommodation

If your employer provides you with accommodation rent free or at a reduced rate and this accommodation is not necessitated by your job, then a taxable benefit arises. This benefit is normally the market rate of the annual rent which could be obtained on a yearly letting of the accommodation. In practice, 8% of the current property value of the accommodation may be taken plus any expenses paid by the employer.

Any amounts paid by the employee to the employer by way of rent are deductible from the taxable benefit.

Share schemes

More and more employers are looking at Share Schemes as a way of rewarding their employees. Some, of these schemes attract favourable tax treatment provided certain conditions are met.

Approved profit share scheme

An Approved Profit Sharing Scheme allows a full or part time employee or a full time director to receive shares tax free from their employer up to an annual limit of £10,000 provided certain conditions are met.

A trust is set up by the company, this trust must purchase shares in the company on behalf of the employees with funds received from the company. The trust must hold the shares for two years before transferring them to the employee, who must then hold the shares for three years after receiving them. If the shares are disposed of by the employee before the end of the three year period income tax is charged on the lower of:

- the market value of the share at the date they were initially apportioned to the employee

  or

- the sale proceeds from the sale of the shares

However, if the employee/director ceases employment or reaches retirement age within the three year period income tax will be payable at 50% of the lower of the above.

Approved Profit Sharing schemes are tax efficient for both the employee and employer as the employee can receive shares tax free up to an annual limit of £10,000 and the employer can offset the cost of the shares against the company's profits.

Employee Share Ownership Trusts

Employee Share ownership Trusts (ESOT's) were first introduced in Finance Act 1997. A company can place shares for a maximum of 20 years in an ESOT. They are designed to work in conjunction with profit sharing scheme as shares can be released from the ESOT each year into the company's profit sharing scheme.

The IR£10,000 tax free limit which applies to Profit Sharing Scheme (see page 235) can be increased to a once-off IR£30,000 after 10 years in respect of shares previously held in an ESOT provided;

- The shares have been transferred to the Trustees of an approved profit sharing scheme by the Trustees of an ESOT;

  and

- In the first five years of the establishment of the ESOT, 50% of the shares retained by the Trustees were pledged as security on borrowings.

- No shares which were pledged as security for borrowings by Trustees of the ESOT were previously transferred to the Trustees of a profit sharing scheme.

Stock Options

A Stock Option arises where a company grants to its employees or directors an option to subscribe for shares in the company at a preferential price. A taxable benefit arises when the predetermined share price is less than the market value.

The amount liable to tax is the difference between the market value of the shares at the exercise date and the price you actually pay. This liability arises at the date you exercise the option.

If the options are capable of being exercised more than seven years after they were granted, income tax also arises on the date the option is granted. The amount liable to income tax is the difference between the market value of the shares at the date the option was granted and the option price. Any tax paid at this early stage can be offset against the total tax liability when the option is eventually exercised.

Capital Gains Tax may also be payable on the shares if they increase in value from the date you exercise the option. Any amounts assessable to income tax are deemed to be part of the cost for Capital Gains Tax purposes.

Example

You are granted an option in August 1998 to purchase 2,000 shares in your employer's company at a future date for £7 per share. When you exercise your options in August 2000 the share price was £9 per share.

The amount liable to income tax in 2000/01	£	€
Market Value of shares in August '00	£9 x 2,000 = £18,000	€22,855
Less: Option Price	£7 x 2,000 = £14,000	€17,776
Benefit liable to Income Tax	£4,000	€5,079

This tax would not be payable until 30th April 2002 unless you already exercised share options in the previous tax year. In these circumstances your preliminary tax liability would be due on 1st November 2000.

Deferment of tax liability

From 6th April 2000 if you exercise stock options, but don't sell the shares immediately i.e. exercise and hold the shares, you may elect to defer the income tax due. This election must be made in writing to your Inspector of Taxes before the normal filing date for your tax return. For 2000/01 the tax return filing date will be the 31st January 2002 and for the tax year 2002 onwards the return filling date will change to the 31st October following the end of the tax year.

If you opt for this deferment, income tax will not be payable until the earlier of

- The 1st November after the end of the tax year in which the shares are sold.

   or

- 1st November after the end of the tax year that begins 7 years after the options were originally exercised.

Note: From 1st January 2002 the tax year will change to a calendar year. As a result of this the 1st November payment date (see previous page) will change to 31st October .

Although you can defer the tax for up to 7 years, the tax payable will be based on the tax rates applicable at the time you originally exercised the options.

If you sell part of your stock options then income tax will be payable only on the shares options sold.

Stock options and non resident

If you are resident in Ireland when the option is granted you are liable to income tax when you exercise the option regardless of whether or not you are resident in Ireland at that time.

If you acquired an option before you came to Ireland, but exercised it after your arrival here no income tax liability would arise in Ireland provided there was no connection between the Irish employment and the granting of the option and no tax planning or avoidance scheme was involved.

Returns by employers

Employers must provide certain information to the Revenue Commissioners about the stock options granted and exercised by employees.

Stock Options and Self-Assessment

If you receive stock options from your employer, you are liable to tax under self-assessment in respect of the profit arising from the stock options. Under self-assessment you must pay your preliminary tax by the due date and also submit your income tax return by the relevant filing date. For the year 2000/01 the return filing date is 31st January 2002 and for the tax year 2001 (9 months from 6th April 2001 - 3rd December 2001) the return filing date is 31st October 2002.

If you don't adhere to these dates, surcharges and interest will apply. The onus lies with you to submit your tax return and to pay your tax on time.

Note: If you'd like a consultation with one of our advisors to discuss the tax implication of your share options, please contact us at 00353 1 6768633 or tab@eircom.net to arrange a private consultation. We have a fixed private consultation fee of £50 (+ 20% VAT) for readers of this Guide.

Relief for new shares purchase by employees/share subscription schemes

When an employee or director of a company subscribes for new shares in a company, they are entitled to a deduction from their total income, up to a maximum lifetime deduction of £5,000, provided certain conditions are met.

• The individual subscribes for new ordinary shares in the company.

• The deduction is granted for the tax year in which the shares are issued.

• The company in which the shares are issued must be resident and incorporated in Ireland and must be a trading or a holding company.

• If the employee sells the shares within three years of the date of acquiring the shares any income tax relief granted is withdrawn by reference to the tax year in which it was originally given.

• The relief will not be withdrawn where the employee ceases employment with the particular company, or where the employee ceases to be a resident for tax purposes or ceases to be a full time employee.

• When the shares are sold the amount of the tax deduction granted is excluded from the base cost of the shares when calculating the Capital Gains Tax liability on the sale of the shares.

Save as you earn scheme (SAYE)

Save As You Earn (SAYE) share option schemes were introduced in the 1999 Finance Act. Under a SAYE scheme a company grants options over shares to its employees. The share options are granted at a price which is fixed by the directors at the time of the grant. This may be at the full market price value or at a discount of up to 25% on the market value.

SAYE schemes operate by allowing the employee to save between £10 - £250 per month out of their net income for a three or five year period in order to finance the purchase of the shares. The employee must save in a special savings scheme which has been set up for SAYE schemes, with a qualifying savings institution. Any interest or bonus paid on the savings contract will be exempt from tax including deposit interest retention tax.

Example

5 Years Saving Contract	£	€
Monthly Savings	£50.00	€63.49
Share Price At Grant	£3.33	€4.23
Discounted Option Price (75% of Market Value)	£2.50	€3.17
Savings on Maturity	£3,000.00	€3,809.21
Interest on Maturity	£250.0	€317.43
Total Savings & Interest	£3,250.00	€4,126.64
Options Granted Over 1,300 Shares		

Normally when an employee exercises a share option, a charge to income tax will arise based on the excess value of the shares over the option price regardless of whether or not the shares are retained, however, options granted through a SAYE scheme approved by the Revenue Commissioners will not be liable to income tax on either grant or exercise provided the option is not exercised before the third anniversary of the grant. After this time any disposal of the shares will trigger a charge to capital gains tax based on the excess of the net sales proceeds over the actual option price.

Share incentive schemes/employee share purchase plans

These are schemes whereby a fixed amount is deducted from your salary every month. After the end of a fixed period, say six months, you purchase shares in your employer's company at a discounted price.

This discount is a taxable benefit for you and is liable to income tax. If you sell the shares immediately on acquiring them no further liability to tax arises. However, Capital Gains Tax may be payable if you keep the shares and sell them at a profit at a later stage.

Example

As part of a Share Incentive Scheme, John saves £200 per month from January to June 2000. At the end of 6 months he has saved £1,200.

Shares in John's employer's company are £10 per share at June 2000. John buys 140 shares at 30th June 2000 at £8.50, at 15% discount, total cost of £1,190. He keeps the shares until November 2000 when he sells them for £2,100.

	£	€
Income Tax Liability at 30th June 2000 - (Date Shares Acquired)		
Market Value of Shares Acquired (140 x £10)	£1,400	€1,778
Price Paid (140 x £8.50)	£1,190	€1,511
Taxable Benefit	£210	€267

A liability to Capital Gains Tax may arise when the shares are sold in November 2000.

		£	€
	Sale Proceeds	£2,100	€2,666
Less:	Cost - (including amount assessed to income tax)	£1,400	€1,778
	Gain	£700	€889
	CGT Exemption	£1,000	€1,270
	Chargeable Gain	Nil	€Nil

As Share Incentive Schemes are designed to encourage employees to invest in their employer's business, many schemes prohibit the sale of shares immediately after they are acquired. Where the employee is prohibited from disposing of the shares for a number of years, the revenue will allow an abatement in the income tax charge depending on the number of years of the prohibition on the disposal.

The abatement is as follows:

No. of Years	Abatement
1 Year	10 %
2 Years	20 %
3 Years	30 %
4 Years	40 %
5 Years	50 %
Over 5 Years	55 %

14

Maximising your redundancy options

Redundancy payments are regulated by the 1967-1991 Redundancy Acts.

As an employee, you are covered under these Acts if you meet the following requirements.

- You are between the ages of 16 and 66.

- You are normally expected to work at least eight hours per week and your employment is terminated because of redundancy.

- 104 weeks continuous service, between the ages of 16 and 66 for regular part-time employees who are also expected to work at least eight hours per week for the same employer.

When does redundancy arise?

Redundancy normally arises where employees are dismissed and this dismissal can be attributed to:

- The employer ceasing to carry on business for the purposes for which the employee was employed or the employer ceasing to carry on the business in the place where the employees were employed.

- Where the employer has decided to carry on business with fewer employees or complete the work in a different manner than that for which the employee is sufficiently qualified or trained.

Voluntary redundancy

Voluntary redundancy occurs when an employer requires a smaller work force and asks for volunteers for redundancy. The person or persons who volunteer for redundancy are also entitled to the statutory lump sum payment.

Notice of redundancy

An employer who, because of redundancy, intends to dismiss an employee who has at least 104 weeks continuous service with the firm must give notice in writing to the employee of the proposed dismissal. This notice must be given at least two weeks before the date on which the dismissal is due to take effect. Form RP1 must be used for this purpose.

Time-off to look for work

An employee is entitled, during the two weeks period of redundancy notice, to reasonable time-off (paid) to look for new employment or to make arrangements for training for future employment.

Redundancy certificate

An employee who is dismissed by reason of redundancy must be given a redundancy certificate by the employer. This certificate must be on a prescribed form **RP2. The employer** must supply the original certificate to the employee who has been dismissed due to redundancy.

Effects of change of ownership of a business on a redundancy lump sum payment

Where there is a change in the ownership of a business and you continue, by arrangement, to work for the new owner with no break in your employment, you are not entitled to any redundancy payments at the time of the change of ownership. Your continuity of employment is also preserved for the purpose of the redundancy payments in the event of your dismissal or redundancy by the new employer at any future date. You are not entitled to a redundancy payment if an offer of employment by the new owner is unreasonably refused by you.

If the new owner merely buys the premises in which you were employed, this will not constitute a change of ownership of the business and your former employer will be liable to pay any redundancy payment which may be due to you.

Calculation of statutory redundancy lump sum payments

The amount of the lump sum payment which a qualified redundant employee is entitled to receive from their employer is calculated as follows:

* A half-week's pay for each year of employment, continuous and reckonable, between the ages of 16 and 41 years.

* A week's pay for each year of employment, continuous and reckonable over the age of 41 years

    and

* In addition, the equivalent of one week's normal pay.

For the purpose of calculating statutory redundancy, a week's pay is limited to a maximum of £300.

Time limit on redundancy claims

A dismissed employee will not be entitled to a lump sum unless within 52 weeks after the date of termination of employment:

* The payment has been agreed and paid

    or

* The employee has given a written claim to the employer

    or

* A question as to the right of the employee to the payment or its amount, has been referred to the Employment Appeals Tribunal.

The Employment Appeals Tribunal has discretion to extend the 52 week time limit, provided that it receives the necessary claim within 104 weeks of the date of dismissal and it is satisfied that the delay by the employee in making the claim was reasonable.

Lump sum payments to employees from the social insurance fund

- If an employee claims that their employer is liable to pay a lump sum

  and

- The employee has taken all reasonable steps, including a written application (**Form RP77** may be used for this purpose) but excluding legal proceedings, to obtain the payment and the employer refuses or fails to pay the whole or part of the lump sum

  or

- The employer is insolvent and the whole or part of the lump sum remains unpaid,

  or

- The employer has died and the lump sum cannot be paid to the employee until the employer's affairs have been settled the employee can apply to the Minister for Enterprise and Employment, Davitt House, Adelaide Road, Dublin 2 for the lump sum payment from the Social Insurance Fund. (**Form RP14** may be used for this purpose).

For further information or relevant forms, contact the Department of Enterprise and Employment, Davitt House, Adelaide Road, Dublin 2 or FÁS, at any of their offices throughout the country.

Taxation of lump sum redundancy payments

Lump sums such as redundancy payments, ex-gratia payments or compensation payments may or may not be liable to tax. Payments can be:

- Totally exempt from tax.

- Relieved from tax.

- Subject to tax.

Totally exempt from tax

- Payments made under the Redundancy Payments Acts 1967-1991.

- Payments made on account of an injury or disability.

- A lump sum payment from an approved pension scheme but excluding a refund of an employee's contributions to that pension scheme.

Relieved from tax

If you receive a lump sum payment from your employer which is not exempt from tax, you may be entitled to claim an extra tax-free amount. The amount is the highest of the following three exemptions:

Basic exemption

The basic exemption is £8,000 together with an additional £600 for each complete year of service.

Increased exemption

The basic exemption may be increased by £4,000 to a maximum of £12,000 plus £600 for each complete year of service provided:

- You have not already made a claim for the increased exemption amount in respect of a previous employment i.e. this increased exemption can only be claimed once

  and

- No tax-free lump sum has been received or is receivable under an approved pension scheme. If a tax-free amount is received or receivable and is less than £4,000 then the increased exemption amount will be £12,000 (£8,000 + £4,000) plus £600 for each complete year of service less the tax-free amount received or receivable from your pension scheme.

Standard capital superannuation benefit (S.C.S.B.)

The third exemption is the Standard Capital Superannuation Benefit. This is arrived at using the following formula:

$$\frac{A \times B}{15} - C$$

A	=	Average yearly remuneration from the employment for the last 36 months ending on the date of termination.
B	=	Number of complete years of service.
C	=	The value of any tax-free lump sums received or receivable under an approved pension scheme.

For the purpose of calculating the increased exemption and the S.C.S.B. amount, the tax-free lump sum receivable from the pension scheme is the present day value of any deferred tax-free lump sum receivable at retirement from the existing pension scheme. A refund of pension contributions which were subject to tax at 25% are excluded.

Note: If you sign a waiver letter i.e. a letter confirming you will not avail of any tax-free lump sum from your current pension scheme now or at retirement, the value of any deferred tax-free lump sum receivable will be Nil. (See C above).

Example

John commenced employment with company XYZ Ltd. on 6th December 1978.

He opted for early retirement on 5th November 2000 and he received a lump sum of £60,000 (excluding statutory redundancy).

He receives a tax free lump sum of £15,000 from his pension scheme.

The tax-free amount of this £60,000 is the highest of the following:

Basic exemption

£8,000 + (£600 x 21) = £20,600

Note: Only complete years count for the purpose of the additional £600. So even though John had 21 years 11 months service he only receives £600 x 21.

Increased exemption

As John received a tax-free lump sum from the pension scheme in excess of £4,000, the increase exemption would not apply to him.

Standard capital superannuation benefit (SCSB)

Assuming John's salary for the last 36 months was as follows:

	£	€	
06/04/00 - 05/11/00	£17,500	€22,220	(7 months)
06/04/99 - 05/04/00	£28,000	€35,553	(12 months)
06/04/98 - 05/04/99	£26,200	€33,267	(12 months)
04/11/97 - 05/04/98	£10,083	€12,803	(5 months)
Total salary for 36 months	£81,783	€103,843	
Average for 12 months	£27,261	€34,614	

Calculation of SCSB

$$\frac{A \times B}{15} \text{ less C} = \frac{£27,261 \times 21}{15} \text{ less } £15,000 = £23,165$$

The highest of the above three exemptions is the SCSB amount of £23,165. This is the amount which John can receive tax-free.

A summary of John's position, assuming he pays tax at 44%, is as follows:

		£	€
	Gross Lump Sum	£60,000	€76,184
Less:	SCSB Amount	£23,165	€29,413
	Taxable	£36,835	€46,771
	Tax @ 44%	£16,207	€20,579
	Levies @ 2%	£737	€936
	Net Lump Sum	£43,056	€54,670

Foreign Service and Redundancy

Your redundancy lump sum may be completely tax free provided;

- 75% or more of your entire period of employment, ending on the date of termination was foreign service

  or

- your period of service exceeded 10 years but the whole of the last 10 years was foreign service

  or

- one half of your period of service including any ten of the last twenty years was foreign service, provided your period of service exceeded 20 years.

Foreign service is defined as a period of employment the emoluments of which were not chargeable to Irish tax, or if chargeable to Irish tax were chargeable on the remittance basis.

Foreign service not sufficient to exempt

If you have foreign service but don't qualify for full exemption from income tax your redundancy payment, as reduced by the basic/increased or SCSB exemption may be further reduced by the following formula;

$$P \times \frac{FS}{TS}$$

P = Payment (as reduced by SCSB or/basic increased exemption)

FS = No of years of foreign service

TS = No of years of total service

Example

Using the example on page 249 and assuming that John had spent 6 years working in the U.S foreign service relief would be;

$$\frac{£36,835 \times 6}{21} \quad = \quad £\,10,524$$

John's taxable lump sum is now £ 10,524

	£	€
Gross lump sum	£60,000	€76,184
Less: SCSB	£23,165	€29,413
	£36,835	€46,771
Less: Relief for foreign service	£10,524	€13,363
Taxable	£26,311	€33,408
Tax @ 44%	£11,577	€14,700
Levies @ 2%	£526	€668
Net lump sum	£47,897	€60,817

Top slicing relief

This relief is available after the end of the tax year in which you received a lump sum. Top Slicing Relief works by calculating your average rate of tax for the five years prior to the tax year in which you received a lump sum. If this average rate is lower than the rate of tax which you paid on your lump sum, the tax will be recalculated at the lower rate and you can get a refund.

The amount of the relief due to you is calculated by the following formula:

$$A-(P x T/I)$$

Where

A   =   The tax which you paid on your lump sum.

P   =   The taxable lump sum after deduction of exempt amount.

T   =   The aggregate of tax payable in respect of the total income of the payee for the five preceding years of assessment.

I   =   The aggregate of the taxable incomes of the payee for the five preceding years of assessment.

Example

Catherine's taxable income and tax paid for the last 5 years was as follows;

	Taxable income		Tax paid	
	£	€	£	€
1996/97	£18,650	€23,681	£5,036	€6,394
1997/98	£18,900	€23,998	£4,914	€6,239
1998/99	£19,400	€24,633	£5,436	€6,902
1999/00	£17,200	€21,839	£4,128	€5,241
2000/01	£20,200	€25,649	£4,444	€5,643
	£94,350	**€119,800**	**£23,958**	**€30,420**

Assuming Catherine received a lump sum in April 2001, the taxable lump sum was £40,000 and she paid tax @ 44% on this, amounting to £ 17,600. Her top slicing relief would work out as follows;

	£	€
A = Tax paid on lump sum	£17,600	€22,347
P = Taxable lump sum	£40,000	€50,790
T = Total of tax paid in the last 5 years	£23,958	€30,420
I = Total of your taxable income for the last 5 years	£94,350	€119,800

Top Slicing Relief due to Catherine;
$$£17,600 - \left(£40,000 \times \frac{£23,958}{£94,350}\right) = £7,443$$

Catherine would have to wait until the end of the 2001 tax year (i.e. the tax year in which she received the lump sum in order to claim the Top Slicing Relief.

15

Foreign income - bringing it home

Generally, your liability to Irish Income Tax on foreign income depends on:

• Whether you are resident in Ireland.

• Whether you are ordinarily resident in Ireland.

• Whether you are domiciled in Ireland.

Residence

You will be regarded as being resident here for tax purposes in the current tax year:

• If you spend 183 days or more here

   or

• If the combined number of days you spend here in the current tax year and the number of days you spent here in the last tax year exceeds 280. In applying this two year test, a period of less than 30 days spent in Ireland in a tax year will be ignored.

Your presence in the State for a day, means your presence at midnight.

Electing to be resident

If you come to Ireland and are not regarded as resident here for tax purposes but you can show that you intend to remain and to be resident here next year, you may elect to be treated as resident for tax purposes from the date of your arrival.

Electing to be non-resident

This is not possible in any circumstances.

Ordinary residence

The term "ordinary resident" as distinct from "resident", relates to your normal pattern of life and denotes residence in a country with some degree of continuity.

When does ordinary residence begin?

If you have been resident here for three consecutive tax years you become ordinarily resident from the beginning of the fourth tax year.

When does ordinary residence cease?

If you have been ordinarily resident here, you will cease to be ordinarily resident at the end of the third consecutive year in which you are not resident. For example, if you are resident and ordinarily resident here in 1999/00 and leave the State in that year, you will remain ordinarily resident up to the end of the tax year 2002.

Domicile

Domicile is a complex legal concept. It is generally the country which you consider to be your natural home. When you are born you obtain a domicile of origin which is normally the domicile of your father.

Tax summary

Individual	Liability To Irish Income Tax
Resident and domiciled in Ireland	On worldwide income from all sources
Resident but not domiciled or ordinarily resident in Ireland	On all Irish and UK income and foreign income remitted to Ireland
Ordinarily resident but not resident here in the relevant tax year.	On World-wide income. However, employment or income from an employment trade or profession which is exercised wholly abroad or income from other sources which does not exceed £3,000 will be ignored for tax purposes. Double taxation agreements may exempt some foreign income.
Not resident or ordinarily resident.	Taxed on income arising from Irish sources.

Double taxation

Generally, Irish residents are liable to Irish income tax on world-wide income and non-residents are liable to Irish income tax on income arising in Ireland. As similar provisions apply to residents of other countries, this can give rise to double taxation. The purpose of Double Taxation Agreements is to prevent this double taxation of income. This may be achieved either by:

• Exempting certain income from tax in one country

   or

• By offsetting the tax paid on income in one country against the tax liability arising on that same income in another country.

Full personal allowances and reliefs

• If you are a resident here you are entitled to full personal allowances and full tax reliefs.

• If you are not resident here but are resident in another Member State of the European Union and 75% or more of your world-wide income is taxable here you will also be entitled to full personal allowances and full tax reliefs here.

255

Partial personal allowances and reliefs

- If you are a citizen of Ireland or a citizen, subject or national of another Member State of the European Union

  or

- If you are a former resident of the State who is now resident outside of this country because of your health or because of the health of a member of your family resident with you,

  or

- If you are a resident or national of a country with which Ireland has a Double Taxation Agreement which provides for such allowances.

If any of the above applies and you are non-resident here for tax purposes you will be entitled to a certain proportion of personal allowances and tax reliefs. The exact proportion of these allowances is determined by the relationship between your income which is subject to Irish tax and your income from all other sources.

Example

In 2000/01 John who is single and an Irish citizen not resident here, had the following sources of income:

	£	€
Rental income in Ireland	£10,000	€12,697
US Dividends	£3,000	€3,809
Rental Income in UK	£4,000	€5,079
Total Income	£17,000	€21,585

As John is not resident here, he is liable to Irish tax only on income arising in Ireland and entitled to partial personal allowances as follows:

		2000/01	
		£	€
	Irish Income	£10,000	€12,697
Less:	Personal Allowances £4,700 x 10,000 / 17,000	£2,765	€3,510
	Taxable	£7,235	€9,187
	Tax £7,235 @ 22%	£1,592	€2,021
	Net Income	£8,408	€10,675

Year of arrival/return

If you return to Ireland but you are not already resident here for tax purposes and if you can show that you intend to remain here and to be resident here for tax purposes next year, you may elect to be treated as a resident here for income tax purposes from the date of your arrival and your tax position will work out as follows:

Example

Patrick returned to Ireland on 1st November 2000 after spending 3 years abroad. His earnings in Ireland from 1st November 2000 to 5th April 2001 will be £16,000.

		2000/01			
		£		€	
	Irish Income		£16,000		€20,316
	Tax Payable £16,000 @ 22%		£3,520		€4,469
Less:	Tax Credits				
	Personal 4,700 @ 22%	(£1,034)		(€1,313)	
	PAYE 1,000 @ 22%	(£220)	(£1,254)	(€279)	(€1,592)
	Net Tax Payable		£2,266		€2,877

Note: Patrick will be liable to Irish tax on any foreign income which may accrue to him after the date of his return, subject to any relevant double taxation agreement.

Year of departure

If you plan to spend a period of time abroad (other than for temporary purposes) and you will not be resident in Ireland for the year after your departure, you may be granted "emigrant status" when you depart. If you are granted "emigrant status", your earnings from an employment exercised outside the State after the date of your departure in the current tax year will be ignored for Irish tax purposes.

Example

John will leave Ireland on the 30th September 2000 to take up a 2 year contract in the USA. From the 6th April 2000 to the date of departure he will earn £15,000 in Ireland and pay PAYE of £4,103. His income in the USA from 1st October 2000 to 5th April 2001 will be £8,000.

John's position in 2000/01 will be as follows:

	Emigrant		Resident	
	£	€	£	€
Salary - Ireland	£15,000	€19,046	£15,000	€19,046
Salary - USA	-	-	£20,000	€25,395
Taxable	£15,000	€19,046	£35,000	€44,441
Tax Payable				
£15,000/£17,000 @ 22%	£3,300	€4,190	£3,740	€4,749
£ 18,000 @ 44%			£7,920	€10,056
			11,660	€14,805
Less: Tax Credit				
Personal Allowance				
£4,700 @ 22%	(£1,034)	(€1,313)	(£1,034)	(€1,313)
PAYE Allowance				
£1,000 @ 22%	(£220)	(€280)	(£220)	(€279)
Tax Liability	£2,046	€2,598	£10,406	€13,213
Less: PAYE Paid	(£4,103)	(€5,210)	(£4,103)	(€5,210)
Refund Due	(£2,057)	(€2,612)		
Additional Tax Due			£6,303	€8,003

Foreign earnings deduction (FED)

If you are resident here for tax purposes and you spend 90 qualifying days working abroad: -

- In a tax year
  or

- In a continuous period of 12 months straddling two tax years

you will be entitled to special tax reliefs provided your employment duties were performed outside of Ireland and the U.K. This relief does not apply to public sector employees.

Qualifying days

Qualifying days are those days on which you are absent from the State and which are part of a continuous period of absence of 11 days or more (14 days prior to 29th February 2000). Each period of absence must be substantially devoted to the duties of employment. While it is not necessary to work at weekends or public holidays spent abroad, other days spent abroad must be devoted to work.

How is foreign earnings deductions (FED) calculated:

This special relief reduces your total income for the year and is calculated in accordance with the following formula:

$$\frac{D \times E}{365}$$

D = The number of qualifying days in a tax year or 12 month period.
E = Total earnings for the year from Ireland and abroad.

From 29th February 2000 the maximum amount of Foreign Earnings Deduction you can claim is £ 25,000.

Example

John works in Ireland from 6th April 2000 to 31st December 2000 (270 days). He goes on a foreign assignment to Germany on 1st January 2001, where he will work up to the 5th April 2001 (96 days). His income for 2000/01 will be £15,000 in Ireland and £10,000 in Germany.

	£	€
Irish Income	£15,000	€19,046
German Income	£10,000	€12,697
Total Income	£25,000	€31,743
Less: Foreign Earnings Deduction		
96 x £25,000 = / 365	(£6,575)	(€8,349)
Taxable Income in Ireland	£18,425	€23,394

John's tax position will work out as follows:

	Before £	Before €	After Claiming F.E.D. £	After Claiming F.E.D. €
Taxable Income	£25,000	€31,743	£18,425	€23,395
Tax Payable				
£17,000 @ 22%	£3,740	€4,749	£3,740	€44,749
£8,000 @ 44%	£3,520	€4,470		
£1,425 @ 44%			£627	€796
	£7,260	€9,218	£4,367	€5,545
Less: Tax Credits				
Personal £4,700 @ 22%	(£1,034)	(€1,313)	(£1,034)	(€1,313)
PAYE £1,000 @ 22%	(£220)	(€280)	(£220)	(€280)
Tax Payable	£6,006	€7,626	£3,113	€3,953
Tax Refund Due			£2,893	€3,673

Claiming foreign earnings deduction (F.E.D.)

You claim this relief at the end of the tax year by submitting your tax return and enclosing a statement showing:

- A breakdown of your total income between Irish and Foreign Income.

- The days and the dates you spent abroad.

- Relevant backup information.

Seafarer allowance

A new allowance of £5,000 is available for seafarers. This allowance can be offset against the seafaring employment. It is conditional on the seafarer being at sea on a voyage for a least 169 days in a tax year. This allowance does not apply in any year where the individual claims the Foreign Earnings Deduction.

Budget 2001: From 6th December 2000 the number of days a seafarer is required to be at sea is reduced from 169 days to 161.

Spouses

Your spouse's resident status is not governed by your residence status. If the residence status of your spouse differs from yours, you may choose to be treated as single people for tax purposes if it is to your advantage to do so.

Right of appeal

If you disagree with your tax inspector's decision relating to your taxation in the year of your arrival or departure or to the special tax reliefs applicable to foreign assignments, you have a right to appeal the decision to the Appeal Commissioners.

Renting while abroad

Many homeowners going abroad for a limited period will rent their homes while they are abroad. This income is taxable in Ireland regardless of your residence status.

Example

John rents his home for £1,000 p.m. He has a mortgage of £85,000, mortgage interest of £4,800 p.a. and outgoings (agency fees, insurance, repairs etc.) of £1,600.

	First renting before Second Bacon Report (23/04/98)		First renting after Second Bacon Report (23/04/98)	
	£	€	£	€
Gross Rental Income	£12,000	€15,237	£12,000	€15,237
Less: Mortgage Interest	(£4,800)	(€6,095)	n/a	n/a
Outgoings	(£1,600)	(€2,032)	(£1,600)	(€2,032)
Taxable Income	£5,600	€7,111	£10,400	€13,205

Note: As a result of the Second Bacon Report if you rent your home for the first time while abroad after 23rd April 1998, any mortgage interest paid in respect of the property cannot be offset against the rental income. See Page 59.

Capital gains tax (CGT)

When you sell your main private residence it is normally exempt from CGT. However, if you have rented your main private residence for a number of years, at the date of sale, the CGT exemption will be restricted on a time basis.

For CGT purposes, certain periods of absence are regarded as periods of occupation e.g.

•   The last 12 months of ownership.

•   Any period of absence throughout which you worked in a foreign employment or any period of absence not exceeding 4 years during which you were prevented from occupying the residence because of employment, provided you occupy the residence before and after the period of absence.

Example

Mary, who is single, bought her home in January 1988 for £50,000. She rented it out from 31st December 1995 to 31st December 1999 while she worked abroad. She sold it in December 2000 for £150,000. Mary's CGT liability will be calculated as follows:

Period of Ownership:

1st January 1988 - 31st December 1995	= 7 Years Principal Private Residence (PPR)
1st January 1996 - 31st December 1999	= 5 Years
1st January 2000 - 31st December 2000	= 1 Year Deemed PPR - last 12 months of ownership

		Mary's position	
		£	€
	Sale Price	£150,000	€190,461
Less:	Selling Costs	(£2,000)	(€2,540)
	Purchase Price	£50,000	€63,487
	Indexation @ 1.384	£19,200	€24,379
	Indexed Purchase Price	£ 69,200	€87,866
	Capital Gain	£78,800	€100,055
Less:	Capital Gains Exemption	(£1,000)	(€1,270)
	Taxable Gain	£77,800	€98,786
	Tax @ 20%	**£15,560**	**€19,757**

However, Mary may claim CGT exemption for the eight years while the property was her main private residence. So, Mary's CGT liability will be £5,985 (5/13 x £15,560).

Mary could also claim total exemption from total CGT, provided she returned and live in her former home for a period before she sold it.

Tenants tax obligations

When you work abroad and rent your home, your tenant is obliged to deduct tax at the standard rate from the rental income and pay this tax over to the Revenue Commissioners. When you complete your Irish tax return you will get credit for this tax.

This obligation on your tenant to deduct tax from your rental income is removed if you appoint an agent to look after your tax affairs here in Ireland while working abroad.

Comment: If you work abroad, TAB can provide a comprehensive tax and financial advice service to minimise your tax obligations here while you work aboard.

Coming to live in Ireland

Ireland has become an increasingly popular place for foreign nationals to work and live. If you become a resident, you will only be liable to Irish income tax from the date of your arrival, provided you were non-resident here in the previous year. Even though you will only be taxed in Ireland on income for part of the year, you will receive a full year's tax free allowances. If you arrive in Ireland and are not resident here for tax purposes, any income arising in Ireland will be liable to Irish tax. However, you will only receive allowances for the portion of the year that you are actually here.

Emergency tax

If your employer does not receive either a certificate of tax-free allowances or a P45 for you, then he will be obliged to deduct tax on an emergency basis from your salary. Under emergency tax, a temporary tax-free allowance is given for the first month of employment and after the first month the rate of tax increases (see Page 223). In order to get a tax-free allowance certificate your must first get a Personal Service Number (PSN). This replaces the RSI number. In order to obtain a PSN number you must present yourself at your local social welfare office together with some form of ID e.g. your passport and they will issue you with a PSN Number. You must then complete a Form 12a which is available in any tax offices. When your employer receives a tax-free allowance certificate for you, you will receive a refund of any tax which you may have overpaid.

You can expect to pay tax on all income, which may include:

- Gross salary.

- Bonuses and commissions.

- Cash allowances for housing, school fees, cost of living , etc.

- Benefit-In-Kind (BIK).

- Share incentives, though various rules apply depending on the scheme.

If you have earnings from other sources, such as rental income, share dividends, deposit interest, it too will be subject to tax, whether it has been earned here or in the UK, though in the case of UK income special rules may apply. Income earned outside of Ireland or the UK may only be taxable in Ireland if it is brought into this country.

On the plus side, business and relocation expenses, pension contributions, shares taken as part of an approved profit sharing scheme and even severance payments can result in important tax relief and opportunities to reduce your overall tax bill.

Capital gains tax (CGT)

Once you are resident here, any assets you still hold abroad, but dispose of could be subject to Irish Capital Gains Tax (currently 20%), though this would not include your principal, private residence. An annual CGT exemption of £1,000 applies in Ireland. The amount of tax you will have to pay will also be affected by whether or not you are legally domiciled here and by how much, if any, of the gain from assets outside of Ireland and the UK is brought into Ireland. Consult your tax adviser for a clear picture of your particular circumstances.

Leaving Ireland

When you leave Ireland, providing you had been resident here for tax purposes, you will be taxed on your income up to the date of your departure, though you can offset a full years tax-free allowance against this income. Depending on when you leave Ireland you may be entitled to a refund upon departure.

In order to claim a refund, you must complete a Form 12, and submit it to your tax office together with your P45 and details of all your allowances, e.g. mortgage interest, health insurance etc.

Relief for trans border workers

This allowance which was introduced in 1998/99 and is aimed mainly at Irish residents who commute to work in Northern Ireland. However, it also applies to individuals who travel to the UK and elsewhere to work and return to Ireland at the weekends. It applies to individuals who commute daily or at weekends to work outside Ireland, to a country with which Ireland has a Double Taxation Agreement.

The relief means that such residents will not pay tax in Ireland on income from the foreign employment. Tax however, may be payable in the foreign country in which the individual is working.

To claim this relief you must comply with the following conditions;

* The work is outside the State in a country with which Ireland has a double tax treaty.

* Employment is held for a continuous period of 13 weeks.

* The duties of the employment must be performed wholly outside the State.

* The income must be taxed in the other country.

* The employee must be at least one day per week in the State.

* The employment must not be with the Government or an authority set up by the State or under Statute.

The final amount of the tax payable is calculated using the following formula;

$$\frac{A \times B}{C}$$

Where

A = The tax payable without this relief and before any credit for foreign tax paid.

B = Your income for the year excluding any income for a qualifying employment.

C = Total income for the year.

Example

John is single, lives in Donegal. He went to work in Derry in September 2000 and his income from Northern Ireland in the 2000/01 tax year is Stg. £15,000. He also earned £12,000 in Ireland from 6th April 2000 to 30th August 2000.

The tax payable by John in the UK is as follows;

2000/01 Northern Ireland		Stg. £	€
	Salary	£15,000	€19,046
Less:	Single Allowance	£4,385	€5,568
	Taxable	£10,615	€13,478
	£1,520 @ 10%	£152	€193
	£9,095 @ 22%	£2,001	€2,541
	UK Tax Payable	£2,153	€2,734

Exhange Rate: IR £1 = .80p Stg.

If John did not qualify for Trans Border Relief his tax would be calculated as follows;.

			£	€
	Income from Employment - Northern Ireland		£18,750	€23,808
	Income from Employment - Ireland		£12,000	€15,237
	Taxable		£30,750	€39,045
	Tax Payable			
	£17,000 @ 22%	£ 3,740		
	£13,750 @ 44%	£ 6,050	£ 9,790	€12,431
Less:	Tax Credits			
	Personal 4,700 @ 22%		(£1,034)	(€1,313)
	PAYE 1,000 @ 22%		(£220)	(€279)
	Total tax due without Cross Border Relief		£8,536	€10,838

Exchange Rate IR £1 = .80p Stg.

Cross Border Relief would reduce this tax bill to £ 5,484 (£2,153 in Northern Ireland + £3,331 here). Calculated as follows;

*   A = £ 8,536 $\underline{£8,536 \times £12,000} = £3,331$
        B = £12,000   £30,750
        C = £30,750

UK employments income

Unfortunately, many of the benefits applicable to foreign employment income outlined earlier are not applicable to U.K. employment income. We here outline the general principles applicable to income earned in the U.K. while you are treated as resident here for tax purposes.

Paid by UK company while working and living in Ireland

If you are resident in Ireland and are employed by a UK resident company, you are normally liable to tax in Ireland on this income, under the Self Assessment System. Usually, the UK company will pay you gross, less a PRSI deduction.

Paid by an Irish company while working and living in the UK

If you are working short-term in the UK and paid from Ireland then there is normally no UK income tax payable and your tax position will be effectively ignored by the UK tax authorities.

PAYE in the UK

When you commence work in the UK you will be asked to complete a Residence Enquiry Form P86 and a Tax Coding Form P15. How you will be taxed on your employment income in the UK will to a large extent be determined by your own personal plans: for example, how long you intend to stay or work in the UK?

If it is your intention to work and take up short-term residence in the UK, your UK employment income will normally be taxed under PAYE on a "week one" basis. However, if it is your intention to work and take up long-term residence in the UK you may be taxed on a PAYE cumulative basis i.e. the UK tax authorities will issue you a tax-free allowance from the 6th of April preceding your arrival.

UK-personal income tax summary
tax allowances

	1998/99	1999/00	2000/01
	Stg. £	Stg. £	Stg. £
Personal Allowance - Under 65	£4,195	£4,335	£4,385
- 65 to 74 Note 1	£5,410	£5,720	£5,790
- 75 and over Note 1	£5,600	£5,980	£6,050
*Married Couple's Allowance-minimum amount Note 2	£1,900	£1,970	£2,000
- 65 and 74 Note 1+2	£3,305	£5,125	£5,185
- 75 and over Note 1+2	£3,345	£5,195	£5,255
*Additional Personal Allowance for Children Note 2	£1,900	£1,970	£2,000
*Widow(er)'s Bereavement Allowance Note 2	£1,900	£1,970	£2,000
Blind Person's Allowance	£1,330	£1,380	£1,400
Income Limit for Age-Related Allowances	£16,200	£16,800	£17,000

Notes:

1. The higher personal and married couples allowances for tax payers aged 65 and over are reduced by £1 for every £2 of income above the income limit (£17,000). However, they cannot be reduced below the basic level of allowances available to those aged under 65.

2. These allowances give relief at 10% rate of tax and reduce the tax payers tax bill by a set amount. For example, those receiving the married couples allowance of £2,000 will have their tax bill reduced by up to £200 (10% of £2,000).

U.K. tax rates

1999/00	2000/01
10% on first £1,500	10% on first £1,520
23% on next £26,500	22% on next £26,880
40% over £28,000	40% over £28,400

Average rates of exchange between Ireland and the U.K.

Tax Year Ending	IR £1
05/04/98	Stg. £0.9016
05/04/99	Stg. £0.8695
05/04/00	Stg. £0.8128

If you are a student in the UK for the summer, you will normally be taxed under PAYE on a week one basis. On your return to college here, you will probably be due a tax refund. In order to get this refund from the UK tax authorities you should complete the following:

•   Tax Repayment Form P50.

•   Residence Enquiry Form P85.

and send both together with your UK P45 to your tax inspector (address available from your UK employer).

It is also advisable to provide some evidence of your imminent return to college here on a full-time basis if you wish your UK tax inspector to speed up your tax refund. Normally, refunds of PAYE tax will only be made after the 5th April.

16

Self assessment & the self-employed

If you are self-employed or if you are in PAYE employment but have non-PAYE income exceeding £2,500, you will be liable to tax under the self-assessment system, which require you to;

- Pay your preliminary tax on the due date in the year of assessment e.g. your preliminary tax for 2000/01 is due on the 1 November 2000.

- Submit your completed Income Tax Return - (Form 11) to your Inspector of Taxes on/before the 31st January following the year of assessment e.g. your 1999/00 tax return must be submitted on/before the 31st January 2001.

Preliminary tax

Preliminary tax is your estimate of income tax payable for the year. It is payable on the 1st November in the year of assessment e.g. on 1st November 2000 you pay your Preliminary Tax for 2000/01.

The amount payable is the lower of;

- 90% of your final liability for the current year

    or

- 100% of your liability for the previous year

Payment by direct debit

If you choose to pay your preliminary tax, by direct debit, payments can commence on the 9th January, 9th February or 9th March in the relevant tax year. Your direct debit payments will be based on 105% of your final tax liability for non PAYE income in the pre-preceding year. e.g. if your final tax liability for non PAYE income in 1998/99 was £6,000 - your 2001 preliminary tax liability can be paid by 12 monthly instalments of £525 (£6,000 x 105% ÷ 12) starting in January 2001 or 11 monthly instalments of £573 starting in February 01 or 10 monthly instalments of £630 starting in March 01.

Surcharge

If you don't submit your tax return by the 31st January, a surcharge will be added to your tax bill. The amount of the surcharge will depend on when your tax return is eventually submitted.

A surcharge of 5% of the total tax due (up to a maximum of £10,000) is added where your tax return is submitted before the 31st March following the year of assessment or 10% (up to a maximum of £50,000) where the return is submitted after the 31st March following the year of assessment. Under self assessment this surcharge only applies from your second filing date.

Change in tax year

At present the tax year runs from 6th April to the following 5th April. With effect from 1st January 2002 the tax year will move to a calendar year. The first tax year under the new system will run from 1st January 2002 to 31st December 2002.

Because of this changeover there will a short transitional year which will run from the 6th April 2001 to 31st December 2001. As the short tax "year" is only for nine months, self employed tax payers will pay tax on 74% (270 days ÷365 days) of the profits from their trade or profession for the 12 month period ending in the short tax "year" also. Income tax allowances credits and bands for the short tax "year" will only be 74% of the normal annual amounts.

New payment and return filing dates

The move to a calendar year will mean changes to the payment and return filling dates which apply under the self assessment system. The return filing date for the short tax "year", i.e. the period from 6th April 2001 to 31st December 2001 will be 31st October 2002. The balance of tax due for the short tax "year" will be payable on the 31st October 2001. Preliminary Tax for the tax year 2002 will also be due on the 31st October 2001.

Pay Preliminary Tax	31st October in year of assessment e.g. 31st October 2002 pay preliminary tax for tax year 2002.
File Tax Return	31st October following the end of the tax year of e.g. tax return for 2002 (year ended 31st December 2002) must be filed by the 31st October 2003.
Pay balance of tax	31st October following the return filing date. Balance of tax due for 2002 (year ended 31st December 2002) must be paid by 31st October 2003.

Contract of service Vs contract for service

If you work for an employer for more than eight hours a week you are entitled to a contract of employment. This contract gives you the benefit of protective legislation, including the Holiday's Act 1973, the Unfair Dismissal Acts 1977 and 1993, the Minimum Notice and Terms of Employment Act 1973 and many others. As an employee you pay PAYE and PRSI.

As a contractor you have an independent business and your contract for work is a contract for services so you are not protected under the employment legislation mentioned earlier.

Setting up as a contractor

There are a number of issues you must face as a contractor. These include, do you operate as a Sole Trader / Partnership or Limited Company ? should you register for VAT?

Limited company

Limited companies prepare audited accounts annually, which may be more costly than preparing accounts as a sole trader.

Corporation tax charged on non-manufacturing company's profits is 20% (from 1st January 2001). The taxable profit is computed in the same way as the taxable profit for a sole trader. Preliminary tax is due six months after the company's year end and its tax return form CT1 should be submitted to the Inspector of Taxes within nine months of the company's year end.

If you operate as a company, you can decide the level of salary you will receive under the PAYE system.

From a pension point of view, a company can make more generous pension contributions to your retirement fund and have these contributions offset against its taxable profits.

If a director owns a car and pays his/her own car insurance, motor tax and petrol costs, he/she can claim a mileage allowance for any business miles they travel on behalf of the company in accordance with the Civil Service Mileage Rates and have this cost offset against profits.

Sole trader

As a sole trader you are liable to income tax at 22% (20% from 6th April 2001) or 44% (42% from 6th April 2001) on the profits earned by the business in each year, regardless of the actual cash you may withdraw from the business. Tax is due for payment on November 1st each year. (31st October for the 2002 tax year onwards).

Cars

As a sole trader the cost of running a car can be apportioned between your business and private use on a basis agreed with your Tax Inspector.

VAT

If you provide a service and your sales are in excess of £20,000 p.a. you must register for VAT. If you provide goods this VAT limit is increased to £40,000.

The implications of VAT registration are as follows;

- VAT must be charged on all invoices.

- VAT on business expenses (other than entertainment and motor expenses can be reclaimed).

- Proper VAT records must be kept and returns completed every two months.

Insurance

If you are operating a business from your own home , you need to be aware your home is also now a business premises and can be treated as such for insurance purposes.

Insurance companies have become increasingly aware of the dual use of private homes and expect clients to inform them when their home is being used for business purposes. This may not necessarily result in a higher annual insurance premiums, but it may affect your right to make a successful claim if equipment is stolen or damaged or if somebody is injured on your premises.

Capital gains tax

Using your house for business purposes means you can claim some of the running costs against your annual income tax bill. These can include electricity, gas, telephone, insurance, etc. However, a drawback could occur on the sale of your home and you may face a Capital Gains Tax bill for that part in respect of which you were claiming tax reliefs. So, check out the details in advance.

Calculation of your profit

Income tax is charged on taxable profits. Taxable profits are your gross income less expenses which are allowed for income tax purposes.

The following expenses are specifically disallowed:

- Any expenses which are not wholly and exclusively made for the purpose of the trade.

- Entertainment expenses - this would include the provision of accommodation, food or drink or any other hospitality for clients. Entertainment provided for staff within reason would be an allowable expense.

- Personal Expenses.

- Capital expenditure incurred on improvements to the business premises.

- Any debt except bad debts and doubtful debts that are not expected to be recouped.

- Motor Expenses
  Motor expenses incurred after 1st December 1999 on a car costing £16,500 or less are allowed in full.

If the car cost more than £16,500 the allowable expenses are reduced by the lower of

(A)   1/3 of (cost of car less £16,500)

or

(B) $\underline{\text{Motor expenses x cost of car - £16,500}}$
          Cost of car

Budget 2001 change: For cars bought and running expenses incurred in accounting periods ending on or after 1st January 2001 the £16,500 limit is increased to £17,000. Also in calculating the allowable motor expenses the formula at (A) above will no longer be used.

Example

John runs a small business. His car cost £ 20,000 which he uses 75% for business and 25% for private use. The annual running cost of the car, including petrol, repairs, motor tax etc. comes to £ 7,600.

	£	€
Total Running Expenses	£7,600	€9,650
Less: Private Portion 25%	£1,900	€2,413
Business Portion 75%	£5,700	€7,238
Business expenses are restricted by lesser of		
1/3 (20,000 - 16,500) = 1,167	(£1,167)	€1,482
or		
5,700 x $\underline{20,000 - 16,500}$ = 1,209 *		
16,500		
Allowable expenses	£4,533	€5,756

Leased cars

Where the car is leased and the list price of the car exceeds £16,500 a portion of the lease expenses is disallowed. The allowable lease expense is calculated as follows:

$$\frac{\text{Leasing cost x £16,500}}{\text{List price of car}}$$

Capital allowances

Depreciation as such is not allowable for tax purposes but Capital Allowances in the form of Wear and Tear Allowances are allowed for plant and machinery, fixtures and fittings and motor vehicles which are used for the trade or profession. The rate of Wear and Tear allowance for plant and machinery is 15% for the first six years and 10% in year seven. The allowance is given on a straight line basis. After seven years the cost of the asset is completely written off. For motor vehicles the annual rate of Wear and Tear is 20% each year on a reducing balance basis.

Budget 2001 change: For expenditure incurred on or after 1st January 2001 the rate of wear and tear for plant and machinery will be 20% per annum for 5 years.

Withholding tax on payments for professional services

Tax at the standard rate - 22% in 2000/01 (20% in 2001) is deducted by Government Departments, State Bodies, Health Boards, etc. from payments made for professional services.

The tax deducted can be claimed in the year in which it is withheld, i.e. tax withheld in 2000/01 can be offset against your tax liabilities for 2000/01 and any excess can be reclaimed.

Basis of assessment - new business

First Year   Actual profits from commencement to following 5th April.

Second Year   Profits for first twelve months trading. Where actual profits of the second year (6th April to the following 5th April) are less than the assessment for the second year, the difference may be used to reduce the assessment for the third year.

Third and following years
Profits for accounts period ending in the actual tax year.

Note: From 1998/99 onwards the second years profit are to be assessed as follows:

(i)   If there is one set of accounts made up to a date within that tax year and these accounts are for 12 months, these accounts will form the basis period for the second year of assessment.

(ii)   If the accounts are for less than one year or if there is more than one set of accounts ending within the tax year, then the basis of assessment is the full amount of the profits for the 12 months ending on the latest of these dates.

(iii)   In all other cases, the actual profits for the tax year.

Basis of assessment - cessation of business

Final   Actual profits from the 6th April to date of cessation.

Penultimate   Where the actual profits (6th April to 5th April) of the
(2nd last)   penultimate tax year exceed the profits assessed for that tax year, the assessment will be increased to the amount of the actual profits.

Note: The rules shown above are based on the tax year running from 6th April - 5th April. As a result of the change in the tax year to a calendar year basis, the basis of assessment for commencement and cessation of a business will also change. However at the time of publication the final details for the new arrangement were not available. This information will be on our Web Site (www.tab.ie) as soon as it becomes available.

Partnership

A partner is assessed on their share of the partnership profits as adjusted for tax purposes, by reference to the profit sharing ratio in force during the period.

Capital allowances on plant and equipment are split between the partners according to their profit sharing ratio in the tax period.

The profits of a trade or profession carried on by a partnership are not assessed for income tax on the partnership as such, but each partner is deemed to be carrying on a separate trade and, thus, each is assessed for tax individually.

Relevant period

For trades or professions carried on by a partnership, there is what is referred to as the "relevant period". This begins when two or more persons commence to carry on a trade or profession in partnership, continue as partners or join or leave the partnership, provided at least one person who is a partner before a change in the partnership remains on after the change. The relevant period ceases only in any of the following circumstances:

- The cessation of a trade.

- Where all the partners but one retire.

- Where a completely new group of partners replaces the old partners.

When the relevant period commences, the partners are assessed on the basis that they have set up new trades and each partner is assessed for tax under the commencement rules for Cases I and II. For the duration of the relevant periods, the partners are treated as continuing these separate trades and are assessed for tax accordingly.

The self-employed and PRSI

With few exceptions, all self-employed people between the ages of 16 and 66 must pay PRSI contributions on their reckonable income, if their gross income exceed £2,500 in a year.

Reckonable income can be both earned and unearned and includes the following:

- Income from a trade or profession.

- Income from which tax has been deducted at source such as annuities, bank interest or building society interest and dividends.

- Irish rents and income from foreign property.

However, the following are excluded for PRSI purposes:

- Any non-cash income i.e. benefits-in-kind.

- Any sum received by way of benefit, pension allowance or supplement from the Department of Social, Community and Family Affairs.

- Any sums received from FÁS for training courses.

Self assessment & the self employed

- Any payments received by way of occupational pension, also income continuance plans payable in the event of loss of employment due to ill health where the scheme has been approved by the Revenue Commissioners.

- Redundancy payments (either statutory or non-statutory), "golden handshake" type payments and early retirement gratuities.

- Health Board payments by way of Infectious Diseases Maintenance Allowance or Mobility Allowance.

- Payments received by a person in respect of the following offices; income related to a member of the Dáil, An Seanad or the European Parliament, the judiciary, public offices under the State such as Labour Court members, the Comptroller and Auditor General, Harbour Commissioners etc.

- Prescribed relatives i.e. certain relatives on low income who help out a self-employed person in the running of a family business, assuming they are not partners in the business.

Self-employed individuals including propriety company directors pay PRSI under Class S.

The PRSI contribution

In the 2000/01 tax year the S rate of PRSI is 5% of earnings up to a ceiling of £26,500 or the sum of £215, whichever is the greater.

If your annual reckonable income exceeds £14,560 you are liable to pay Health, Employment and Training Levies of 2% on your reckonable income.

In 2000/01 the first £1,040 of the income of a self-employed person is exempt from PRSI. There is also a special flat-rate contribution of £124 a year for people whose income is so low that they are not required by the Revenue Commissioners to submit a tax return.

If you enter insurance for the first time after the prescribed age (56) and if you will not be entitled to a Contributory or Non-Contributory Old Age Pension, you may be entitled to a refund of the pension element of the PRSI contribution paid by you.

Self-employed PRSI (S1) Rate

Calculated on non-PAYE income less capital allowances

2000/01

Self-employed PRSI contributions	Health levy
5% up to a maximum income of £26,500 (First £1,040 exempt) Minimum contribution £215.	2% (not payable where income for the year is £11,750 or less).

2001

Self-employed PRSI contributions	Health levy
3% of all income Minimum contribution £200	2% (not payable where income for the year is £11,750 or less).

Paying PRSI

If you pay income tax directly to the Collector General, you also pay your PRSI contributions to the Collector General.

If you are on a low income and liable for the £124 annual payment, you will receive a demand from the Department of Social, Community and Family Affairs and you may pay the amount using books of receivable orders.

Class "S" benefits

Self-employed people paying Class "S" PRSI will generally be entitled to the following benefits, assuming they have paid the minimum qualifying contributions:

• Old Age Contributory Pension (after ten years contributions).

• Contributory Widow's/Widower's Pension (after three years contributions).

• Orphan's contributory allowance (after contributions for 26 weeks).

• Maternity and Adoptive Benefits.

281

17

Calculating your capital gains tax

Capital Gains Tax (CGT) is a tax on gains arising from the disposal of capital assets. It was first introduced in 1974. The necessary provisions to extend self assessment to capital gains were introduced in the 1991 Finance Act.

Persons chargeable

All persons resident in the State for tax purposes are liable to Capital Gains Tax (CGT). Individuals who are resident and domiciled in Ireland are chargeable on all gains wherever arising, while those who are resident and non-domiciled are liable in respect of all Irish and UK gains and of other gains to the extent that the gains are remitted to Ireland.

Non-Irish residents are liable only in respect of gains made on the disposal of assets related to Irish property, or mining/exploration rights.

Chargeable assets

All forms of property are assets for CGT purposes including options, debts and foreign currencies, except those specifically exempted.

Disposal

A disposal for CGT takes place whenever the ownership of an asset changes. This includes a part-disposal and also even where no payment is received e.g. a gift or exchange. An exception to this latter rule is on death. In the case of death, no chargeable disposal takes place and the person who receives the asset is treated as acquiring it at the market value at the date of the death.

Married couples

Transfers between spouses do not give rise to a CGT charge - the spouse who received the asset is deemed to have acquired it on the date and at the cost at which the other spouse acquired it.

Capital gains tax rates

From 3rd December 1997 a single rate of 20% applies to most chargeable gains including gains from the sale of development land. From 5th April 2002 the Capital Gains Tax on development land zoned for residential development is due to increase from 60%.

Change in tax year

On 1st January 2002, the tax year will change to a calendar year. Because of this changeover there will be a short transitional "year" which will run from 6th April 2001 to 31st December 2001. For the short transitional "year" you will only be liable to capital gains tax arising in this period. However the normal capital gains tax annual exemption will be scaled back to 74% (270 days ÷ 365 days) of the full amount to take account of the short tax "year".

Exemptions and reliefs

Annual allowance

From 6th April 1998 the first £1,000 of chargeable gains arising to an individual in each tax year is exempt. This is an individual allowance and is not transferable between spouses.

Principal private residence (PPR)

No CGT arises on the disposal of your main residence and grounds of up to one acre, provided it has been occupied by you throughout the entire period of ownership. You are still deemed to occupy the residence where you are absent for any period of employment abroad or during absence imposed by conditions of your employment, provided you live in the house before and after the period(s) spent abroad. If your house was not your principal private residence for the entire period of ownership e.g. if you rented the house for a period, any gain arising on the sale of the house will be apportioned between the period when it was your principal private residence (PPR) and the period when it was not. The gain when it was your PPR is exempt and the balance of the gain is liable to CGT @ 20%.

Tangible moveable assets

A gain arising to an individual on such assets is exempt if the total consideration received does not exceed £2,000.

Life assurance policies/deferred annuities

Disposals of these contracts are exempt from CGT in the hands of the original beneficial owner. A chargeable gain can arise on the disposal of such contracts by a person who is not the original beneficial owner if they acquire them for a consideration of money or money's worth.

Irish government securities

Exempt.

Budget 2001 change: From 6th December 2000 Capital Gains Tax will no longer apply on the transfer of a site from a parent to a child provided it is for the construction of the child's principal private residence and the market value of the site does not exceed £200,000. However, the parent can only transfer one site for the purpose of this exemption.

Retirement relief

Where an individual aged over 55, having owned a farm or business for more than 10 years, disposes of that farm or business for a consideration of less than £375,000 (£250,000 prior to 1st December 1999), the disposal is ignored for CGT. Where the proceeds exceed £375,000 (£250,000 prior to 1st December 1999) the CGT arising is restricted to the lower of, half of the difference between the proceeds and £375,000 (£250,000 prior to 1st December 1999), or the CGT as computed in the normal way.

Complete exemptions can be claimed by an individual meeting the above conditions if they dispose of their farm/business to their child (or nephew/niece working in the business). However, this exemption is lost if the recipient disposes of the farm/business within six years.

Roll-over relief

Under this relief, a person can defer the payment of CGT arising on the disposal of certain assets used solely for business purposes, if the proceeds arising are reinvested in similar assets and used solely for business purposes. The assets which qualify for this relief are plant and machinery, land, buildings, goodwill and in certain circumstances, shares in private companies.

Disposal on emigration

Irish non-residents normally pay Irish Capital Gains Tax on disposals relating to Irish property or mineral/exploration rights only.

So, if you are emigrating and wish to dispose of certain assets before you become non-resident any chargeable gain on such disposals e.g. shares in a company will be liable to Irish Capital Gains Tax.

Capital Gains Tax on such disposals can be reduced if the disposal takes place after you become non-resident for Irish tax purposes. It is also important to note that the date of disposal for Capital Gains Tax purposes is the date of contract.

Computation of gains and losses

Basically, this is done by deducting from the proceeds received the cost of the disposed asset and, where the asset is held for more than 12 months, "indexation relief" as measured by the increase in the consumer price index. This is done by multiplying the cost of the asset by the index factor relative to the tax year in which the purchase took place.

Indexation relief

When you sell an asset, the original cost and enhancement expenditure may be increased by indexation before any CGT liability is calculated.

Where an asset is acquired prior to 6th April 1974, the "cost" to be indexed is the market value at 6th April 1974, rather than the original cost. Indexation relief does not apply to Development Land.

Capital gains tax indexation factors

Year of purchase	Year of Disposal					
	1995/96	1996/97	1997/98	1998/99	1999/00	2000/01
1974/75	5.899	6.017	6.112	6.215	6.313	6.582
1975/76	4.764	4.860	4.936	5.020	5.099	5.316
1976/77	4.104	4.187	4.253	4.325	4.393	4.580
1977/78	3.518	3.589	3.646	3.707	3.766	3.926
1978/79	3.250	3.316	3.368	3.425	3.479	3.627
1979/80	2.933	2.992	3.039	3.090	3.139	3.272
1980/81	2.539	2.590	2.631	2.675	2.718	2.833
1981/82	2.099	2.141	2.174	2.211	2.246	2.342
1982/83	1.765	1.801	1.829	1.860	1.890	1.970
1983/84	1.570	1.601	1.627	1.654	1.680	1.752
1984/85	1.425	1.454	1.477	1.502	1.525	1.590
1985/86	1.342	1.369	1.390	1.414	1.436	1.497
1986/87	1.283	1.309	1.330	1.352	1.373	1.432
1987/88	1.241	1.266	1.285	1.307	1.328	1.384
1988/89	1.217	1.242	1.261	1.282	1.303	1.358
1989/90	1.178	1.202	1.221	1.241	1.261	1.314
1990/91	1.130	1.153	1.171	1.191	1.210	1.261
1991/92	1.102	1.124	1.142	1.161	1.179	1.229
1992/93	1.063	1.084	1.101	1.120	1.138	1.186
1993/94	1.043	1.064	1.081	1.099	1.117	1.164
1994/95	1.026	1.046	1.063	1.081	1.098	1.144
1995/96	-	1.021	1.037	1.054	1.071	1.116
1996/97	-	-	1.016	1.033	1.050	1.094
1997/98	-	-	-	1.017	1.033	1.077
1998/99	-	-	-	-	1.016	1.059
1999/00	-	-	-	-	-	1.043

Computation of liability on sale of investment property

In August 2000, a married couple sold a house for £255,000. Sales costs amounted to £3,500. They had bought the house in August 1973 for £25,600. The market value of the house at 6th April 1974 was £26,000. The couple had added an extension costing £10,000 to the house in March 1987.

The house was not their principal residence and they had no other chargeable gains in the tax year 2000/01.

Capital gain computation 2000/01

	£	€
Sales Price	£255,000	€323,783
Less: Selling Costs	£3,500	€4,444
Deduct:	£251,500	€319,339
Value on 6th April 1974 adjusted for inflation: i.e. £26,000 x 6.582	£171,132	€217,293
1986/87 Expenditure, adjusted for inflation: i.e. £10,000 x 1.432	£14,320 £185,452	€18,183 €235,475
Capital Gain	£66,048	€83,864
Less: Exemption (House in Joint Name)	£2,000	€2,539
Taxable @ 20%	£64,048	€81,324
Tax Payable	£12,810	€16,265

Note: The Capital Gains Tax of £12,810 will be payable on 1st November 2001.

18

Marriage matters

Tax and financial issues arising from marriage are spread throughout our tax and financial system. To make everything as simple and as straightforward as possible, we shall look at marriage under a number of different headings:

- Legal Impact.

- Income Tax.

- Capital Gains Tax.

- Capital Acquisition Tax.

- Stamp Duty.

- Probate Tax.

- Social Welfare.

Legal impact

Marriage changes the legal status of two people from a couple to spouses, with many consequential and financial implications. For example, a surviving spouse's legal entitlements under the 1965 Succession Act are as follows:

If there is a Will - Irrespective of what's in it, the minimum legal entitlements of a surviving spouse are;

| Spouse and No Issue | - | One-half of Estate to the surviving Spouse |
| Spouse and Issue | - | One-third of Estate to the surviving Spouse |

No Will in Existence

| Spouse and No Issue | - | Whole Estate to the surviving Spouse |
| Spouse and Issue | - | Two-thirds to the surviving Spouse, one-third to issue in equal shares. |

Succession Act rights may be voluntarily renounced by a prenuptial agreement.

Income tax

A marriage ceremony in itself does not give rise to any income tax advantage. To obtain these benefits, a couple must be married and "living together".

Under the income tax rules, a married couple are deemed to be "living together" unless

- They are separated under an order of a Court of competent jurisdiction or by Deed of Separation,

   or

- They are in fact separated in such circumstances that the separation is likely to be permanent.

A married couple living together may choose to be taxed jointly, separately or as single people.

The significant tax advantages for a married couple living together and claiming joint assessment under Income Tax rules are as follows:

- A married allowance which is double the single person allowance.

- Home carer's allowance.

- Double the rate bands of tax which are available to a single person.

- Double the mortgage interest relief available for a single person for a principal private residence.

- Trading losses incurred by one spouse can be set against income of other spouse.

- Tax relief is available to a spouse for VHI/BUPA and other qualifying payments made for the other spouse.

- Double the age allowance even though only one spouse may be over the age of 65 years.

- Medical expenses incurred or defrayed by one spouse can be claimed by the assessable spouse.

- Increased blind person's allowance where both spouses are blind.

- Tax relief can be obtained by one spouse in respect of a person employed to take care of the incapacitated other spouse.

Individualisation

In the 1999 Budget the Minister announced a radical development of doing away with the double rate tax bands for married couples and moving towards 'individual' standard rate tax bands over this and the next two budgets.

To achieve this he increased the standard rate band in the 2000/01 tax year for the single person from £14,000 to an 'individual' £17,000. This 'individual band' was further increased in the 2001 Budget to a maximum of £40,000 for a married couple with two incomes, which comprises of two 'individual bands' (£20,000 x 2 = £40,000). The standard rate tax band for a single income family is at £ 29,000 in the 2001 tax year. To gain the maximum benefit from the new 'individual' band increases for a two income couple, each spouse must have an minimum 'individual' income of £11,000 in the year 2001.

For example, a two income couple where one spouse earns £35,000 in the year 2001 and the other earns £6,000, the maximum married couple standard rate band of £29,000 can be utilised by the higher earning spouse but only £6,000 of the £11,000 band can be utilised by the lower earning spouse. The balance of £5,000 is left unused.

Year of marriage

In the year of marriage, you and your spouse are treated as two single people for income tax purposes for the entire tax year. However, if you pay more tax than that which would have been payable as a married couple, you can claim a refund. This refund will be the excess of the tax paid as two single people over the tax payable as a married couple jointly assessed, reduced in proportion to the part of the tax year in which you were not married.

Example

Sean and Anne were married on 1st July 2000. Sean's annual salary is £30,000 and Anne's salary is £15,000. Their tax liability for 2000/01 will be as follows:

	Sean			Anne	
	£	€		£	€
Salary	£30,000	€38,092		£15,000	€19,046
Tax Payable					
£17,000 @ 22%	£3,740	€4,749	15,000 @ 22%	£3,300	€4,190
£13,000 @ 44%	£5,720	€7,263			
	£9,460	€12,012			
Less: Tax Credits					
Personal £4,700 @ 22%	(£1,034)	(€1,313)		(£1,034)	(€1,312)
PAYE £1,000 @ 44%	(£220)	(€279)		(£220)	(€279)
Net Tax	£8,206	€10,419		£2,046	€2,598
Total Tax as Single People			£10,252	€13,017	

At the end of the year, Sean and Anne may apply for a reduction in their tax liability on the basis of joint assessment as illustrated below:

	2000/01	
	£	€
Total Salaries	£45,000	€57,138
Tax Payable		
£34,000 @ 22%	£7,480	€9,498
£11,000 @ 44%	£4,840	€6,146
	£12,320	€15,643
Less: Tax Credits		
Personal £9,400 @ 22%	(£2,068)	(€2,626)
PAYE £2,000 @ 22%	(£440)	(€559)
Net Tax	£9,812	€12,459
Less: Tax Paid (See Previous Page)	(£10,252)	(€13,017)
Excess of single over joint basis of assessment.	£440	€559
Restriction for Pre Married Period £440 x 3/12	(£110)	(€140)
Tax Refund Due	£330	€419

The tax refund due to each spouse will be in proportion to the amount of tax each has paid.

Married couples/income tax options

After the year of marriage, you have three options as to how you are taxed.

Joint assessment

Joint assessment is automatic, unless either spouse gives notice of election for separate or single assessment to the Revenue Commissioners. Up to 1993/94, where a wife was living with her husband. The husband was automatically the assessable spouse and was chargable to tax on the joint income of the couple.

However, if you married in 1993/94 or later, the assessable spouse will be the spouse with the higher income and will continue to be so unless you jointly elect to change it.

Repayments made are allocated between each spouse according to the amount of tax they paid in the year.

Separate assessment

A claim may be made for separate assessment of income tax liability where the joint assessment basis applies. The claim must be before the 6th July in the year of assessment, or before 6th July in the following year in the case of marriage. Where separate assessment is claimed the allowances are divided between the spouses. If at the end of the tax year, the total tax payable under separate assessments is greater than the amount payable if an application for separate assessment had not been made, you can apply for a tax refund.

Single assessment/(separate treatment)

As a married couple, you may each elect for single assessment. Each spouse is treated as a single person with no right of transfer of allowances or reliefs between spouses. Single assessment is normally only beneficial where one spouse has foreign employment income.

Tax options -

Example: 2000/01

John and Mary are married with two children, with salaries of £28,000 and £16,000 respectively. John pays mortgage interest of £5,000 and £500 pension contribution. Their tax options are illustrated on Page 295.

Married Couples Tax Options Illustration 2000/01

Method of assessment	Joint assessment £		Separate assessment John £		Mary £		Single assessment John £		Mary £	
	Amount	Tax	Amount	Tax	Amount	Tax	Amount	Tax	Amount	Tax
Salary	44,000		28,000		16,000		28,000		16,000	
Less: Pension	(1,000)		(1,000)				(1,000)			
Taxable Income	43,000		27,000		16,000		27,000		16,000	
Tax Payable 22%	34,000	7,480	17,000	3,740	16,000	3,520	17,000	3,740	16,000	3,520
44%	9,000	3,960	10,000	4,400			10,000	4,400		
Total		11,440		8,140		3,520		8,140		3,520
Less: Tax Credits										
Personal £9,400/£4,700 @ 22%		(2,068)		(1,034)		(1,034)		(1,034)		(1,034)
PAYE £2,000/£1,000 @ 22%		(440)		(220)		(220)		(220)		(220)
Mortgage Interest £4,000/£2,000 @ 22%		(880)		(880)		-		(440)		-
				6,006		2,266		6,446		2,266
Total Payable		£ 8,052		£ 8,272				£ 8,712		

Notes:

1. Separate assessment results in an additional tax bill of £220 which can be reclaimed at the end of the tax year as Mary didn't use all of her £ 17,000 standard rate threshold.

2. The claim under single assessment results in an additional tax bill of £660 due to the loss of £ 2,000 mortgage interest relief. This loss of relief could be avoided if the mortgage was in joint names or if Mary also contributed to the mortgage repayments.

Capital gains tax (CGT)

A couple must be married and "living together" in order to maximise their benefits under Capital Gains Tax which include:

- Entitlement to dispose of assets to each other without being subject to CGT.

- Capital losses available to one spouse can be used by the other spouse.

Capital acquisitions tax (CAT)

The "living together" rules do not apply to Capital Acquisition Tax and all gifts and inheritance given by one legally married spouse to the other are exempt from Capital Acquisitions Tax regardless of their "living together" status.

Pensions benefits

Section 56 of the CAT Act 1976 provides that any pension benefit taken by a person, other than the pension member, will be treated as a gift or inheritance for tax purposes.

However, the spouse exemption from Capital Acquisition Tax means any lump sum death benefit or dependent's pension benefit received by your spouse from a pension scheme of which you were a member will be exempt from tax.

Life assurance policies

Section 32 of the CAT Act 1976 provides that an interest in possession in life assurance policies is only deemed to occur when a benefit becomes payable under the policy. So if you effect a Life Assurance policy on your own life for the benefit of someone else, no gift or inheritance tax will arise until the benefit becomes payable under that policy. Any sums received by you or your spouse from a life assurance policy, of which you or your spouse were the original beneficial owners, will be exempt from tax.

Stamp duty

Transfer of all assets between spouses is exempt from stamp duty. This exemption includes a direct transfer of assets from one spouse to another or a transfer from one spouse into the joint names.

Probate tax

If your spouse receives assets absolutely, no Probate Tax is payable. However, if assets are left to your spouse by way of a trust for life, then the payment of Probate Tax is deferred until your spouse dies.

Social welfare

Social Welfare Widow(er)'s Contributory Pension is payable to the widow(er) following the death of their spouse, for as long as the widow(er) does not remarry or cohabit with someone else as man and wife. A spouse may qualify for this pension either on their own PRSI contribution record, or on that of the other spouse.

A Non-Contributory Social Welfare Widow(er)'s Pension is payable to a widow(er) who passes a means test, following the death of the other spouse, for as long as the widow(er) does not remarry or cohabit with someone else as man and wife.

Qualified adult dependent payment

A qualified payment may be payable in addition to the basic benefit in respect of a claimant's spouse/partner, where the claimant's spouse/partner is wholly or mainly maintained by him/her. There are, however, certain exemptions, e.g. if the spouse has income of more than £70 - £135 per week or is receiving some other Social Welfare Benefit this supplement may not be paid.

PROVIDING A BETTER FUTURE

- Pensions
- Savings
- Investment

For Independent advice on all your Pension, Savings and Investment requirements talk to your broker

Talk to your broker today!

Scottish Provident - Providing a better future

www.scotprov.ie

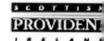

SCOTTISH
PROVIDENT
IRELAND

PENSIONS | INVESTMENTS |

19

Separation and divorce

To make everything in this section as simple as possible, we will look at each of the issues relating to "Separation and Divorce" under the same heading as those used in the previous chapter entitled "Marriage Matters". To get a better understanding of the tax implications of "Separation and Divorce", we advise you to first read the previous chapter outlining the tax issues arising on marriage.

Marriage breakdown is a major and traumatic event for couples and it is best approached in a logical and non-confrontational manner. A brief checklist of points to consider in relation to separation and divorce is included at the end of this section.

When a married couple decide to separate, they will normally go about it in one of the following ways:

• They decide to live apart.

• They seek a Legal Separation.

• They seek a Judicial Separation.

Living apart

Legal impact

Living apart does not change the legal status of your marriage.

Succession rights

There is no automatic loss of your Succession Act entitlements if you live apart from your spouse. However:

- A spouse who is guilty of desertion, which continues for two years or more up to the death of the other spouse , is precluded under the Succession Act from taking any share in the estate of the deceased, either as a legal right or on intestacy.

- If a surviving spouse is deemed to be "guilty of conduct which justified the deceased separating and living apart", then the surviving spouse could be deemed to be guilty of desertion and hence precluded under the Succession Act from taking a share in the deceased spouse's estate, for example where a wife leaves home because of violent behaviour on the part of her husband, he could be found guilty of desertion and lose his Succession Act rights to her estate while, conversly, she could in fact, retain her rights to his estate.

- Any spouse who has been found guilty of a serious offence against the deceased spouse or against a child of the deceased spouse, is also precluded, under the Succession Act, from taking any legal right under the estate of the deceased.

Income tax

A couple's Income Tax position following separation is determined by three main factors:

- Whether the separation is likely to be permanent.

- Whether maintenance payments are being made by one spouse to the other.

- If maintenance payments are being made, whether these payments are *legally enforceable.*

If the separation is not likely to be permanent, there is no change in the Income Tax position and you can elect for Joint, Separate or Single Assessment.

If the separation is likely to be permanent and if there are no legally enforceable maintenance payments, the spouses are assessed for Income Tax under Single Assessment. Any Voluntary maintenance payments are ignored for income tax purposes.

If the separation is likely to be permanent and if there are legally enforceable maintenance payments being made, then the couple may generally opt for either Single Assessment or if both spouses remain resident in Ireland, Separate Assessment. If Single Assessment applies, maintenance payments are tax-deductible for the payer and are taxable in the hands of the recipient. Under Separate Assessment, maintenance payments are ignored for income tax purposes.

Capital gains tax (CGT)

If the separation is not likely to be permanent, there is no change in the spouse's status for CGT purposes.

If the separation is likely to be permanent, the spouses are treated as two unconnected persons for CGT purposes:

- Transfers between spouses are no longer exempt from CGT. However, any transfer by virtue of, or in consequence of, the Separation will not trigger a CGT liability.

- No transfer of unused CGT losses is permitted between spouses .

Capital acquisition tax (CAT)

Spouse's exemption from Capital Acquisition Tax will continue to apply.

Pensions/death-in-service benefit

If a member of a pension scheme dies while still working for an employer, *Death in Service Benefits* may be paid to the member's dependants. Many pension schemes give discretion to the pension trustees as to how these death-in-service benefits may be paid e.g. the pension rules may require a spouse to be living with, or ordinarily residing with, their spouse at date of death.

Life assurance

The proceeds are normally exempt from tax provided you or your spouse were the original beneficial owners of the relevant policy.

Stamp duty

Exemption from Stamp Duty will continue to apply on relevant property transactions.

Probate tax

Spouse's exemption from Probate Tax will continue to apply.

Social welfare

The Contributory Widow(er)'s Pension is payable to the widow(er), following the death of their spouse, for as long as the widow(er) does not remarry and does not cohabit with someone else as man and wife. A widow(er) may qualify for this pension either on their own PRSI contribution record or that of their late spouse.

Qualifying adult dependent payment

A qualifying adult dependent payment is generally payable to a claimant who is separated, provided their spouse is wholly or mainly maintained by the claimant.

Legal separation

Under a Legal Separation, both spouses voluntarily enter into a legal agreement. This legal agreement is often referred to as a "Deed of Separation".

A Deed of Separation will usually include:

- An agreement to permanently live apart.

- Arrangements for custody of, and access to, children.

- Provision for maintenance to be paid by one spouse for the benefit of the other spouse and/or children.

- Succession Act rights: one spouse may voluntarily renounce their rights to the other's estate, etc.

Legal impact

A Deed of Separation will not change the legal status of your marriage.

Succession rights

- There is no automatic loss of your entitlements under the Succession Act.

- Your entitlements under the Succession Act may be voluntarily renounced under a Deed of Separation

- Any specific bequest in your Will to your spouse will stand until you make a new Will or change your existing Will.

Income tax

A couple's Income Tax position following separation is determined by three main factors:

- Whether the separation is likely to be permanent.

- Whether maintenance payments are being made by one spouse to the other.

- If maintenance payments are being made, whether these payments are *legally enforceable.*

If the separation is not likely to be permanent, there is no change in the Income Tax position and you can elect for Joint, Separate or Single Assessment.

If the separation is likely to be permanent and if there are no legally enforceable maintenance payments, the spouses are assessed for Income Tax under Single Assessment. Any Voluntary maintenance payments are ignored for income tax purposes.

If the separation is likely to be permanent and if there are legally enforceable maintenance payments being made, then the couple may generally opt for either Single Assessment or if both spouses remain resident in Ireland, Separate Assessment. If Single Assessment applies, maintenance payments are tax deductible for the payer and taxable in the hands of the recipient. Under Separate Assessment, maintenance payments are ignored for income tax purposes.

Assessable spouse

Heretofore, the husband was the assessable spouse. However where couple were married after 6th April 1993, the spouse with the greater income in the year of marriage will generally be deemed to be the assessable spouse from year to year.

The assessable spouse may be changed provided both spouses elect jointly for an alternative option. The assessable spouse is generally responsible for submitting the annual return and paying any tax due.

Year of separation

The Married Allowance and Double Rate Tax Band can be claimed for the year of separation by the assessable spouse providing:

• Separation does not occur on 6th April

  or

• The non-assessable spouse has not submitted a claim for single assessment prior to separation.

The assessable spouse is liable to Income Tax for the tax year of separation on his/her own income under joint assessment if they were previously taxed jointly for the full year, and on the other spouse's income up to the date of separation. A tax deduction will be available for legally enforceable maintenance payments.

Example

John and Mary separated on 5th October 2000 on a basis that is likely to be permanent. In the tax year 2000/01 their tax position will work out as follows: We assume John is the assessable spouse and no maintenance is payable. In the interest of simplicity, we are using the same figures in this example as were illustrated on Page 295 for John and Mary as a married couple.

	£	€
John's Assessable Income	£28,000	€35,553
Mary's Income to 5th October 2000	£8,000	€10,158
	£36,000	€45,711
Mary's income from 6th October 2000	£8,000	€10,158

	John			Mary	
	£	**€**		**£**	**€**
John's Salary	£28,000	€35,553			
Mary's Salary	£8,000	€10,158		£8,000	€10,158
	£36,000	€45,711		£8,000	€10,158
Less: Allowances					
Pension	£500	€635		-	-
Taxable	£35,500	€45,076		£8,000	€10,158
Tax Payable					
£34,000/£8,000 @ 22%	£7,480	€9,498		£1,760	€2,235
£1,500 @ 44%	£660	€838			
Less: Tax Credits					
Personal 9,400 @ 22%	(£2,068)	(€2,626)	4,700 @ 22%	(£1,034)	(€1,313)
PAYE 2,000 @ 22%	(£440)	(€559)	1,000 @ 22%	(£220)	(€279)
Mortgage Interest					
4,000 @ 22%	(£880)	(€1,117)			
Tax Payable	£4,752	€6,034		£506	€642
After Tax Income	£31,248	€39,677		£7,494	€9,515

Note: John & Mary's total tax bill in 2000/01, the year of separation, worked out at £5,258 compared to £8,052 as a married couple living together (see page 295).

Year of separation/Single assessment

If John & Mary were paying tax under Single Assessment before the separation, each spouse would have been responsible for submitting their own tax returns and paying their own tax. No change in their status for income tax purposes would have occurred on separation and they would pay same tax bill as illustrated on page 295 under Single Assessment.

Subsequent tax years

How you will be taxed in subsequent tax years will depend on a number of factors e.g.

- Voluntary Maintenance Payments.

- Legally Enforceable Maintenance Payments.

- Single Parent Allowances.

- Mortgage Repayments etc.

Maintenance payments

Tax is not deducted at source from legally enforceable maintenance payments from one spouse to the other. Such payments may be allowed for tax purposes as a deduction against the income of the payer and may be chargeable to income tax, in the hands of the recipient. A spouse will not be entitled to the marriage allowance where he/she claims a deduction for maintenance payments made.

Where maintenance is received for the benefit of a child:

- The payment is to be made without deduction of income tax,

- The amount is to continue to be treated as the income of the payer,

    and

- The payer's income tax liability is calculated without any allowance for the payments made.

PRSI & levies

If you are legally separated and you receive maintenance payments from your spouse, PRSI & levies will be payable on the maintenance received if you are taxed as a single person. If you have opted for separate assessment, maintenance payments are ignored for income tax purposes and PRSI and levies are not payable on the maintenance.

The PRSI payable would be the Class S1 rate, which in 2000/01 is 5% of the gross income up to a maximum income of £26,500. However, the first £1,040 of your gross income is exempt from PRSI. Also, if your total income for the year is below £2,500, no PRSI is payable. (See page 279 for rates in 2001).

Health levies of 2% are also payable on the maintenance your receive. However, an exemption from these levies is given if your total gross income, including maintenance, is below £14,560. If the paying spouse has already paid PRSI/levies on the maintenance, there is an element of double taxation. However, the paying spouse may be entitled to a refund of these levies. If the spouse receiving the maintenance pays PRSI as an employee, no PRSI is payable in respect of the maintenance. However, if they are self- employed then PRSI will be payable on all maintenance payments received.

Voluntary maintenance payments

If you wholly or mainly maintain your spouse by voluntary maintenance payments, you will be entitled to the married couple's allowance. The Revenue generally accepts that you wholly or mainly maintain your spouse if the voluntary maintenance paid to him/her exceeds his/her earned income.

Example

Mary and Patrick agree to separate.

- Mary's income is £20,000 p.a. Patrick is unemployed.

- Mary agrees to pay Patrick £100 per week.

The arrangement is informal and nothing is legally enforceable.

Mary's tax position

	2000/01				
	Joint assessment married		Single assessment separated		
	£	€		£	€
Salary	£20,000	€25,395		£20,000	€25,395
Tax Payable					
20,000 @ 22%	£4,400	€5,587	17,000 @ 22%	£3,740	€4,749
			3,000 @ 44%	£1,320	€1,676
				£5,060	€6,425
Less:Tax Credits					
Personal 9,400 @ 22%	(£2,068)	€2,626	9,400 @ 22%	(£2,068)	€2,626
PAYE 1,000 @ 22%	(£220)	€279	1,000 @ 22%	(£220)	€279
	£2,112	€2,682		£2,772	€3,520
The £100 p.w. Maintenance which Mary pays is not tax deductible, her additional tax payable as a Separated person under Single Assessment is				£ 660	€838

Notes

- The marriage allowance will be granted because Mary's husband is wholly or mainly maintained by her. She is not entitled to deduct the maintenance payments as these are voluntary and not legally enforceable.

- Mary's husband is not living with her and she is not entitled to the benefit of the double tax bands because the maintenance payments are not enforceable.

Legally enforceable maintenance payments

Legally enforceable maintenance payments are tax-deductible from the income of the paying spouse and are taxable in the hands of the receiving spouse.

Example
Mary and Patrick agree to separate. Patrick is unemployed.

- Mary's salary is £26,000 p.a.

- Mary agrees to pay Patrick £100 per week and the arrangement is legally enforceable.

Mary's Tax Position

	Joint assessment married			Single assessment separated	
	£	€		£	€
Salary	£26,000	€33,013		£26,000	€33,013
Less: Maintenance	-	-		£5,200	€6,603
Taxable	£26,000	€33,013		£20,800	€26,411
Tax Payable					
£26,000 @ 22%	£5,720	€7,263	17,000 @ 22%	£3,740	€4,749
			3,800 @ 44%	£1,672	€2,123
	£5,720	€7,263		£5,412	€6,872
Less: Tax Credits					
Personal £9,400 @ 22%	(£2,068)	(€2,626)		(£2,068)	(€2,626)
PAYE £1,000 @ 22%	(£220)	(€279)		(£220)	(€279)
Net Tax Payable	£3,432	(€4,358)		£3,124	(€3,967)

As legally enforceable maintenance payments are tax-deductible, reduction in tax payable by Mary under single assessment is: £308 or €392.

Maximising mortgage interest relief

Maintenance payments and mortgage repayments may be made more tax-efficient if they are treated as two separate items, as both spouses will be entitled to claim Mortgage Interest Relief as illustrated in Option 1 & 2 for Anne on Page 310 and for Sean Page 311. However, maintenance payments will have to be substantially adjusted to take account of the different arrangements.

Example

Sean's income is £25,000 and Anne's income is £9,000 p.a. They have a mortgage of £70,000, monthly repayments of £440. Under Option 1 Anne has maintenance payments of £ 5,000 p.a. and does not Under Option 2 Anne's maintenance payments increased to £ 9,100 p.a. and she makes half the mortgage repayments.

Mortgage interest relief is as follows in 2000/01.

Mortgage interest	Total £	Sean £	Anne £
Interest Paid	£4,000	£2,000	£2,000
Allowable Interest	£4,000	£2,000	£2,000
Tax Relief @ 22%	£800	£440	£440

Capital gains tax (CGT)

Normally, under a legal separation the spouses are treated as two unconnected persons for CGT purposes:

- Transfers between spouses are no longer exempt from CGT. However, any transfer by virtue of, or in consequence of, the Deed of Separation will not trigger a CGT liability.

- No transfer is permitted between spouses of unused CGT losses.

Option 1
Sean agrees to pay maintenance payments of £5,000 p.a. to Ann and that Sean meet all the mortgage repayments.

Option 2
Sean agrees to pay maintenance payments of £9,100 p.a. to Ann and that the mortgage repayments are split 50/50.

Anne's position	Option 1		Option 2	
	£	€	£	€
Salary	£9,000	€11,428	£9,000	€11,428
Maintenance	£5,000	€6,349	£9,100	€11,555
(A)	£14,000	€17,776	£18,100	€22,982
Tax Payable				
£14,000 @ 22%	£3,080	€3,911		
£17,000 @ 22%			£3,740	€4,749
£1,100 @ 44%			£484	€615
Total	£3,080	€3,911	£4,224	€5,363
Less: Tax Credits				
Personal £4,700 @ 22%	(£1,034)	(€1,313)	(£1,034)	(€1,313)
PAYE £1,000 @ 22%	(£220)	(€279)	(£220)	(€279)
Single Parent				
£4,700 @ 22%	(£1,034)	(€1,313)	(£1,034)	(€1,313)
Tax Payable **(B)**	£792	€1,006	£1,936	€2,458
Net Income **(A less B)**	£13,208	€16,771	£16,164	€20,524
Net Mortgage **(C)** Repayment Less Mortgage Interest Relief @ 22%	(£Nil)	(€Nil)	(£2,280)	(€2,895)
Disposable Income **(A less B + C)**	£13,208	€16,771	£13,884	€17,629

Sean's position	Option 1		Option 2	
	£	€	£	€
Salary	£25,000	€31,743	£25,000	€31,743
Maintenance	(£5,000)	€6,349	(£9,100)	(€11,555)
(A)	£20,000	€25,395	£15,900	€20,189
Tax Payable				
17,000 @ 22%	£3,740	€4,749		
15,900 @ 22%			£3,498	€4,442
3,000 @ 44%	£1,320	€1,676	_____	_____
Total	£5,060	€6,425	£3,498	€4,442
Less: Tax Credits				
Personal 4,700 @ 22%	(£1,034)	(€1,313)	(£1,034)	(€1,313)
PAYE 1,000 @ 22%	(£220)	(€279)	(£220)	(€279)
Single Parent * (Balance of Allowance)				
4,700 @ 22%	(£1,034)	(€1,313)	(£1,034)	(€1,313)
Tax Payable (B)	£2,772	€3,520	£1,210	€1,536
Net Income (A less B)	£17,228	€21,875	£14,690	€18,652
Net Mortgage (C) Repayment Less Mortgage Interest Relief @ 22%	(£4,560)	(€5,790)	(£2,280)	(€2,895)
Disposable Income (A less B + C)	£12,668	€16,085	£12,410	€15,757

Capital acquisition tax (CAT)

Spouse's exemption from Capital Acquisition Tax will continue to apply.

Pension benefits

Pension rights negotiated under a Deed of Separation may not be enforceable, unless the agreement is backed up by a formal court order.

Life assurance

Specific rights obtained under a Deed of Separation in relation to life assurance policies may not be legally enforceable - to avoid problems make sure that your interest in a life assurance policy is backed up by a relevant court order e.g. *Financial Compensation Order,* under the Family Law Act 1995.

Stamp duty

Exemption from Stamp Duty will continue to apply on relevant property transactions.

Probate tax

Spouse's exemption from Probate Tax will continue to apply.

Social welfare

The Social Welfare Contributory Widow(er)'s Pension is payable to the widow(er) following the death of their spouse, for as long as the widow(er) does not remarry and does not cohabit with someone else as man and wife. The surviving spouse may qualify for a Widow(er)'s Pension either on their own PRSI contribution record, or that of their late spouse.

- A Qualified Adult Dependent supplement may not be payable to a claimant if that claimant's spouse is no longer wholly or mainly maintained by the claimant.

Judicial separation

A decree of judicial separation can be obtained by a spouse applying to the courts under the Judicial Separation and Family Law Reform Act 1989. The application may be made on one or more of the following grounds:

- The other spouse has committed adultery.

- That the other spouse has behaved in such a way that the applicant spouse cannot reasonably be expected to live with the other spouse.

- That the other spouse has deserted the applicant spouse for a continuous period of at least one year immediately preceding the application and that the spouses have lived apart from one another for a continuous period of at least one year immediately preceding the application and that the other spouse consents to a decree being granted.

- That the spouses have lived apart from one another for a continuous period of at least three years immediately preceding the application and that the marriage has broken down to the extent that the court is satisfied in all circumstances that a normal marital relationship has not existed between the spouses for at least one year immediately preceding the application.

Ancillary orders

On the granting of, or following, a decree of Judicial Separation, the Circuit or High Court can make a number of orders relating to maintenance or specific assets. These orders are known as Ancillary Orders.

Under a Judicial Separation either spouse, or, in some cases, a person acting on behalf of a dependent child, can apply to the courts to have one or more Ancillary Orders made in relation to:

- Maintenance.

- The family home.

- Property.

- Pension benefits.

- Life assurance policies.

- Succession rights etc.

While the Courts retain the discretion to grant an Ancillary Order sought by a spouse, or a person acting on behalf of a dependant child, the Family Law Act 1995 does provide specific factors which the Court is obliged to take into account before making a decision.

- The income, earning capacity, property and other financial resources which each of the spouses has, or is likely to have in the foreseeable future. The financial needs, obligations and responsibilities which each of the spouses has or is likely to have in the foreseeable future (whether in the case of remarriage of the spouse or otherwise).

- The standard of living enjoyed by the family concerned before the proceedings were instituted or before the spouses separated, as the case may be.

- The age of each of the spouses and the length of time during which the spouses lived together.

- Any physical or mental disability of either of the spouses.

- The contributions which each of the spouses has made or is likely in the foreseeable future to make to the welfare of the family, including any contribution made by each of them to the income, earning capacity, property and financial resources of the other spouse and any contribution made by either of them by looking after the home or caring for the family.

- The effect on the earning capacity of each of the spouses of the marital responsibilities assumed by each during the period when they lived together and, in particular, the degree to which the future earning capacity of a spouse is impaired by reason of that spouse having relinquished or foregone the opportunity of remunerative activity in order to look after the home or care for the family.

- Any income or benefits to which either of the spouses is entitled by or under statute.

- The conduct of each of the spouses, if that conduct is such that in the opinion of the court it would in all the circumstances of the case be unjust to disregard it.

- The accommodation needs of either of the spouses

- The value to each of the spouses of any benefit (for example, a benefit under a pension scheme) which by reason of the decree of judicial separation that spouse will forfeit the opportunity or possibility of acquiring.

- The rights of any other person, other than the spouses but including a person to whom either spouse is remarried.

Enforcing maintenance orders

Experience has shown a relatively high rate of defaulting on regular maintenance payments; a court can enforce these payments in one of two ways:

- *Secured Payments* here the periodic payments are secured on some capital asset or investment. For example, the court could order the sale of an investment property to generate the necessary funds.

- *Attachment of earnings order* where the court may order an employer to deduct the periodic payments from the earnings of one spouse and pay it to the other spouse.

Payments orders will normally specify the period, or periods, during which the payments are to be made, which can be a fixed number of years, or for the lifetime of either spouse. However, payments orders will generally cease on:

- The death of either spouse.

- The date of remarriage of the applicant spouse.

Legal impact

A Judicial Separation does not change the legal status of your marriage.

Succession rights

- There is no automatic loss of entitlements under the Succession Act.

- Your entitlements under the Succession Act may be voluntarily renounced under a Judicial Separation.

- Any specific bequest in your Will to your spouse will stand until you make a new Will or change your existing Will.

Income tax

If there are no legally enforceable maintenance payments being made, the spouses are assessed for Income Tax under Single Assessment. Any voluntary maintenance payments are not tax-deductible for the paying spouse and are not taxable in the hands of the receiving spouse.

If there are legally enforceable maintenance payments being made, then the couple can generally either opt for Single Assessment or if both spouses remain resident in Ireland, Separate Assessment. If Single Assessment applies, maintenance payments made for the benefit of the spouse are tax deductible for the payer and taxable in the hands of the recipient. Under Separate Assessment, maintenance payments are ignored for tax purposes.

Note: If you have a Judicial Separation, your income tax position is the same as under a Legal Separation. See page 302.

Capital gains tax (CGT)

Normally, under a judicial separation the spouses are treated as two unconnected persons for CGT purpose:

- Transfers between spouses are no longer exempt from CGT. However, any transfer by virtue of, or in consequence of, a decree of Judicial Separation will not trigger a CGT liability.

- No transfer of unused losses is permitted between spouses.

Capital acquisition tax (CAT)

Spouse's exemption from Capital Acquisition Tax will continue to apply.

Pension benefits

The Family Law Act 1995 envisages a number of ways in which a spouse's pension benefits might be taken into account in the event of a judicial separation:

- Earmarking.

- Pension Splitting.

- Offsetting.

Earmarking — A charge is set against a spouse's pension benefits, so that when they become payable a designated part of these benefits are payable to the other spouse.

Pension Splitting — The relevant pension benefits are split on an agreed basis between both spouses.

| Offsetting | - | If proper financial provision can be made by other orders (e.g. a financial compensation order), or a property adjustment order the court may decide to offset these benefits against any relevant pension rights rather than "splitting everything down the middle". |

Life assurance

Once a decree of Judicial Separation is granted, a spouse or a person acting on behalf of a dependent child may seek a Financial Compensation Order which can compel either or both spouses to:

- Effect a policy of life insurance for the benefit of the applicant or the dependent child.

- Assign the whole or a specified part of the interest in a life insurance policy effected by either, or both, spouses to the applicant or for the benefit of a dependent child.

- Make or continue to make the payments which either, or both, of the spouses is, or are, required to make under the terms of the policy.

A Financial Compensation Order will generally cease on the death or remarriage of an applicant spouse.

Stamp duty

Exemption from Stamp Duty will continue to apply on relevant property transactions.

Probate tax

Spouses' exemption from Probate Tax will continue to apply.

Social welfare

The Social Welfare Contributory Widow(er)'s Pension is payable to the widow(er) following the death of their spouse for as long as the widow(er) does not remarry or does not cohabit with someone else as man and wife. The surviving spouse may qualify for a Widow(er)'s Pension either on their own PRSI contribution record, or that of their late spouse.

An Adult Dependent Supplement may not be payable to a claimant if that claimant's spouse is no longer wholly or mainly maintained by the claimant.

Divorce

The grounds on which a court may grant an application for a decree of divorce are those set out in Article 41.3.2 of the Constitution:

- At the date of the institution of the proceeding, the spouses must have lived apart from one another for a period of, or periods amounting to, at least four years during the previous five years.

- There is no reasonable prospect of a reconciliation between the spouses

   and

- Such provisions as the court considers proper, having regard to the circumstances that exist, will be made for the spouses, any children of either or both of them and any person prescribed by law

   and

- Any further conditions prescribed by law are complied with.

Ancillary orders

The courts, on application by either spouse or by someone acting on behalf of a dependent child, can issue one or more of a number of Ancillary Orders including the following:

- Periodical payments and secured periodical payments order.

- Lump sum payments order.

- Property adjustment order.

- Order regarding occupation or sale of family home.

- Order regarding title of property.

- Variation of benefit of either spouse, or any dependent family member, of any pre or post nuptial agreement.

- Order regarding partition of property.

- Financial compensation orders.

- Pension adjustment orders.

- Order extinguishing succession rights.

- Order for sale of property, except the family home where a remarried spouse ordinarily resides with their spouse.

- Maintenance Pending Relief Order.

- Order for provision for one spouse out of the estate of the other spouse.

Legal impact

Divorce legally dissolves the marriage and each spouse may legally remarry after the decree.

Succession rights

Each spouse's succession rights are automatically extinguished by the decree of divorce. Any specific bequest in a Will to a former spouse will stand until a new Will is made or an existing Will is changed.

Income tax

If there are legally enforceable maintenance payments being made then the couple can generally either opt for Single Assessment or if both spouses remain resident in Ireland, Separate Assessment. If Single Assessment applies, maintenance payments for the benefit of the spouse are tax-deductible for the payer and are taxable in the hands of the recipient. Under Separate Assessment, maintenance payments are ignored for Income Tax purposes.

Note: If you are divorced, your income tax position is the same as that under legal separation. See page 302.

Capital gains tax

Divorced spouses are treated as two unconnected persons for CGT purposes:

- Transfers between spouses are no longer exempt from CGT. However, transfers by virtues of, or in consequence of, the divorce will not trigger a CGT liability.

- No transfer of unused losses between spouses.

Foreign divorce

If you obtain a foreign divorce which is not legally recognised in Ireland and you remarry, this marriage will not be legal in Ireland. However, it is current Revenue practise that when a marriage certificate is produced to accept it at face value from an Income Tax or Capital Gains Tax point of view.

Note: If the second marriage is legally challenged by one of the parties, the true legal position will then generally be enforced by the Revenue for Income Tax or Capital Gains Tax purposes.

Capital acquisitions tax

After divorce, you are no longer legal spouses and the spouse exemption ceases to apply in respect of any future gifts or inheritances and for CAT purposes. The "stranger threshold" will apply for CAT purposes after the divorce. However, property transfers between former spouses on foot of a court order governing a decree of divorce will be exempt from Capital Acquisition Tax.

Pensions

The Family Law (divorce) Act 1996 envisages a number of ways in which a spouse's pension scheme benefits might be taken into account in the event of a decree of divorce:

- Earmarking.

- Pension Splitting.

- Offsetting.

Earmarking   -   A charge is set against a spouse's pension benefits, so that when they become payable a designated part of these benefits is payable to the other spouse.

Pension Splitting -   The relevant pension benefits are split on an agreed basis between both spouses.

Offsetting   -   If proper financial provision can be made by other orders, e.g. financial compensation order or property adjustment order, the court may decide to offset these benefits against the relevant pension rights rather than "splitting everything down the middle".

Life assurance

After the granting of the decree of divorce, a spouse, or a person acting on behalf of a dependent child, may seek a financial compensation order which can compel either or both spouses to:

- Effect a policy of life insurance for the benefit of the applicant or the dependant child.

- Assign the whole or a specified part of the interest in a life insurance policy, effected by either or both spouses, to the applicant or for the benefit of a dependent child.

- Make or continue to make the payments which either, or both, of the spouses is, or are, required to make under the terms of the policy.

Such an order will cease on the death or remarriage of an applicant's spouse.

Probate tax

When an ex-spouse dies the surviving ex-spouse, provided they have not remarried, can apply for provisions out of the estate of the deceased ex-spouse.

No Probate Tax will be payable on assets transferred to a spouse following an order under the 1996 Family Law Divorce Act.

Social welfare

There is no change in either spouse's entitlement to a Social Welfare Widow(er)'s Pension following decree of divorce provided that the other spouse has not remarried or is not cohabiting with someone else as man and wife.

A Qualified Adult Payment is generally not paid to a claimant in respect of a former spouse.

A quick reference guide

A legal separation can be finalised by entering into a mutually agreed Deed of Separation or by obtaining a Decree of Judicial Separation from a court.

Legal separation

Normally, the least expensive and the most dignified way of finalising a separation is by both parties voluntarily entering into a Deed of Separation. If agreement cannot be reached, either party can still apply to the Court for a Judicial Separation. There are two important services available to spouses who want to agree their own terms of separation:

- A free mediation service, which is not means tested, is provided by the Government sponsored "Family Mediation Service".

- The Legal Aid Board provides a nation- wide legal aid service for applicants of modest means and all applicants in receipt of Social Welfare Assistance are eligible. A contribution is required for the service provided.

The main areas to be addressed in a Deed of Separation are:

Arrangements regarding children, maintenance, issues concerning the family home and issues concerning other assets.

If one spouse is making a claim in relation to another spouse's pension or life assurance policies then it may be necessary to apply to the Court for a Judicial Separation, as the trustees of a pension scheme or a grantee of a life assurance plan may not be bound by an agreement concluded between two spouses unless the agreement is also made a formal order of a court.

Judicial separation

If an application is made to the Court for a Judicial Separation the court will rule on:

Arrangements regarding children

The Court will give paramount consideration to the welfare of the children and, generally, any decision made will be based on the children residing with the same parent throughout each week, while the other parent may see the children at weekends and during holidays.

Maintenance

A dependent spouse will be entitled to seek maintenance if they can establish that there is a financial need and that the other spouse has the financial ability to pay. In any claim for maintenance, it is essential to prepare a comprehensive weekly or monthly estimate of your requirements to support the claim. A dependent spouse who is guilty of serious matrimonial conduct (e.g. desertion) could be refused maintenance by the Court. However, a spouse's conduct will have no bearing on their claim for maintenance in respect of the children. Any amount of maintenance payable in respect of the children will depend on their financial needs and the ability of the other spouse to pay.

The family home

If the family home is very valuable, a court may require that it be sold and the net proceeds of the sale be divided. If the family home is an "average one" with a mortgage attached, the dependent spouse with children is often given the right to reside there for the remainder of the children's dependency, while the other spouse will have to vacate it.

Other assets

Depending on the circumstances of each case, a fair and proper division of these assets will be determined. If the assets are substantial, it would not be unusual to expect a lump sum payment from one spouse to the other and there would be no Income Tax or Capital Acquisitions tax liability in respect of these payments.

Pensions and life policies

It is essential that proper arrangements are put in place so that if the spouse who is paying the maintenance dies before the other spouse, there will be sufficient money available from a pension or life policy, or both, to enable the dependent spouse maintain themselves and any dependent children.

Divorce

The Court will only grant a Decree of Divorce if the parties have lived separate and apart from each other for at least four years prior to issuing the proceedings and that proper provision is made for any dependent spouse and children.
This quick reference guide was supplied by:
Eugene Davy Solicitors,
16-18 Harcourt Road,
Dublin 2.
Tel: 4754766

In a land of opportunity,

you still need expert guides.

Ulster Bank Business & Corporate Banking offers local expertise in all business sectors combined with international knowledge as part of the Royal Bank of Scotland Group.

Whatever your goals, we have the people to help you get there.

★ Banking relationship teams ★ Inward investment teams
★ Property Finance teams
★ Asset Finance teams ★ Commercial Services teams

Ulster
Bank

Business & Corporate
Banking

20
Death - what to do about taxes

While Tax and Financial matters are not the foremost consideration when somebody dies, they are nevertheless areas that must be sorted out before a deceased person's estate can be finalised.

The Revenue Commissioners have published a very useful book "What to do about tax when somebody dies" and they have kindly allowed us to reproduce certain sections of it here.

Before looking at the tax consequences arising on a death it might be helpful to look briefly at some key terms, at the ways in which property passes on a death to the beneficiaries and at certain procedures that must be gone through before assets are handed over to the beneficiaries.

What is an "estate"?

A deceased's estate consists of whatever assets (e.g. bank accounts, stocks and shares, house, land, livestock, jewellery, car, etc.) can be passed on to beneficiaries following the deceased's death.

How does the estate pass on to the beneficiaries?

The assets, which make up the deceased's estate, can be passed on in a number of ways. Assets left by Will pass to the beneficiaries in accordance with the terms of the Will. If there is no Will (a situation known as intestacy), assets that would otherwise have passed by Will pass instead under special rules laid down by law. In addition, assets can also pass outside of the Will or intestacy.

Examples of assets which pass under the will or intestacy

* Assets owned in the deceased's sole name.

- Assets owned by the deceased but placed in the name of another person for convenience or some similar reason.

- Assets placed by the deceased in the joint names of the deceased and another person without the intention of benefiting that other person.

Examples of assets which pass outside of the Will or intestacy

- Assets passing by nomination, e.g. the deceased may have instructed An Post to pay Saving Certificates on his or her death to a particular person, called the nominee.

- Death benefits passing under a life insurance policy or pension scheme where the beneficiaries are particular family members named in the policy or scheme.

- Assets passing in which the deceased had an interest for his or her life only.

- Assets placed by the deceased in the joint names of the deceased and another person with the intention of benefiting that other person on the deceased's death.

The personal representative

The **Personal Representative** is the person who is responsible for finalising the deceased's affairs. He or she must, within a reasonable time, collect the assets passing under the **Will** or **intestacy**, pay any debts and distribute the surplus assets to the beneficiaries entitled to them.

If there is a Will, it is likely that the Personal Representative has been appointed by being named in the Will as its **executor** and has taken on the responsibility, because he or she is the deceased's spouse or one of the next-of-kin. A Personal Representative who has not been appointed by Will is known as an **administrator**.

Beneficiary

A **Beneficiary** is a person who inherits either the whole or part of the deceased's estate whether passing under the Will or intestacy or outside of the Will or intestacy.

Trustee

Instead of providing for property to be given directly to the beneficiary, the deceased's Will may provide that, for a specified period, the property is to be held on trust on behalf of the beneficiary by **trustees** named in the Will. Such trusts may arise because the beneficiary concerned is very young, or because the deceased wishes the property to be held for the benefit of one person for life and, on the death of that person, to be transferred to another beneficiary. The trustees will take over the management of the trust property only after the estate has been administered by the personal representative. The trust will then continue until the time specified in the Will for the ultimate handling over of the property.

Note: The same person can have more than one role; for example, a Personal Representative can also be a Beneficiary.

Assets passing outside of the Will or intestacy

Before assets are handed over to the beneficiaries certain procedures must be gone through. Broadly, these are as follows:

Before assets are handed over to the beneficiaries

In the case of an asset passing outside of the Will or intestacy, production of a death certificate by the beneficiary is often all that is required to establish the beneficiary's entitlement to receive the asset in question.

Assets passing under the Will or intestacy

In order to get legal confirmation of his or her appointment, the Personal Representative must apply to the Probate Office of the High Court for a document known as a **Grant of Representation**. The Grant of Representation acts as an assurance to financial institutions (e.g. banks, building societies, credit union, etc.) and to others that they can safely place the deceased's assets in the hands of the person named as Personal Representative in the grant. The Grant of Representation is also known as a Grant of Probate (where there is a Will) or Letters of Administration (where there is no Will).

The application for the Grant of Representation will normally be made by a solicitor acting on behalf of the Personal Representative. In straightforward cases, it may be possible to make a personal application for the grant through the Personal Application Section of the Probate Office.

Special additional procedure relating to money in joint names

In the absence of a letter of clearance from the Revenue Commissioners, banks, building societies and other financial institutions are prohibited by law from releasing monies (other than current accounts) lodged or deposited in the joint names of the deceased and another person or persons. This applies if, at the date of death, the total of all the amounts standing with the institution in the joint names of the deceased and that other person or persons exceeds £5,000. It does not apply, however, to monies which have only been held in the joint names of the deceased and his or her surviving spouse.

Applications for letters of clearance for production to financial institutions should be made to the Capital Taxes Office of the Revenue Commissioners.

If you are a personal representative

In summary this is what you should do about tax and when you should do it.

Sorting out the deceased's pre-death tax affairs

As personal representative, you are responsible for settling any outstanding tax matters for the period up to the date of death. Depending on the circumstances, you may need to pay additional taxes or claim a repayment.

Notifying the tax office

The deceased's tax office should be advised as soon as possible of the date of death and the name and address of the personal representative. This will ensure that correspondence will be addressed to the personal representative until such time as the administration of the estate is finalised.

The address of the deceased's tax office can be found on any correspondence from that office to the deceased. If you are in any doubt as to which tax office to contact, get in touch with your local tax office - or call the Central Telephone

Information Office (CTIO) at 01 - 8780000.

Remember that:

• If you distribute the estate without paying any outstanding tax liabilities, you may have to pay the tax out of your own pocket.

• If you fail to claim a tax rebate due to the estate, you may have to make good the loss to the estate.

If the deceased was *self-employed*, you will most likely get the deceased's accountant to file any outstanding Income Tax returns and business accounts with the deceased's tax office. As well as Income Tax, you will also need to ensure that any outstanding VAT, employer's PAYE/PRSI, or other taxes in respect of the period up to the date of death are fully paid.

If the deceased was an employee, there may be a PAYE tax rebate due, as the deceased's tax-free allowances for the year of death may not have been fully used up. The deceased's employer will send Form P45 to the tax office which dealt with the deceased's tax affairs. Any tax rebate will form part of the deceased's estate. As personal representative, it is your responsibility to file any outstanding tax return on behalf of the deceased.

Paying probate tax

A 2% tax, known as Probate Tax, is payable by the personal representative on the entire net value of the deceased's estate (insofar as it passes under the Will or intestacy) where that net value is above the relevant threshold. The payment is made to the Capital Taxes Office.

A number of exemptions and reliefs are available. For example, in arriving at the net value of the deceased's assets the value of agricultural land is reduced by 90%. Probate Tax referable to assets transferred to a surviving spouse is reduced to nil.

It is important to bear in mind that:

- The tax must be paid within 9 months of the date of death. If you pay the tax later than that, interest will be payable; if you pay it earlier, a discount is available.

- The personal representative is responsible for paying the tax.

A one-page self-assessment return must be completed and sent to the Capital Taxes Office with the Probate Tax due. This will normally be done at the same time as an account of the deceased's estate, known as the Revenue Affidavit, is being submitted to that Office.

Completing the Revenue affidavit

The Revenue Affidavit is an account of the deceased's estate that has to be completed and sworn by the personal representative in order to get a Grant of Representation from the Probate Office. Before being presented to the Probate Office it must be submitted to the Capital Taxes Office for certification.

What information is looked for in the affidavit?

The Revenue Affidavit looks for:

- A full account of the deceased's assets and liabilities at the date of death;

- Information on, among other things, assets passing outside of the Will or intestacy.

  and

- Details of the beneficiaries and of the value of the benefits taken.

To complete the Affidavit, you will need to establish whether the beneficiaries have received any other gifts or inheritances - either from the deceased or from any other person - at any time on or after 2 June, 1982.

What happens to the affidavit?

The Capital Taxes Office having examined the Affidavit will certify it once satisfied that (i) the correct amount of Probate Tax has been paid and (ii) Inheritance Tax due by the beneficiaries will be paid. A copy of the certified Affidavit will then be returned to your solicitor or - if you are making a personal application for the Grant of Representation - to the Probate Office or to the appropriate District Probate Registry. The certified Affidavit is part of the documentation required by the Probate Office when processing the application for the Grant of Representation.

Income and capital gains during the administration period

It may take the personal representative some time to administer the estate during which time income may be earned or capital gains may be made. Broadly the position is as follows.

Income tax

- The personal representative is liable to pay Income Tax at the standard rate on income earned during the administration period. There is no entitlement to personal allowances or to any of the reliefs otherwise available to individual taxpayers.

- In certain circumstances, the tax office may concessionally agree to treat the beneficiary as succeeding to the inheritance from the date of death. In such circumstances, the beneficiary will take full responsibility for paying Income Tax on the post-death income as if he or she had been entitled to the asset - and the income - from the date of death.

Capital gains tax (CGT)

- Death does not give rise to a Capital Gains Tax liability. For example, if the deceased bought share for £10,000 and they were worth £15,000 at the date of death, the £5,000 capital gain is not taxable.

If the personal representative sells any property during the administration period, there may be a liability to Capital Gains Tax - but only to the extent that the value of the property in question has increased between the date of death and the date of sale. Following on from the example above, if the personal representative sells the shares during the administration period for £17,000, the relevant capital gain is £2,000 and is taxable. The distribution of property by the personal representative to the beneficiaries does not give rise to a Capital Gains Tax liability.

You should be aware that, in addition, the personal representative has secondary liability for the payment of any Inheritance Tax due by the beneficiaries in respect of the benefits they take under the Will or intestacy. This means that if a beneficiary should fail to pay, the personal representative will have to do so.

If you are a surviving spouse

This section gives an outline of the main tax exemption and reliefs specifically for surviving spouses.

Main tax exemptions reliefs for surviving spouses

In summary these are covered under the following headings;

- Inheritance Tax;

- Probate Tax;

- Income Tax;

Inheritance tax

If you take an inheritance from your late spouse you don't have to pay Inheritance Tax on that inheritance. The exemption is unlimited - it doesn't matter how much you inherit, it is entirely exempt. There is no necessity to claim this exemption and you don't have to fill in any Inheritance Tax forms.

Probate tax

There is also a complete relief from the 2% Probate Tax for the part of the deceased's estate that is transferred to the surviving spouse. The personal representative will claim this relief when sending in the Probate Tax return together with the Revenue Affidavit to the Capital Taxes Office.

Income tax - for the year in which your spouse has died

Your Income Tax treatment for the tax year (i.e. the year to 5th April) in which your spouse has died will depend on how you and your spouse were treated before your bereavement.

Your tax office will help you to do the calculations and make sure you have the right tax-free allowances. Broadly, the position is as follows:

- If your late spouse was the "assessable spouse", i.e. the person responsible for making a joint tax return on behalf of both of you, then you will be entitled to a special increased widowed person's allowance from the date of your spouse's death up to the following 5th April. The single person's rate bands will apply for this period.

- If you yourself were the "assessable spouse", you will continue to get the married person's allowance and double rate bands for the remainder of the tax year. You will be taxable on your own income for the full tax year in which your spouse's income from 6th April to the date of death.

- If you were both taxed as single persons, you will get the special increased widowed person's allowance

- and single rate bands for the year.

Special allowance for surviving spouse with a dependant child

If you have any dependent children you may be entitled to a special Income Tax allowance (called "widowed parent's allowance") for the 5 tax years after the year of your spouse's death. You may also be entitled to the "one-parent family allowance" for as long as you have any dependent children.

Widowed person's allowance

A widowed person whose spouse has died in a given tax year is entitled to the widowed person's bereaved allowance, for that year only. This allowance is the same as the married person's allowance but is not available to a surviving spouse who is the subject of a joint assessment for the same year. A widowed person with dependent children is also entitled to;

(i) The one parent family allowance

332

and

(ii) Widowed Parent Allowance

Widowed parent allowance

This allowance is available for the five years following the year of death.

The amount of the allowance is as follows;

£10,000 in first tax year after death.

£ 8,000 in second tax year after death.

£ 6,000 in third tax year after death.

£ 4,000 in fourth tax year after death.

£ 2,000 in fifth tax year after death.

The above allowance is allowed at the standard rate of tax.

Widow(er) in year of bereavement

The tax treatment for individuals in the year of death depends on whether they were taxed under joint or separate assessment and whether it was the assessable spouse who died.

- If your late spouse was not the accessable spouse, i.e. the person responsible for making the joint tax return on behalf of both of you, then you will be entitled to a special increased widowed person's allowance from the date of your spouse's death up to the following 5th April. The single person's rate bands will apply for this period.

- If your late spouse was not the "assessable spouse", you will continue to get the married person's allowance and double rate bands for the remainder of the tax year. You will be taxable on your own income for the full tax year in which your spouse died plus your late spouse's income from 6th April to the date of death.

- If you were both taxed as single persons, you will get the special increased widowed person' allowance and single rate bands for the year.

See example on Page 335.

Note: The surviving spouse can elect for joint assessment for the year of death before the end of that tax year.

Widow(er) in subsequent tax years

The tax position of a widow or widower in subsequent tax years is as follows;

- A reduced Personal Allowance.

- A single person's Tax Band.

- A single person's PAYE Allowance.

- Reduced Mortgage Interest Allowance, if applicable.

- Single Parent Allowance.

- Widowed Parent Allowance (for 5 years following bereavement).

Example

A married Couple/Widow(er) with one dependent child and a salary of £30,000 p.a. (only one spouse working). Mortgage Interest of £4,000.

Widow(er) in subsequent year

	2000/01			
	Married £		**Widow(er) £**	
Gross Salary		£30,000		£30,000
Taxable Income		**Tax**		**Tax**
Taxable @ 22%	£28,000	£6,160	£20,150	£4,433
@ 44%	£2,000	£880	9,850	£4,334
Total Tax Payable		£7,040		£8,767
Less: Tax Credits				
Married Person £9,400 @ 22%		(£2,068)		
PAYE £1,000 @ 22%		(£220)		(£220)
Widowed Person £4,700 @ 22%				(£1,034)
Single Parent £4,700 @ 22%				(£2,200)
Mortgage Interest £4,000@ 22%		(£880)		(£880)
		£3,872		£3,399

Income tax for the year in which your spouse has died

John and Mary Jones annual earnings were £ 25,000 p.a. each. **John is the assessable spouse** dies on 31st December 2000. Mary is entitled to a widow's pension of £ 6,000 p.a. or £ 500 p.m. from 1st January 2001.

	John £ (9 months)	Mary £ (3 months)
Salary-John (to date of death)	£18,750	
Salary-Mary	£18,750	£6,250
Pension		£1,500
Taxable Income	£37,500	£7,750
Tax Payable		
£34,000/7,750 @ 22%	£7,480	£1,705
£3,500 @ 44%	£1,540	
Less: Tax Credits		
Personal £9,400 @ 22%	(£2,068)	
PAYE £2,000/£1,000 @ 44%	(£440)	(£220)
Widow £9,400 @ 22% *(in year of death)*	n/a	(£2,068)
Net Tax Payable	£6,512	Nil

At the end of the tax year Mary could apply for a refund if the total amount of tax paid by herself and John for the full tax year exceeded £ 6,512.

John and Mary Jones annual earnings were £ 25,000 p.a. each. Mary dies on 31st December 2000. **John is the assessable spouse.** John is entitled to a widow's pension of £ 6,000 p.a. or £ 500 p.m. from 1st January 2001.

	John £ (12 months)	Mary £ (9 months)
Salary-John	£25,000	N/A
Salary-Mary (to date of death)	£18,750	N/A
Pension	£1,500	N/A
Taxable Income	£44,500	N/A
Tax Payable		
£34,000 @ 22%	£7,480	N/A
£10,500 @ 44%	£4,620	
Less:Tax Credits		
Personal £9,400 @ 22%	(£2,068)	N/A
PAYE £10,000 @ 22%	(£220)	N/A
Net Tax Payable	£9,812	N/A

Any unused allowances which Mary had at the date of her death could be transferred to John before the end of the tax year.

Where there's a Will there's a relative!

This old proverb is never out of date. It has also been said that nothing is more inevitable than death and taxes. While, good financial planning cannot lessen your sense of loss on the death of a loved one, it can reduce your tax bill.

Issues that need to be considered when you have assets to pass on include:

- Making a Will.

- Testate and Intestacy.

- The Succession Acts.

- Capital Acquisition Tax.

- Probate.

Anyone who owns property or other assets such as a life assurance policy, savings plan or even a simple deposit account, should make a Will. A Will not only ensures that you can distribute your wealth as you wish, but it also means that your family and beneficiaries are spared the expense and distress of a complicated and drawn-out administration of your estate, as set out by the Succession Act 1965.

Wills should be drawn up with the assistance of a solicitor. The simpler the terms of the Will, the less work involved and the lower the fee. However, it will be money well spent.

Many people do not realise that a Will is revoked on marriage unless it is clearly made with the marriage in mind. An important time to make a Will, if you haven't done so already, or to review an existing one, is when you have children. This is in order that you name a legal guardian for the child(ren) in the unlikely event that both you and your spouse should die together, or soon after each other.

When you make a Will you will have to name an executor, someone who has the responsibility of seeing that your wishes are carried out and your assets distributed. Married couples often name each other, or an adult child or a family advisor - a solicitor or accountant - to act as executor. Others choose a business partner, bank manager or friend. Even if you, as a spouse, are named as Executor, your family advisor can assist with the various procedures involved.

Planning ahead

Before you meet your solicitor gather up a list of your assets and the names and addresses of the people whom you wish to be beneficiaries and make sure your Executor consents to being named in your Will.

- A Will must be in writing - verbal ones are not valid.

- A Will must be witnessed by two people, neither of whom can be beneficiaries.

- You cannot disinherit your spouse.

- Your Will will remain in force until death or marriage unless it is clearly made with the marriage in mind. If a new Will is made, it automatically revokes any previous Wills you may have made.

- You should always keep a copy of your Will in a safe place - a strongbox or bank safety deposit facility. Let your Executor and family know where it is and where your other valuable papers are kept.

Dying "intestate"

If you die without making a Will, this is known as dying "intestate" and all your property will be distributed according to the 1965 Succession Act. (See page 338).

Since there is no official Executor, the personal representative of the deceased - who can be a spouse, relative or even friend, will need to obtain what is known as a grant of Letters of Administration, in order to distribute the proceeds of your estate to your beneficiaries.

Death and taxes

Capital Acquisition Tax (CAT) and Probate Tax are the two taxes the State levies on a deceased person's estate.

Inheritance tax

If after your death the beneficiaries of your estate receive sums in excess of the Thresholds for Capital Acquisitions Tax (CAT) purposes Inheritance Tax will be payable.

Gift tax

A liability to gift tax arises when a person receives a benefit liable to capital acquisitions tax other than on a death.

Death - what to do about taxes

SUCCESSION ACT 1965	
Relatives surviving	**Distribution of estate where the deceased dies intestate**
Spouse and Issue	Two thirds to spouse, one-third to issue in equal shares. Children of a deceased son or daughter take their parent's share.
Spouse and no Issue	Whole estate to spouse.
Issue and no Spouse	Whole estate to Issue in equal shares. Children of a deceased son or daughter take their parent's share.
Father, mother, brothers and sisters	One-half to each parent.
Parent, brothers and sisters	Whole estate to parent.
Brothers and sisters	All take equal shares. Children of a deceased brother or sister take their parent's share.
Nephews and nieces	All take equal shares.
Remoter next-of-kin	All take equal shares.

338

Tax-free threshold for CAT

There are three tax free thresholds which apply for CAT purposes. From 1st December 2000 these threshold amounts were as follows:

Class A: £300,000 where the recipient is a child, or minor grandchild of the benefactor, if the parent is dead. In some cases this threshold can also apply to a parent, niece or nephew who have worked in a family business for a period of time.

Class B: £30,000 where the recipient is a brother, sister, niece, nephew or linear ancestor/descendent of the benefactor or where the gift is made by the child to the parent.

Class C: £15,000 in all other cases.

Budget 2001 change: Class A Threshold of £300,000 applies to gifts/inheritance taken on/after 6th April 2000 from a foster parent to a foster child provided the foster child was cared for and maintained from a young age up to the age of eighteen for a period of 5 years. The foster child must also have lived with the foster parent for the period.

CAT rates

Amount	Before 1st December 1999 rate	After 1st December 1999 rate
Below Threshold	Nil	Nil
Next £10,000	20%	20%
Next £30,000	30%	20%
The Balance	40%	20%

Some benefits are not subject to CAT:

• Any inheritance or gifts made between spouses;

• The first £1,000 (£500 prior to 1st January 1999) of all gifts received from a benefactor in any calendar year;

• Any inheritance received from a deceased child which had been given to that child as a Gift by the parent;

- Irish Government stock given to a non-Irish domiciled beneficiary, so long as it had been held by the beneficiary for at least three years previously;

- After 1st December 1999 a family home provided the following conditions are met;

- It is the principal private residence of the disponer and/or the recipient;

- The recipient had been living in the home for the three years prior to the transfer;

- The recipient does not have an interest in any other residential property;

The relief will be withdrawn if the recipient disponer of the home within 6 years of the transfer.

Agricultural land

Agricultural lands which are passed on as part of an inheritance enjoy some additional CAT reliefs. Instead of the land being assessed for CAT purposes at its full market value, it is assessed at 10% of its value. The relief will be disallowed, however, if the property is disposed of within six years of the inheritance (or gift) and partly disallowed if disposed of within six to 10 years.

Legal rights of spouse under a will

Irrespective of what the deceased leaves to his Spouse, the Spouse has a legal entitlement as follows:

Relatives surviving	Spouse's share by legal right
Spouse and Issue	One-third of estate.
Spouse and no Issue	One-half of estate.

Since Capital Acquisition Tax in the form of an Inheritance or Gift are subject to aggregation - a rolling up of benefits from various sources - the relevant thresholds can be affected. The calculations can be very complicated and you should always consult your financial or tax advisor.

Business relief

Relief from CAT is available where business property is acquired under a gift or inheritance. This relief works by reducing the value of the qualifying asset which pass under a gift or inheritance by 90%.

The following condition apply to this relief;

• The business must be carried on in the State.

• The qualifying business assets must have been owned by the disponer for at least 5 years in the case of a gift or at least 2 years in the case of an inheritance.

• Qualifying business assets;
    - unquoted shares or securities of an Irish company.
    - land, buildings, machinery or plant owned by the disponer but used by a company controlled by the disponer.
    - quoted shares or securities of an Irish company which were owned by the disponer prior to them being quoted.

The relief will be clawed back is the assets are disposed of within 10 years of the gift/inheritance. If a disposal takes place between 6 and 10 years 75% of the relief will be clawed back.

CAT payments

As a recipient of gift or inheritance you are obliged to file a return within four months of the valuation date (date of benefit) where 80% of your threshold amount is exceeded.

Inheritance/gift from a child to a parent

If a "child" gives a gift to a parent the Class II threshold of £30,000 applies. However, the Class I threshold of £300,000 applies if a parent receives an inheritance from "a child".

Probate tax

Probate tax is payable at 2% of the value of the net estate - that is, after all liabilities and expenses have been paid.

Probate Tax does not apply on an estate left to a surviving spouse, on an estate worth less than £40,000, or on a dwelling house, or portion of a house left to a dependent child or relative, such as an elderly sister or brother who shared the property with the deceased. Also Probate Tax will not apply to;

- Property passing to charity.

- Heritage property.

- Proceeds of Section 60 life assurance policies taken out to defray a CAT bill.

- Exempt Government securities.

Budget 2001 change: Probate tax has been abolished in respect of deaths occuring on or after 6th December 2000.

Section 60 policy

CAT can be avoided by a beneficiary if a Section 60 life assurance policy was taken out for the purpose of paying CAT. Policies like these appeal to people who are leaving large estates to their families or other beneficiaries in assets that are not cash rich.

Death - capital gains tax

A liability to Capital Gains Tax does not arise on death. When you inherit an asset you are treated for Capital Gains Tax purposes as receiving the asset at the date of death at the market value at that time.

A quick reference guide to the information required when somebody dies

When a person dies the Revenue Commissioners require an affidavit (Form CA24) to be completed setting out certain information about the deceased. Form CA24 is submitted in duplicate and its main requirements are:

- The name, address and RSI No. of the deceased person.

- Date of birth, death and place of death.

- Occupation.

- Marital Status.

- A copy of the deceased's Will, if any. If no Will exists the Revenue Commissioners will require information on the surviving relatives.

- A complete statement of the deceased's assets, both inside and outside the State, together with a valuation of each of these assets.

- A statement of all debts owing by the deceased including the funeral expenses.

- The official Death Certificate of the deceased.

If the deceased was in receipt of Social Welfare assistance a Social Welfare claim number must also be provided.

Inheritance tax

Generally speaking, if somebody stands to inherit more than 80% of their Capital Acquisitions Tax (CAT) threshold, the Revenue Commissioners will also require following information relating to this person:

- Their name and RSI number.

- Information about their relationship to the deceased (son, niece etc.).

- A statement of all previous gifts or inheritances (including their value) that they have received, together with the name and address of the provider(s), plus information about their relationship to the provider(s).

When the Revenue Commissioners are satisfied with the valuation of the estate, they will return one copy of Form CA 24 to the applicant. At the same time that Form

CA24 is completed a Probate Tax Self-Assessment Form (Form PT1) is also completed and submitted to the Revenue Commissioners in order to discharge any Probate Tax that is due.

After the valuation of the estate is confirmed and Probate Tax is paid an application can be made to the Probate Division of the High Court for a Grant of Probate, where there is a Will. Where there is no Will an application is made to the Probate Division of the High Court for Letters of Administration. The Probate Division will require both the Revenue Affidavit Form CA24 and the Probate Tax receipt issued by the Revenue Commissioners to accompany application.

It will also require the original Will (if any) plus a photocopy of the Will, the original Death certificate and the agreement of the party applying for the grant to faithfully administer the estate. Once the Probate Office is satisfied that all the papers are in order it will issue a Grant of Probate to the applicant (if there is a Will) of Letters of Administration to the applicant (where there is no Will). When the Grant of Probate/Letters of Administration issue, the assets in the Estate can be realised and the Estate can be administered.

Either one of these documents entitles the person administering the estate to realise all the assets of the deceased and deal with these assets in accordance with the instructions of the deceased's Will, or, where there is no Will, in accordance with the legal rules of intestacy.

Insurance bond

If the deceased did not make a Will then it is a requirement that the person administering the estate obtain a bond from an insurance company for double the amount of the gross value of the assets in the estate so, if the administrator does not properly administer the estate, then the beneficiaries can rely on the insurance bond to pay any money that is due to them in law.

Naturally, insurance company bonds will vary in price according to the size of the estate and other circumstances. The cost of a bond, however, is usually far more expensive than the actual cost of preparing a Will. And it is for this reason alone that is more financially prudent for people to prepare a Will rather than burdening their estate with the cost of a bond after their death.

This quick reference guide to the information required when somebody dies was supplied by;   *W. Terence Liston & Co.,*
Solicitors,
103/5 Morehampton Road,
Donnybrook,
Dublin 4.   Tel: 01-6685557

21

An easy step-by-step guide to completing your tax return

Form 12 is completed by employees and pensioners if their main source of income is under PAYE.

Form 12 Directors is completed by company directors who pay all their income tax under PAYE.

If you pay income tax by direct assessment you should complete **Form 11**.

A simpler version of the Form 11 is called **Form 11 Short**. However, if you pay income tax under self assessment and you have received dividends from an Irish company, you should complete Form 11.

Your tax return

Here we take you through each section of your tax return, we follow the layout of Form 11 and include details of backup documents that may be required by your tax inspector. A model Form 12 is reproduced on Pages 364.

Income details for the year ended 5th April 2001

1. Income from Trade, Profession or Vocation

If you are self-employed, you must submit the accounts for the business, together with a computation of your profit or loss, balancing charges and capital allowances.

For more details see Chapter on Self Assessment and the Self Employed, Page 271.

2. Credit for withholding tax on payments for professional services

Credit may be claimed in 2000/01 in respect of withholding tax deducted in the year 2000/01. If your accounting period ends on a date other than 5th April, credit for withholding tax is given by reference to the withholding tax deducted during the accounting period ended in the year 2000/01.

Backup Documents That May Be Required: Original F45 Forms. No credit will be given for tax paid unless original F45's are submitted.

3. Fee, commissions etc. not included elsewhere

This is the place on the return for giving details of any income received in the year to 5th April 2001 from whatever source for which specific provision is not made elsewhere in the return, for example:

- A second source of income from a trade, profession or vocation.

- Sums received after discontinuance of a trade or profession.

Backup Documents That May Be Required: Copies of accounts.

4. Income from land & property in the State

This includes rent, premiums key money and income from advertising. Income from foreign property should be included in the section Foreign Income. Enclose a statement on renting property. See Page 47.

Backup Documents That May Be Required: An inventory of the fixtures and fittings should be submitted in order to claim capital allowances.

5. Untaxed income arising in the State

This would include income from Government gilts etc. Enclosed the relevant certificate with your return. See Page 35.

Backup Documents That May Be Required: Original vouchers for the relevant year showing interest paid to you.

6. Income from which Irish tax was deducted

While liability to tax at the higher rate no longer applies on deposit interest, which is subject to DIRT, the interest must nevertheless be returned. Levies may be charged on this interest.

346

Backup Documents That May Be Required: Copies of accounts.

Give details of deposit interest from which standard rate DIRT was deducted. Deposit interest form "Special Savings Accounts" - subject to 20% DIRT - should not be returned, unless you are entitled to claim a refund of DIRT (if you or your spouse is either 65 years or over or permanently incapacitated).

Backup Documents That May Be Required: Deposit interest certificate showing the gross and net interest and the DIRT deducted.

7. Royalties from "Qualifying Patents"

To be exempt from income tax, patent royalties must meet the following conditions:

- The original inventor must be the recipient of the royalty

- The royalty must be in respect of a manufacturing activity (other than IFSC and certain Shannon Free Zone activities) carried on in the State or elsewhere, or a non-manufacturing activity and it must be paid by a person unconnected with the recipient.

- Where the royalty payment is between connected persons the exemption is restricted to an amount which would have been payable between parties at arm's length.

Although exempt from income tax you could still be liable to PRSI/Levies depending on the level of your income.

8. Settlement, covenant etc. issue.

If you receive income under an Irish Settlement covenant maintenance you should include details here.

Backup Documents That May Be Required: Form 185 which you should receive from the person paying the Covenant to you.

9. Distributions of companies resident in the State

Enter the totals for all distributions and the amount of dividend withholding tax deducted.

Backup Documents That May Be Required: Dividend vouchers showing the gross and the dividend withholding tax deducted.

10 a. Employments/pensions/directorships

Show all income from employments (including directorships) and pensions. Also include Disability Benefit/Occupational Injury Benefit and Unemployment Benefit paid by the Department of Social Welfare if you are in receipt of any of these payments.

Backup Documents That May Be Required: Your P60 for the year which you should receive from your employer after the end of the tax year or your P45 if your employment ceased before the end of the tax year.

10 b. If income arose from any other Irish sources (e.g. Disability Benefit, Unemployment Benefit)

Note: Child benefit elements included in Disability Benefit and Unemployment Benefit are exempt from tax for 2000/01. In addition, the first £10 per week of Unemployment Benefit is exempt.

Backup Documents That May Be Required: The Taxation section of the Department of Social, Community & Family Affairs can provide you with a certificate showing the amount of taxable Unemployment and disability Benefit which you received.

10 c. Other payments

Give details of any sum (not already included above) received by you in the year ended 5th April 2001 from an employer as a result of:

- Commencing employment
  or

- The termination of an office or employment
  or

- Any change in its functions premoluments
  or

- The commutation of annual or periodic payments
  or

- Consideration for entering into restrictive covenants
  or

- Any other matter related to an employment.

See Chapter 14, Page 243.

Backup Documents That May Be Required: Your P45 if you ceased employment

11. Allowable deduction incurred in employment

Give details of any (i) allowable expenses, (ii) capital allowances or (iii) superannuation contributions (other than those deducted by your employer) incurred in the office or employment.

(i) Expenses in employment

An allowance may be claimed only for an expense arising in the course of the carrying out of the duties of an employment. See Page 224.

(ii) Capital allowances

If you must use your car in carrying out the duties of your employment, you can claim an allowance for wear and tear of the car (in addition to the running costs, which should be given under "expenses" above. The allowance is based on 20% of the written down value of the car, but where the car is also used for private purposes, only the proportion attributable to its used for the purpose of your employment may be claimed. Travelling to/from work is private travel.

(iii) Superannuation contributions

These should be shown only if they have not already been deducted in arriving at the figure for earnings shown in the return.

12. Benefits from employments

In calculating the amount of any Benefits-in Kind, you should include Company Cars, preferential loans, stock options received etc. Deduct any contributions, which you make to your employer- For more details see Page 229.

Backup Documents That May Be Required: For preferential loans an interest statement showing the interest paid by you for the year.

13. Foreign income (dividends, pensions, rents etc.)

The amounts shown for foreign income should be shown in IR£. If you cannot get the rate of exchange applicable at a particular date, you may show the foreign currency amount but be sure that you state clearly the foreign currency concerned.

Income from the U.K. (including Northern Ireland) should be shown here.

Backup Documents That May Be Required: Original dividend vouchers.

14. Foreign bank accounts

Individuals who opened foreign bank accounts during the year ended 5th April 2001 are required to give certain information in relation to such accounts - including the amount of the initial deposit.

15. Offshore funds

Individuals resident or ordinarily resident in the State must include details of acquisitions of material interests in offshore funds during the year ended 5th April 2001. An offshore fund is:

- A company which is resident outside the State, or

- A unit trust scheme the trustees of which are not resident in the State, or

- Any arrangements, which do not fall within paragraph (a) or (b), which take effect by virtue of the law of a territory outside the State and which, under the law, create rights in the nature of co-ownership.

16. Annual payments, charges and interest

Rents etc. payable to non - residents

Payments under Deed of covenant

Backup Documents That May Be Required: If this is your first Covenant, a copy of the deed should be submitted with the return. Only covenants in favour of certain individuals qualify for tax relief.

17. Other charges, e.g. annuities/maintenance payments

Any annual payments, whether or not tax is deductible before payment, should be shown here.

18. Retirement annuities

An R.A.C. certificate, should be submitted with your Tax return. This will normally be given to you by the insurance company when you pay the premium. For more details see Page 209.

19. Interest paid in full

Relief for 2000/01 in respect of interest paid on a loan used to acquire your principal private residence is subject to certain maximum limits. For more details see Page 204.

Where the interest was paid on a loan applied to acquire an interest in a company, relief may be claimed in respect of the amount paid in the year of assessment.

Backup Documents That May Be Required: If your mortgage is with a building society or loan authority, you should fill in your account number. If your loan is with someone else e.g. Bank, you should submit the Mortgage Interest Certificate.

20. Artists exempt income

Income derived from qualifying works on which the Revenue Commissioners have granted exemption from Income Tax must be returned. Although this income is exempt from Income Tax you are still liable to pay PRSI & Levies on it.

Personal Circumstances and Claims for Allowances and Reliefs

The information requested in this section of your Income Tax Return is required to give your correct tax allowances and to correctly compute your PRSI/Levy liabilities.

21. Children

If your income is below a certain figure, you will not have to pay income tax for that year. However, if you have dependent children, you are entitled to an increase in the exemption limit. This increase operates only to increase the exemption limit for low-income taxpayers. It is not a general tax allowance for all taxpayers. See Page 199 for more details

Generally speaking, a dependent child is any child under 16 years and any child over 16 years who is going to school or college full-time or is in training as an apprentice.

22. One-parent family allowances and incapacitated child allowance

You may be entitled to a **one-parent family allowance** if you are a widowed, parent if you are a single parent (deserted spouse, separated spouse or unmarried person) and you have the custody of a child who is:

- born at any time between 6th April 2000 and 5th April 2001 or

- under 16 years of age at 6th April 2000 or

- 16 years or over at 6th April 2000 and receiving full-time education, instruction or apprenticeship or

- 16 years or over at 6th April 2000 and permanently incapacitated either before reaching 21, or had become permanently incapacitated after 21 while receiving full-time education, instruction or apprenticeship.

The allowance is reduced by £1 for every £1 by which any child's income exceeds £720. You may be entitled to an incapacitated child allowance if you have a child, (including stepchild, legally adopted child or informally adopted child) who is:

- under 16 years of age at any time between 6th April 2000 and 5th April 2001 and permanently incapacitated, or

- 16 years or over at 6th April 2000 and had become permanently incapacitated in the circumstances outlined above. The incapacity must be such as to make it unlikely that the child will be able to maintain himself or herself.

Backup Documents That May Be Required: Birth Certificate for your child.

23. Widowed parent allowance

You may claim a Widowed Parent Allowance for 2000/01 if you were widowed in a year prior to 2000/01. For more details see Page 201.

Backup Documents That May Be Required: Death certificate for your deceased spouse. Birth Certificate for your dependent child(ren).

24. Dependent relative allowance

If you maintain at your own expenses:

- a relative, including a relative of your spouse, who is incapacitated by old age or infirmity or

- your own or your spouse's widowed father or widowed mother, whether incapacitated or not, you may be entitled to this allowance. See Page 203.

25. Medical insurance

Relief is available at the 22% rate for 2000/01 in respect of qualifying premiums paid in the year ended 5th April 2000.

Backup Documents That May Be Required: Medical Insurance Certificate showing the amount of insurance paid.

26. Permanent health insurance

A deduction not exceeding 10% of your total income may be claimed in respect of premiums paid.

Backup Documents That May Be Required: You should attach form PH1 if this is your first claim and the form has not already been submitted.

27. PAYE allowance

A PAYE allowance of £1,000 at the standard note of tax (22%) may be claimed in the 2000/01 by employees and non- proprietary directors who pay tax under the PAYE system. If PAYE earnings are less than £1,000 in any tax year, the allowance is reduced to the amount of the PAYE earnings.

The following Social Welfare payments also qualify for the PAYE allowance:

Survivor's Contributory Pension; Orphan's Contributory Allowance; Retirement Pension; Old Age Contributory Pension; Disability Benefit and Occupational Injury Benefit and Unemployment Benefit.

The PAYE allowance may also be claimed by taxpayers who are employed abroad and who pay tax abroad on their earnings under a PAYE system (or similar system where tax is deducted at source from the earnings of the employment). To qualify for relief, the earnings from the foreign employment must be subject to Irish tax.

The PAYE allowance cannot be claimed:-

• By a proprietary director or his/her spouse, in respect of emoluments received from the company in which the director has a proprietary interest. (A proprietary director of a company is a director who controls either directly or indirectly 15% or more of the share capital of that company).

• By a spouse of an individual in respect of emoluments paid by the individual (or by a partnership in which the individual is a partner).

28. Relief for investment in corporate trades

Relief may be claimed up to a maximum of £25,000 for eligible shares issued in the year ended 5th April 2001. Where the subscription is made through a Designated Fund, but the fund does not invest monies within the year of assessment, you can elect to claim relief on such a subscription in the year in which you subscribe to the fund, rather than in the year in which the fund invests in eligible shares PROVIDED the fund invests the moneys subscribed in eligible shares within the next year of assessment.

Backup Documents That May Be Required: RICT forms should be submitted, however these RICT forms are normally slow to issue from the investing company, so, the Revenue will accept a receipt showing your investment in a BES fund and you can submit the RICT form at a later stage.

29. Tax relief for tuition fees paid to approved colleges / gifts to approved third level institutions

Relief at the 22% rate is available for tuition fees paid to approved colleges for the 2000/01 academic year in respect of approved undergraduate courses of at least 2 years duration.

Relief is also available for gifts with a net value of £1,000 or over made to approve third level institutions.

Backup Documents That May Be Required: Receipt for the third level fees.

30. Residence/domicile

Income Tax: In general, residents are taxable on the full amount of income and profits from all sources, Irish and foreign.

Residents who are either not domiciled in the State or are citizens of Ireland who are not ordinarily resident in the State are taxable on the full amount of income and profits from Irish and U.K. sources, and on amount remitted to the State from any other sources. See Chapter 15, Page 253.

31. Capital gains and chargeable assets capital gains tax

Capital Gains Tax is subject to self-assessment principles. If you have acquired or disposed of shares or other assets, you should keep the contract notes or other documents relevant for computing your Capital Gains/Losses.

Form 12
1999/2000 Tax Return (Employees and Pensioners)

Please quote this number in all correspondence or when calling at your tax office	Your RSI Number	Employer's Reg. No.	

Office Hours
Monday - Friday
9.30 a.m. - 5.00 p.m.

RETURN OF INCOME AND CAPITAL GAINS FOR YEAR ENDED 5 APRIL 2000

CLAIM FOR ALLOWANCES AND RELIEFS FOR YEAR ENDED 5 APRIL 2000

This form is to be completed by a person (other than a Company Director) whose main source of income is from an employment or pension. It should be sent to the return address shown.

Return address

All amounts returned on this form MUST be expressed in IR£

Use any envelope and write "FREEPOST" above the address

NO STAMP REQUIRED

NOTICE

You are hereby required, under Section 879 Taxes Consolidation Act 1997, by the Inspector of Taxes named above to prepare and deliver, on or before 31 January 2001, a tax return on this prescribed form for the year of assessment ended on 5 April 2000.

NOTES

One-Parent Family Allowance may be claimed by widowed persons or other single parents who have the custody of, and maintain at their own expense, a dependent child, stepchild or adopted child who is under 18 years of age or over 18 years of age but is receiving full-time education at a recognised educational establishment or is receiving at least 2 years full-time training for a trade or profession or is permanently incapacitated. The allowance is not due in the case of a married couple or an unmarried couple who are living together.

Widowed Parent Allowance may also be claimed for 1999/2000 by a parent with a dependent child (see above for "dependent child") whose spouse died between 6 April 1994 and 5 April 1999.

Revenue Job Assist may be claimed by unemployed / disabled / blind persons in receipt of Social Welfare payments for 12 months or more who took up a qualifying job in the tax year.

Exemption limits. Persons with income below the following amounts for 1999/2000 will not be liable for Income Tax.

	Under 65	65 or over
Single or Widowed	£4,100	£6,500
Married Couple (Combined Incomes)	£8,200	£13,000

These limits are increased by £450 each for the first and second child and £650 for each subsequent child.

Where income is not greatly above the exemption limits, marginal relief may apply. Further details can be obtained from the tax office or the Central Telephone Information Office at (01) 878 0000.

All Revenue Forms and Information Leaflets are available from the Revenue Forms and Leaflets Service at (01) 878 0100.

Penalties: There are penalties of up to £10,000 for failure to make a correct return, where required.

YOU MUST SIGN THIS DECLARATION

I DECLARE that, to the best of my knowledge and belief, this form contains a correct return in accordance with the provisions of the Taxes Consolidation Act 1997 of:

- All the sources of my income and of the amount of income derived from each source in the year ended 5 April 2000, **and**
- All disposals and acquisitions of chargeable assets and of the amount of chargeable gains which accrued to me in the year ended 5 April 2000.

I DECLARE that, to the best of my knowledge and belief, all the particulars given as regards allowances and reliefs claimed and as regards outgoings are correctly stated.

Signature		Date	
Address		Telephone No.	

Int. Ver. 2000

Completing your tax return

CLAIM FOR ALLOWANCES AND RELIEFS FOR 1999/2000

SEE PAGE

PERSONAL ALLOWANCE- Tick (✔) appropriate box **K1**

MARRIED	200	02	SINGLE	199	01		
			WIDOWED	201	03	MARRIED but living apart	299	01

If MARRIED enter spouse's name ___   Date of marriage (if after 5/4/99) / /   Spouse's RSI No. ___

If WIDOWED state date of spouse's death (if after 5/4/94) / /   If separated/divorced state date of separation (if after 5/4/99) / /

AGE ALLOWANCE: State Date of Birth (if aged 65 or over in year to 5/4/2000) Self *SEE PAGE 203* **A3** Spouse / /

BLIND ALLOWANCE- Tick (✔) appropriate box *SEE PAGE 204* One Spouse Blind **W6** Both Spouses Blind

REVENUE JOB ASSIST - Tick (✔) if claimed *SEE PAGE 214* Attach Form RJA1 unless already submitted **F2/F3/V9**

DEPENDENT RELATIVE ALLOWANCE

Relative's Name and RSI No. **K6** *SEE PAGE 203* Date of Birth / /

Income for 1999/2000 £ ___ Details of Help given by others ___

		SELF	SPOUSE
INCAPACITATED PERSON - Allowance for employing a carer	(Attach Form HK1 unless already submitted)	Amount paid in year to 5/4/2000 £ *SEE PAGE* **K7**	203
MAINTENANCE PAYMENTS	(If first claim, attach evidence)	Amount paid in year to 5/4/2000 £ *SEE PAGE* **A9**	306
MEDICAL EXPENSES	(Attach Form MED1)	Amount claimed for year to 5/4/2000 £ *SEE PAGE* **H5**	211
MEDICAL INSURANCE Name of Authorised Insurer		Amount paid in year to 5/4/1999 £ *SEE PAGE* **M4**	210
PERMANENT HEALTH BENEFIT Name of Insurer		Amount paid in year to 5/4/2000 £ *SEE PAGE* **M5**	214
RENT RELIEF	(Attach form RENT 1 unless already submitted)	Amount paid in year to 5/4/2000 £ *SEE PAGE* **M9/M8**	214
TUITION FEES paid to an approved college or for an approved training course (Attach receipt)		Amount paid in year to 5/4/2000 £ *SEE PAGE* **A7**	215
OTHER ALLOWANCE specify		Amount paid in year to 5/4/2000, if relevant £	

SEE PAGE *SEE PAGE* *SEE PAGE* *SEE PAGE*
Tick (✔) the appropriate box if you wish to claim any of these allowances and supply the details requested below (see notes on front page).

(a) ONE-PARENT FAMILY ALLOWANCE **M6** 200	(b) WIDOWED PARENT ALLOWANCE **B2** 201	(c) INCAPACITATED CHILD ALLOWANCE **B8** 202	(d) INCREASED EXEMPTION/ DEPENDENT CHILDREN **B5** 199

Child's Name	Date of Birth	Child's Income for 1999/2000 where (a) or (c) is claimed	Name of School if receiving full-time education OR Name of Employer if receiving at least 2 years training for a trade or profession OR Nature of Incapacity, if relevant

One-Parent Family Allowance may not be claimed in the case of a married couple or an unmarried couple who are living together.

EXPENSES IN EMPLOYMENT
If approved "Flat Rate" expenses apply you need not complete this section

Expenses wholly, exclusively and necessarily incurred in the performance of the duties of the employment in year ended 5 April 2000 (details should be set out on a separate sheet).

SELF £ *SEE PAGE 225* **W1/V6** SPOUSE £

Payments Made Under Deeds Of Covenant

If this is a first claim attach copy of the Deed of Covenant **A6**

Date of Deed	To whom paid - Name & Address	Relationship (if any)	Gross Paid 1999/2000
	SEE PAGE 207		£
			£

CAPITAL GAINS TAX

1. In the year ended 5 April 2000, did you or your spouse acquire, sell, exchange or otherwise dispose of any chargeable assets, (e.g. land, shares, paintings, antiques etc.)?

Tick (✔) as appropriate   SELF YES NO   SPOUSE YES NO

2. If the answer is "YES" please attach, as appropriate, a statement showing:
(a) Description of Asset(s); (b) Date of Acquisition; (c) Cost or acquisition value; (d) Date of disposal; (e) Disposal price; (f) Computation of the chargeable gain/loss. In the case of a disposal enter the amount of chargeable gain/loss here

SEE PAGE 283

SELF £   SPOUSE £

OTHER INCOME FOR THE YEAR ENDED 5 APRIL 2000
Where there is no income under a heading write "NONE"

Payments including Social Welfare Pensions

(Include Disability Benefit, Unemployment Benefit, Old Age Pension, Widows'/Widowers' Pension, Retirement and Invalidity Pensions and One-Parent Family Payment)

	SELF	SPOUSE
Type of Payment/Pension	SEE PAGE 190	
Date payment started (if after 5 April 1999)	/ /	/ /
Date payment ceased, if ceased	/ /	/ /
Amount of payment / If amount is not known state weekly amount	£	E4 E7/E9 £

Deposit Interest

Deposit Interest from "Special Savings Accounts" - subject to 20% DIRT - need not be returned unless you are entitled to claim a refund of DIRT

	SELF	SPOUSE
Gross Interest from which Irish tax was deducted	£	£
Name of Bank, Building Society etc.	SEE PAGE 24	C1/G1
Untaxed Interest	£	D5 £
Source (Government Stocks, Credit Union Dividends, Name of Foreign Bank etc.)		

Foreign Bank Accounts

Were you or your spouse the beneficial owner of any foreign Bank Account opened in year ended 5 April 2000? Tick (✔) as appropriate. Include details of interest received from these accounts in panel for **Deposit Interest** above.

SELF		SPOUSE	
YES	NO	YES	NO

Rents

Rents from letting of property, including land (State address(es) of property let, and give details of receipts and expenses on a separate sheet)

	SELF	SPOUSE
Enter Net Rent here	£ SEE PAGE 47	D7 £

Other Income

	SELF		SPOUSE
Other Income not shown above (give details here) Investment Income (Dividends etc.)	£ SEE PAGE 33	D5	£
Trading or Professional Income	£ SEE PAGE 271	D2/H2	£
Patent Royalties (unless you are the original inventor)	£	D2/H2	£
Other Income (including Deeds of Covenant)	£ SEE PAGE 207		£
Maintenance Payments Received	£	A1/H2	£

(Attach accounts or an itemised list as appropriate for each heading)

Profits from Farming (attach details)

		D2/H2
State the location of all lands in the State owned and/or occupied by you or your spouse.		
Acreage		
Profits	£	£

INTEREST PAID

INTEREST PAID ON MAIN RESIDENCE LOANS (attach certificate(s) unless the lender is a Building Society)

Lender's Name		Loan A/C No.		Date of Loan	/ /
If loan is in joint names state Name of other person		His/Her RSI No.			

	Self			Spouse	
Is this your first home loan? tick (✔) appropriate box	YES NO	J4		YES NO	
Is your main residence in a Designated Area? SEE PAGE 204	YES NO			YES NO	
	Self	J5		Spouse	
Interest paid in year ended 5/4/2000	£			£	

OTHER INTEREST PAID - Loans applied in acquiring interest in unquoted trading companies etc.

Name and Address of Lending Agency	Date & Purpose of Loan	Amount of Loan
		£

	Self	J6	Spouse
Interest paid in year ended 5/4/2000	£		£

Completing your tax return

CLAIM FOR ALLOWANCES AND RELIEFS FOR 1999/2000

PERSONAL ALLOWANCE - Tick (✔) appropriate box **K1** *SEE PAGE*

MARRIED	200	02	SINGLE	199	01	WIDOWED	201	03	MARRIED but living apart	299	01

If MARRIED enter spouse's name _____

| Date of marriage (if after 5/4/99) | / / | Spouse's RSI No. _____ |

| If WIDOWED state date of spouse's death (if after 5/4/94) | / / | If separated/divorced state date of separation (if after 5/4/99) | / / |

AGE ALLOWANCE: State Date of Birth (if aged 65 or over in year to 5/4/2000) Self *SEE PAGE 203* **A3** Spouse / /

BLIND ALLOWANCE - Tick (✔) appropriate box *SEE PAGE 204* One Spouse Blind **W6** Both Spouses Blind

REVENUE JOB ASSIST - Tick (✔) if claimed *SEE PAGE 214* Attach Form RJA1 unless already submitted **F2/F3/V9**

DEPENDENT RELATIVE ALLOWANCE

Relative's Name and RSI No. **K6** *SEE PAGE 203* Date of Birth / /

Income for 1999/2000 £ _____ Details of Help given by others _____

			SELF	SPOUSE
INCAPACITATED PERSON - Allowance for employing a carer	(Attach Form HK1 unless already submitted)	Amount paid in year to 5/4/2000 £ *SEE PAGE* **K7**		203
MAINTENANCE PAYMENTS	(If first claim, attach evidence)	Amount paid in year to 5/4/2000 £ *SEE PAGE* **A9**		306
MEDICAL EXPENSES	(Attach Form MED1)	Amount claimed for year to 5/4/2000 £ *SEE PAGE* **H5**		211
MEDICAL INSURANCE Name of Authorised Insurer		Amount paid in year to 5/4/1999 £ *SEE PAGE* **M4**		210
PERMANENT HEALTH BENEFIT Name of Insurer		Amount paid in year to 5/4/2000 £ *SEE PAGE* **M5**		214
RENT RELIEF	(Attach form RENT 1 unless already submitted)	Amount paid in year to 5/4/2000 £ *SEE PAGE* **M9/ M8**		214
TUITION FEES paid to an approved college or for an approved training course (Attach receipt)		Amount paid in year to 5/4/2000 £ *SEE PAGE* **A7**		215
OTHER ALLOWANCE specify		Amount paid in year to 5/4/2000, if relevant £		

Tick (✔) the appropriate box if you wish to claim any of these allowances and supply the details requested below (see notes on front page). *SEE PAGE* *SEE PAGE* *SEE PAGE* *SEE PAGE*

(a) ONE-PARENT FAMILY ALLOWANCE **M6** 200	(b) WIDOWED PARENT ALLOWANCE **B2** 201	(c) INCAPACITATED CHILD ALLOWANCE **B8** 202	(d) INCREASED EXEMPTION/ DEPENDENT CHILDREN **B5** 199

Child's Name	Date of Birth	Child's Income for 1999/2000 where (a) or (c) is claimed	Name of School if receiving full-time education OR Name of Employer if receiving at least 2 years training for a trade or profession OR Nature of Incapacity, if relevant.

One-Parent Family Allowance may not be claimed in the case of a married couple or an unmarried couple who are living together.

EXPENSES IN EMPLOYMENT
If approved "Flat Rate" expenses apply you need not complete this section

Expenses wholly, exclusively and necessarily incurred in the performance of the duties of the employment in year ended 5 April 2000 (details should be set out on a separate sheet).

	SELF		SPOUSE
	£ *SEE PAGE* 225 **W1/V6**	£	

Payments Made Under Deeds Of Covenant

If this is a first claim attach copy of the Deed of Covenant **A6**

Date of Deed	To whom paid - Name & Address	Relationship (if any)	Gross Paid 1999/2000
	SEE PAGE 207		£
			£

CAPITAL GAINS TAX

1. In the year ended 5 April 2000, did you or your spouse acquire, sell, exchange or otherwise dispose of any chargeable assets, (e.g. land, shares, paintings, antiques etc.)?

   Tick (✔) as appropriate

	SELF			SPOUSE	
	YES	NO		YES	NO

2. If the answer is "YES" please attach, as appropriate, a statement showing:
   (a) Description of Asset(s); (b) Date of Acquisition; (c) Cost or acquisition value; *SEE PAGE 283*
   (d) Date of disposal; (e) Disposal price; (f) Computation of the chargeable gain/loss.
   In the case of a disposal enter the amount of chargeable gain/loss here

	SELF		SPOUSE
	£		£

A Worked Example 2000/01

1. John Smith has a salary of £35,000 for the year ended 05/04/2001 and the use of a company car whose original market value was £15,000. PAYE tax deducted per the P60 was £9,152.

2. Mary his wife owns a Boutique and her adjusted profit for the year ended 31/12/2000 was £20,000. Capital allowances amounted to £200 and she paid £6,000 Preliminary Tax.

3. Mary received two dividends from Irish Oil Ltd., amounting to £780 net. withholding Tax amounted to £220. These were received in December 2000.

4. Mary received £400 gross interest from Irish Government loan stock.

5. Mary paid £790 to the VHI in the year ended 05/04/2000.

6. Mary contributed £2,600 to a Pension Fund.

7. John pays £750 (Net) per annum to his mother who is 68 by way of a Deed of Covenant.

8. Mary pays £430 Permanent Health Insurance.

9. John pays £5,000 p.a. mortgage interest (mortgage taken out in 1989).

TAX LIABILITY FOR 2000/01

Income

To arrive at your assessable income for the year ended 5th April 2001 you should examine income arising under the following headings:

1. Wages, salaries or pensions. Year to 5th April 2001.
   Gross pay from employment - (John)   £35,000

   Benefit-in-Kind

	Note 1	£ 4,500	£ 39,500

2. Self-Employment - Year to 5th April 2001 - (Mary). If you are self-employed or a partner then you should include your profit or share of profits arising in your accounts for the financial year ending within the tax year ended 5th April 2001. This should be your adjusted profit for tax purposes and then do not forget to enter under deductions any wear and tear allowances.

	Note 2	£20,000	
Less Capital Allowances		£200	£19,800

3. Irish dividends-year to 5th April 2001

Total of dividends received (gross)	£1,000

4. Investment income - year to 5th April 20001 (untaxed)

(b) Irish Government Loan Stock etc.	£400
Total income C/F	£60,700
Total income B/F	**£60,700**
Deductions	
Pension Contributions	£2,600
Covenants Paid **Note 5**	£962
	£3,562

Permanent Health Insurance	£430	
Taxable Income	£56,708	
Tax Payable		
(£34,000)	£34,000 @ 22%	£7,480
	£22,708 @ 44%	£9,992
Deed of Covenant £ 962 @ 22% **(Note 5)**		£212
	Tax Chargeable	£17,684
Less:	Tax Credits	
	Personal Allowance	
	£9,400 @ 22%	(£2,068)
	PAYE	
	£1,000 @ 22%	(£220)
	Mortgage Interest	
	£4,000 @ 22%	(£880)
	VHI	
	£790 @ 22%	(£174)
		£14,342
	Deduct Tax Paid/Credit	£15,372
	(See Below)	
	Tax Overpaid	(£1,030)

Tax Paid / Credit

John's PAYE Paid	£9,152
Preliminary Tax Paid By Mary	£6,000
Tax credit on dividends	£ 220
	£15,372

Notes:

1. Mr. Smith uses the car supplied by the company and his total mileage for the year was approximately 12,000, of which about 5,000 was for private use. The company paid all the running expenses. The benefit-in-kind is, therefore, £15,000 x 30% = £4,500.

2. Mrs. Smith's income is assessed under Schedule D Case I and is, therefore, assessed on a "current year"basis for 2000/01.

3. The net amount of £750 covenanted to his mother is grossed up and deducted as a charge. (£750 x 100/78 = £962)

The tax deducted (£962 x 22% = £212) must be accounted for to the Revenue.

4. This Balancing Statement does not include PRSI and levies of £1,432 which may be due to the Revenue Commissioners if not already paid (5% of £19,800 +£1,000+£400 less £1,040 income exemption allowance + 2% of (£19,800 + £1,000+ £400)).

INCOME TAX - PAYE AS YOU EARN
Balancing Statement for Tax Year 2000-01

Regarding John & Mary Smith
Reference No: 1234567 F

Taxation Advice Bureau
Eagle House
Wentworth
Dublin 2

Please quote in any correspondence

District/Unit	Employer No.	RSI No
01 967	7654321 B	1234567 F

This matter is being dealt with by:

Dublin PAYE 4, Unit 700
85/93 Lower Mount Street,
Dublin 2

INCOME FROM EMPLOYMENTS/PENSIONS AND OTHER SOURCES

Source/Description	Income Amount IR£	Tax Deducted PAYE and or Tax Credits	
A.N. OTHER – Salary	35,000	9,152	→ 15,372
Benefit in Kind	4,500		Deduct amount if any, in respect of arrears of tax taken into account in your Tax-Free Allowances for this year
Self Employed Income	19,800	6,000	
Dividends & Distributions	1,000	220	
Government Stock	400	–	
Totals IR£	60,700	15,372	0.00 Net Amount for Computation 15,372

ALLOWANCES AND RELIEFS

Permanent Health Insurance	430
Deed of Covenant	962
Retirement Annuity	2,600
Total IR£	3,992

COMPUTATION OF NET TAX PAYABLE BY YOU

Gross Statutory Income		60,700
Less Allowances and Reliefs		3,992
Taxable Income		56,708
Which is chargeable as follows:		
	34,000 @ 22%	7,480
	22,708 @ 44%	9,992
Deed of Covenant	962 @ 22%	212
Total Income Tax Due		17,684
Less: Tax Credits		
Personal Allowances	9,400 @ 22%	2,068
PAYE	1,000 @ 22%	220
Home Loan Interest	4,000 @ 22%	880
Medical Insurance	790 @ 22%	174
Net Tax deducted PAYE/Tax Credits		15,372
Tax Overpaid		1,030

....

DETACH

P.O.   **AP**
BANC
NA hEIREANN
College Green,
Dublin 2

90-14-66

loc le   John & Mary Smith   no Ordu

7 A Cho

100,000	10,000	1,000	100	10	1	p
—	—	One	Zero	Three	Zero	—

1030

No Coimisineiri Ioncaim, an tÁrd Bhallitheoir
Cuntas Tarraingthe, Iumhir 1.

SPECIMEN ONLY

Appendix 1

Funds first accepted into ARF's before 6th April 2000

These ARF's are taxed under three headingss:

- Tax on Profit & Gains within the Fund

- Tax on the withdrawal of the initial "Residue"

- Tax on the death of the beneficial owner

Tax on profit & gains

The profits and gains earned within these ARF are not exempt from Income Tax and Capital Gains Tax and any tax liability arising on profits and realised gains within the fund must include on your Annual Tax Return.

Withdrawing the residue

The general rule in relation to withdrawal of the Residue from these funds is that it is treated as income in the relelvant year and taxed accordingly under the self-assessment system.

Tax payable in respect of withdrawal of the Residue is chargeable under Case IV of Schedule D (where the funds were derived from a Personal Pension Plan) and under Schedule E (where the funds were derived from an Occupatinal Pension Scheme for a proprietary director).

Taxes on death
Income Tax

In general, where "The Residue" is transferred out of these ARF on death, the amount transferred is treated as income of the deceased person in the year of death. The QFM will, be obliged to deduct tax at the top rate 44% in 2000/01 (42% in 2001) from this Residue.

Exemptions

If these ARF funds are transferred into another ARF in the name of the surviving spouse or into an ARF owned by the surviving spouse, no tax liability will arise on this transfer

or

If these ARF funds are transferred to an ARF for the benefit of a child of the deceased, and the child is under 21 years of age, no income tax liability will arise on the transfer.

A surviving spouse will be liable to tax on funds transferred to an ARF in exactly the same way as his/her deceased spouse. When the surviving spouse dies, the rate of tax which the QFM is obliged to deduct on the Residue from the funds (see exemptions above) is reduced to 25%, an no further income tax liability will arise in respect of transfers to other individuals following the death of the surviving spouse. Children over 21 will be exempt from inheritance tax while children under 21 and other beneficaries may be liable to inheritance tax if the normal thresholds are exceeded.

Say YES

Have a look at the following checklist and see if any of these areas in your finances could benefit from professional advice:

- Are you paying too much tax   Yes ◯   No ◯
- Do you – or do you plan to – work abroad?   Yes ◯   No ◯
- Children's Education – Will you plan for this?   Yes ◯   No ◯
- Redundancy/Early Retirement – Is this a likely option?   Yes ◯   No ◯
- Separation/Divorce – does this affect you?   Yes ◯   No ◯
- Buying a House – are you planning this?   Yes ◯   No ◯
- Your Pension – can your benefits be enhanced?   Yes ◯   No ◯
- Savings/Investments – Could they be more efficient?   Yes ◯   No ◯
- Your Livelihood/Health – Is it financially exposed?   Yes ◯   No ◯

Because We Can Help You!

If you tick even one "YES" to the questions above you'll find this Guide a very useful aid to helping you to get the most out of your finances.

If you'd like a consultation with one of our advisors to discuss your specific requirements or to seek advice about which options suit you best, please contact us to arrange a private consultation. We have a fixed private consultation fee of £50 (+ 21% VAT) for readers of this Guide. If you'd like to take advantage of this consultation offer:

Call Catherine McGuirk or Siobháin Usher
to arrange an appointment

Taxation Advice Bureau,
Eagle House,
Wentworth,
Eblana Villas
Dublin 2.

Tel: 01-6768633
Fax: 01-6768641

email: tab@eircom.ie
www.tab.ie

Index

369

Are You Paying Too Much Tax?

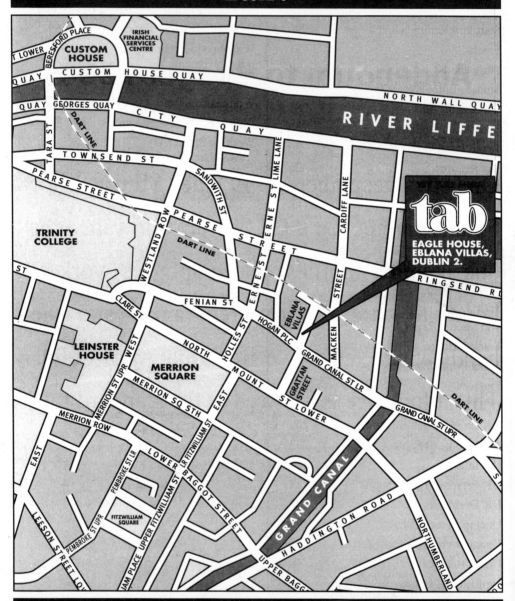

Let TAB Map out Your Financial Options For You!